John Howell

Starting a business
SPAIN

CADOGANguides

Contents

Introduction 1

01

The Big Picture 3
How Many People are
Setting up Businesses
Abroad? 4
How Many People are
Setting up Businesses
in Spain? 4
Who is Doing What –
and Where? 5
Opportunities – Gaps in
the Market 10

02

Getting to Know
Spain 15
Climate and Geography
16
Economy 19
The Governmental
System 20
The Administrative
System 21
Spanish Languages 22

03

Business Ideas 29
The Brilliant Idea –
Eureka 30
Some Common Ideas –
the Pros and Cons 31
Will It Work in Spain? 66

Research 69
Legal Advice 70
Talk to People Who
Have Already Done
It 72
Your Experience 72
Language Skills 73

04

Setting Up a
Business in Spain
75
First Steps 76
Finding Business
Opportunities 76
Your Business Plan 77
Working from Home
80
Relating to Your 'Parent'
Business 81
Should You Set Up Your
Own Business or Buy
Into an Existing
Business? 82
Business Structures 90
Licences and
Registrations 97
Raising Finance 98
Getting Finance into
Spain 101
Spanish Banks 103
Business and Personal
Taxes 105
Acquiring Business
Premises 109
Employing Staff 118

Marketing 123
Final Plan Checklist 124

05

Red Tape 125
Permits and Paperwork
126
NIE 127
Using a *Gestor* 128
Social Security 129
Licences 129
Taxes 130
IAE 130
Ministry of Labour and
Social Affairs 131
Professional and Other
Qualifications 131
Registration with a
Consulate 132

06

Working in Spain 133
Business Practices 134
How to Find a Job 138
Terms and Conditions
of Employment 145
Dismissal and
Redundancy 146
Benefits 149
Unions 151

07

Living in Spain 153
Learning Spanish 154

Moving 158
Finding
  Accommodation 162
Communication and
  the Media 175
Home Utilities 179
Motoring 182
Healthcare 183
Pensions 188
Education 189

08

Legal Matters 193
Business Law 194
Insurance 199
Disputes and Debt
  Collection 204
Bankcruptcy 210

09

References 213
Spain at a Glance 214
Further Reading 215
Contacts 216
Spanish Area Telephone
  Codes 223
Regional Climate
  Chart/Rainfall 224
Largest Cities 225
Dictionary of Useful
  and Technical Terms
  226
Public Holidays and
  Celebrations 233

10

Appendices 249
Appendix 1 250
Sample CV in Spanish
  Format 250
Appendix 2 251
Sample Job Application
  Letter 251
Appendix 3 253
Spanish Format
  Business Plan 253
Appendix 4 259
Types of Spanish
  Business Structure
  259
Appendix 5 261
Wealth and Inheritance
  Tax 261

Maps
Spain *inside front cover*
Spain Touring Guide
  235–46
Spain's Road Network
  247
Spain's Rail Network
  248

About the author

John Howell established John Howell & Co in Sheffield in 1979 and by 1997 it had become one of the largest and most respected law firms in the north of England, employing over 100 lawyers. On moving to London in 1995, John Howell has gone on to specialise in providing legal advice to clients buying a property in France, Spain, Italy and Portugal and more recently Turkey and Croatia.

Cadogan Guides
2nd Floor
233 High Holborn
London WC1V 7DN
info@cadoganguides.co.uk
www.cadoganguides.com

The Globe Pequot Press
246 Goose Lane, PO Box 480, Guilford,
Connecticut 06437–0480

Copyright © John Howell 2005

Cover photographs: © Westend61/Alamy ;Nicholas Stubbs/ Alamy;Stuart Crump/Alamy; Tim Gartside/Alamy; Elizabeth Whiting & Associates/ Alamy
Maps © Cadogan Guides drawn by Maidenhead Cartographic Services
Cover design: Sarah Rianhard-Gardner
Editor: Matthew Tanner
Proofreader: Carla Masson
Indexing: Isobel McLean

Produced by **Navigator Guides**
www.navigatorguides.com

Printed in Finland by WS Bookwell
A catalogue record for this book is available from the British Library
ISBN 10: 1-86011-210-2
ISBN 13: 978-1-86011-210-8

Introduction

Many people are today considering establishing their own business in Spain. The attractions are obvious. From the relaxed lifestyle and temperate climate to the excitement of embarking on a new life in a foreign country, starting a business in Spain has much to offer. However, setting up any business can seem a daunting experience, especially if you are new to it. Add to this the additional complication of getting a business up and running in a foreign country and it can begin to appear positively frightening. This book explains the right way to go about setting up such a venture, and aims to shed some light on the common pitfalls. Knowledge is power, and if you go about the process in the right way then these pitfalls can be avoided.

Many potential problems are common to starting a business anywhere, but we do not worry about these because we feel we are on familiar territory and, more importantly, because we are shielded against contact with most of them by our solicitor. The same is actually true when starting a business abroad. Read this book to get some ideas, understand the background and gain some awareness of Spanish law and what problems may exist. Ask your lawyer to advise about any issues of concern to you and leave him to avoid the landmines!

The first chapter, **The Big Picture**, provides a general overview of the business opportunities available in Spain. Chapter 2, **Getting to Know Spain**, looks at the climate, geography and administrative systems of the country. Chapter 3, **Business Ideas**, takes an in-depth look at how to come up with the right money-making scheme. Chapter 4, **Setting Up a Business in Spain**, gets down to the nitty gritty of working out such essentials as a business plan, licences and registrations, raising finance and acquiring premises. In Chapter 5, **Red Tape**, essential information is provided on areas such as social security, permits and paperwork while Chapter 6, **Working in Spain**, covers more general ground relating to such things as business etiquette and terms and conditions of employment. Chapter 7, **Living in Spain**, looks at everyday aspects including learning Spanish, getting the gas connected and finding the right school for your children. Chapter 8, **Legal Matters**, as its name suggests, relates to business law and legal disputes while Chapter 9, **References**, is where you'll find many of Spain's 'vital statistics'. The final chapter contains **Appendices** and gives, among other things, a sample CV and advice on formulating a business plan.

All prices in the book are given in euros and are usually only rough estimates. This book is intended primarily for people from England and Wales so comparisons have been with English law. Scottish law is somewhat different. Where the points also apply to Scottish law we have tried, depending on the context, to refer to either UK or British law. The law is intended to be up to date as at 1 January 2005.

The Big Picture

How Many People are Setting up Businesses Abroad? 4
How Many People are Setting up Businesses in Spain? 4
Who is Doing What – and Where? 5
Opportunities – Gaps in the Market 10

01

How Many People are Setting up Businesses Abroad?

The British have always had an interest in travelling to different countries. However, in the distant past, foreign travel was only available to a privileged few. In modern times, particularly since the introduction of low-cost air fares, more and more Britons have ventured outside their own country.

People visit different countries for a wide variety of reasons, but mainly for holidays. There is a natural progression from visiting a country for a one- or two-week vacation to wanting to pack up and go and work there. And from this position it is only a small leap to wanting to start up your own business, especially when the country appears to provide better business opportunities than those found at home, or where the climate and standard of living are seen as being preferable.

Many people have already taken the plunge. It is estimated that 768,000 Britons (1.3 per cent of all 'British' workers) are now working abroad in the EU. In addition to this, it is thought that about 280,000 British people are based in the UK but regularly work overseas – often for extended periods of time. In fact, we are all on the move – there are approximately 17 million workers within the EU who are working in a country that they are not from.

How Many People are Setting up Businesses in Spain?

Over the last couple of years Spain has been among the top 10 countries in the world in terms of attracting foreign investment. Small to medium enterprises generate 61 per cent of the country's turnover and provide work for 65 per cent of the population in most sectors of the economy, apart from those that are naturally served by the larger companies. In 2003, 55.8 per cent of companies were classified as small companies – i.e. having fewer than 50 employees. In 2003 there were 2,139,882 companies registered in total.

Statistics about how many new businesses are set up in Spain every year by foreigners are difficult to obtain although undoubtedly the number has increased dramatically over the last few years. A rough indication of where businesses are being set up by non-Spaniards can be seen from the number of foreigners in each area generally.

Obviously, we need to bear in mind that only a percentage of those living in an area will have set up their own business, as many will be working, studying or retired.

Officially, Madrid has the highest number of foreigners of any area in Spain, with approximately 366,000 non-Spaniards living there. This is followed by Catalonia, which has about 310,000 resident foreigners, and Valencia with 218,000. Andalucia has 178,000 resident foreigners, the Canary Islands has 98,000, while Murcia has in the region of 70,000. In addition, there are many thousands of people who live in Spain without declaring themselves as resident, or who are living or working there illegally. Some estimates suggest that there are as many foreigners living in Spain without permission as there are legally, although this is impossible to verify.

Breaking down these figures into statistics for individual countries gives some indication of where people are setting up businesses. Official figures (again unofficial figures are probably much in excess of this) show that there are 30,664 British people living in Andalucia, 27,638 in the province of Valencia and 11,690 in the Canary Islands. These numbers reflect where the British are buying properties and also where they tend to be setting up businesses. The next three largest groupings of British residents are the Balearic Islands (7,944), Catalonia (6,681), Madrid (4,856) and Murcia (4,856). As before, the number of foreigners in other parts of Spain is fairly insignificant.

Who is Doing What – and Where?

The British and other nationalities have been visiting and buying properties in Spain for several decades. Historically, many people started a business in order to get round restrictions on the ability to work abroad. With Spain's accession to the EU, and the free flow of citizens within the EU, this motive has been superseded by people's desire to establish a business in Spain as a way of taking control and improving their lifestyle. As a consequence, a wide variety of businesses have been set up in Spain over the years – some targeted at the British market and others at a wider market.

Bars and Restaurants

Traditionally, the majority of new small-scale foreign business have been bars and restaurants aimed at the foreign holiday market. In fact, in some areas it is now difficult to find a traditional Spanish bar because of the influx of foreign people opening up bars. Many people fail in the first year. This is often because they have never run a bar or restaurant in the UK – let alone such a business abroad, with all the differences and complications that this entails. One false assumption that people make is that just because they have been to many bars and restaurants over their years they will know how to run a successful bar or restaurant themselves. Sadly, people can learn very quickly how difficult running a business of this kind can be. For more information about running these types of business, see 'Bars', p.35, and 'Restaurants', p.38.

For the most part, these types of business have been set up in the popular holiday regions – particularly the Costa del Sol and the Costa Blanca – but as competition in these parts of the country has dramatically increased over the years, people have now started to look for new areas, both in terms of the 'next big tourist area' or by concentrating on a different kind of business that targets a more select number of clientele.

Property

After bars and restaurants, the holiday accommodation business is the next top industry. Over the last few years there has been an explosion of foreigners investing in property abroad – mainly in order to obtain income from renting out these properties. Approximately 1.5 million homes in Spain are owned by foreigners, yet 80 per cent of these owners do not live in their Spanish property. Owning property abroad is often seen as an easy way of making your money work for you, especially when traditional investments such as shares are not performing as well as expected. Spain has in the region of 70 million visitors per year, making it the second most-visited country after France – and even then it is catching up with France rapidly. This boom means that there is money to be made from property in Spain, and in a wide variety of ways.

As you would expect, all these visitors need somewhere to stay. As more people move away from traditional package holidays in favour of privately rented holiday accommodation there is a large market for renting out properties in Spain – particularly in certain parts of the country. Marketing such properties is now fairly straightforward thanks to the internet. Obviously, buying a property to rent out requires careful thought as the property that you might buy for your own use may be very different from one that you would buy to rent out.

In addition to this, some people over the last few years have decided to build up a portfolio of properties for rental. Sometimes people opt to manage the properties themselves – doing everything from advertising to making the bookings, meeting and greeting the guests and cleaning the properties. In other cases the owners of a property will be too busy to manage it themselves, and will engage a management company to look after the property for them. This, in turn, creates a new business opportunity – that of managing properties for other people by setting up as a management agency.

The average annual cost of owning a property in Spain is in the region of €1,500 and many people who originally just bought a property to use as a holiday home are attracted by the idea of renting it out to holidaymakers as a way of retrieving some or all of this sum. This aim is, in itself, a business opportunity for others if they are willing to take on some of the management. Some of the cost of home ownership is taken up by bills, but a significant amount of this annual expenditure is spent on maintentance and a variety of home improvements and this, too, is a business opportunity for someone.

Once you have bought a property in Spain you will invariably require the services of different people to help you manage your property. This might include using a management company to help you rent the property or a marketing company to help you advertise it. Even if you have no intention of renting it out, you may want somebody to cut the lawn and maintain your pool while you are not at the premises. More significant home improvements, such as buying and installing a new swimming pool, sauna or security system, also present business opportunities.

You may consider getting somebody else to do many of the jobs you would normally do yourself in the UK. This might be because the system or regulations are different or because your language skills are not up to the job. Or it might be because you simply haven't got the time to do it yourself or because you are living too far away. These and other reasons present an opportunity for small businesses to be established to provide such services. Obviously the areas where people are buying properties to rent out and where people set up businesses targeting the rental and holiday accommodation market are those areas where there is the largest number of tourist visitors – traditionally the Costa del Sol and the Costa Blanca. But other parts of the country are also becoming popular, especially along the southern coast of Spain – running all the way down from France to the Portuguese border.

In tourist areas there is also a demand for hotels and bed-and-breakfast accommodation and many people have gone into this area. There is also an increasing number of companies offering package holidays. This is basically providing holiday accommodation, but in a different way to the rental properties. The main difference between renting out a property and running a hotel or a B&B is the necessity of providing food in addition to accommodation, which means that those who have set up such businesses must have a wider range of skills in order to run their business, or else employ staff to take on the additional roles. Most people have started hotel and B&B businesses in the tourist areas, but some have decided that they would rather concentrate on doing something slightly different and in a less competitive area. One downside of this latter approach is that more of the budget will probably have to be used in marketing and attracting people to a less well known part of the country.

Tourist Activities

Simple beach holidays are not as popular as they once were and in the last decade or so there has been an increased demand for tourist activities. This presents a good business opportunity and the number of businesses that target this market has increased to cater for the demand. The traditional activities in this market are car-hire services, local guided tours, excursions to different areas and, of course, nightlife (particularly the nightclubs), which has become famous in certain parts of Spain.

However, as holidays have become more sophisticated over the years, so the demands and tastes of the average holiday-maker have also changed and people are now just as likely to hire a jet ski or windsurfer, or take lessons in scuba diving. Other activity-based business opportunities include flying schools, sailing schools, cycling and walking holidays. In many cases, people now go on holiday with a specific activity in mind. Golf is an obvious example of this in Spain (*see* below).

One of the main advantages that Spain has over similar businesses in the UK when considering these types of activities is the weather. The many hours of sunshine allow people to enjoy an outdoor activity in comfort for much of the year. In addition, they can practise or improve their skills for more of the year too. It is no surprise that many athletes fly to Spain in the winter to carry on training, rather that staying in the UK.

Obviously, these activities need specialist equipment and sometimes specific venues or locations – requiring further businesses to cater for them. People who go on this type of holiday will focus on the activity as the main reason for the holiday, but will also normally require some other forms of entertainment nearby. As you would expect, most of these businesses tend to be based in the busy tourist areas.

Golf

As in other parts of Europe, the number of golf courses has risen in Spain and more are being built. In fact, if you drive along the Costa del Sol you will see signs indicating that it is also the Costa del Golf. With so many people wanting to play golf there is always the opportunity of selling golf-based services, and many people have done exactly that without necessarily setting up their own golf course. As more courses are built, so more businesses selling golfing products and golf tuition are established. No prizes for guessing that these are based in areas that have golf courses within easy access.

Construction

Over the last few years property-building has expanded in Spain and this has naturally brought with it the opportunity for people to set up businesses associated with the boom in construction. As more and more construction takes place – particularly in the Costa del Sol, Costa Blanca and the Costa de la Luz – the construction industry requires a wide variety of businesses that can provide related goods or services. These sorts of businesses include architects' firms that specialize in designing properties suitable for the foreign buyer but that also comply with the Spanish building regulations. Many of the new properties are being built by developers who have their own construction companies, or who sub-contract to just one construction company. However, there is a market for small firms to provide peripheral services such as plumbing, electrics, brick-laying and crane operators. These types of services may be required not only by large companies, but also by those individuals who are having their own property built, rather than buying a standard property from a developer.

Over the last couple of years there has also been an increase in the number of firms offering what might be described as 'secondary construction management'. These are businesses that will send you periodic independent reports on the stage your property has reached in terms of construction, or carry out a survey at the end of the build to make sure that everything is to your specifications without you needing to inspect the property yourself. As in any business, these types of activities are normally best located close to where the construction is taking place – traditionally the Costa del Sol and Costa Blanca, but again you must bear in mind that major construction is now taking place in other areas of Spain and at the moment they are not yet well served by such firms.

Estate Agency

Estate agencies have boomed recently in certain parts of Spain, driven by a fast-growing market and the attraction of higher commissions than those charged in the UK. It is relatively easy to set up an estate agency and in some areas it can sometimes seem like almost everybody has a property to sell. Most people tend to stick to the popular tourist coastal areas, but some people have successfully set up estate agencies to concentrate on more specific types of buildings – city, rural or older properties. There are many niche markets for property and although the number of people buying these more specialized types of property is smaller than those buying the typical holiday apartment on the Costas, it can be more rewarding and interesting than doing what everybody else is doing.

Service Businesses

Many businesses are now in operation offering goods and services to those living in or visiting Spain. The kind of services on offer is extremely varied, ranging from transport companies to poodle parlours. The provision of professional services has increased in Spain over the years. This has happened for two main reasons. Firstly, the number of professionals has generally increased as the country has moved from a predominantly agricultural economy to a more service-orientated economy. Secondly, as more foreigners have moved to Spain so the number of 'specialist' services targeting this new community has increased. It is now far more common to find accountants, IT firms, recruitment agencies, architects, doctors and insurance brokers catering for the many foreigners who live or own property in Spain. Any profession, in fact, that is needed in the UK is likely to be needed in Spain, including English-speaking dentists and doctors, taxi firms and yacht brokers. In addition, native English speakers can usually find work teaching English as a foreign language, either freelance or in a language school. Shops supplying non-Spaniards with goods and services they miss from their home country often thrive. An obvious example is food, and there are many stores selling typically 'British' goods such as Marmite or PG Tips, as well as other goods that are not regularly stocked in Spanish shops.

The Internet

In 2001, 33 per cent of households in Spain owned a computer and 14 per cent had access to the internet. By 2003 this had increased to 43.3 per cent of homes owning a computer, with 25.2 per cent of homes having internet access. This gradual increase in access to the world wide web has opened up new avenues for foreign business. Many people are now realizing that having an internet-based company means that they can continue to have clients in their home country while enjoying the benefits of living in a foreign country. Distribution centres and call centres can be in any country where the service-provisions costs are low, while clients for the business can be found in any country where the prices are high. In fact, thanks to the marvels of global communications, more and more people are discovering that there is no real reason why they shouldn't do their job anywhere – and that they might as well be somewhere with pleasant weather and an agreeable way of life. As technology and mobile communications improve, it is not inconceivable that a successful business could be run from a laptop on the beach anywhere in the world.

There are, however, a whole range of issues that need to be considered when setting up an internet-based company. There is as yet no specific legislation to cover such activities, but it is likely that there will be in the future. In the meantime, anyone starting up a business abroad, even if it is an internet-based business, will have to take into account regulations covering where a company is officially based, and therefore which country's laws apply to such things as working practices, consumer protection and taxes.

Opportunities – Gaps in the Market

So far, the majority of British people who have tried to establish a business in Spain have opened a bar or restaurant in one of the main tourist regions, or invested in a business relating to the property market. Although some people have been successful, this well-trodden path is littered with failures for the simple reason that the market is too crowded. Just as in the UK, there are myriad opportunities for new business ventures in Spain and your chances of success will greatly increase if you avoid what has already been done and offer something fresh and distinctive.

A business is most likely to succeed if there is a gap in the market. It is vital that you carry out an analysis of your chosen area to establish where and what the gaps are – and why. If a certain type of business does not exist then it is important to look for reasons. Is it because nobody has thought of it? Or because people have tried before and failed? Ask around. A little research at an early stage could save you from a costly mistake.

Many people go on holiday to Spain and find that they want to eat or drink something that it is not available. They then have the idea of starting up a business to service that need. This is a common occurrence and can be a good way of spotting a new market. But beware! It is important to do your research to make sure that what you have in mind is viable – or even legal. There is a story of a man who identified the need for a mobile ice cream selling business – he had spotted a gap in the market and lost no time in attempting to exploit it. He bought special bikes and organised storage and ice cream-making facilities. It was only at this late stage that he discovered mobile food-vending in his intended area was prohibited by law. It is obvious, therefore, that you need to do your homework before embarking on a new venture.

A Few Ideas

Most people assume that when they set up a business in Spain they are going to target the market that is served by their own nationality. But there are large numbers of foreigners living in the country who also need businesses to provide them with goods and services. According to the Instituto Nacional de Estadistica (National Institute of Statistics in Spain) there are 1.6 million foreign residents in Spain. Of these, 35 per cent come from the EU, 20 per cent come from Morocco, 10.6 per cent are from Ecuador, 6.5 per cent come from Colombia, 3.5 per cent from Peru, 3.4 per cent from China and 3.3 per cent from Romania. That is a lot of people to target!

When dealing with individual nationalities it is important to understand not only the different languages, but also the different expectations and requirements of people from a different culture. This is one good reason why most people stick with the market they know best – their own nationality – but it is important that you at least consider whether you could provide services to different nationalities as this will broaden the appeal of your business and, as a consequence, your chance of success. And do not forget the domestic market. The man who runs a bar in Spain and who cannot speak Spanish is immediately going to exclude any potential Spanish customers coming into his bar – let alone any other nationalities.

Foreign property investors living or based in Spain are now starting to look elsewhere to buy new properties as the profits that can be made from Spanish properties are diminishing. Specialist estate agencies based in Spain may soon start to spring up, selling properties in nearby countries. At present, the majority of estate agents in Spain sell Spanish properties, but there is an emerging market for properties in countries such as Croatia, Turkey, Bulgaria and Hungary.

During your travels to Spain you might have noticed that the disposal of waste can leave a lot to be desired. In fact, despite the 1998 EU directive on waste disposal, some sources claim that Spain may be 10 years behind other EU countries in their treatment of dangerous waste. Add to this the fact that there is a great deal of construction going on and it certainly seems that there is a market for the provision of waste disposal and also the provision of waste disposal products, to the extent that the Australian government has identified this as a potential market for Australians wishing to do business in Spain.

The IT industry is growing in every country and Spain is no exception. The number of households and businesses with computers and internet access increases every year. E-commerce in Spain is expected to grow dramatically over the next few years and the Spanish government has implemented measures to encourage the use of computers. One potential opportunity for starting a new business is to target the increasing IT use in Spain – whether through the sale of IT hardware or software, through IT support or IT training.

As more and more people leave the UK to go and live in Spain, so the DIY culture will follow. Is there a market for providing DIY and building supplies to those foreigners living in Spain? I remember being in Barcelona with a client who needed to go and have a key cut for his property. He could have explained through a series of signals and facial expressions what he required, but it soon became obvious that, as I happened to be there, it would be useful for me to go along and explain to the locksmith what he needed. If there was a business targeting this type of client they might do well in certain areas. How many of us know what a self-tapping screw is in Spanish? (*Un tornillo que golpea ligeramente del uno mismo.*)

The US Commercial Service at the US Embassy in Spain carried out some research into different types of business in Spain and identified the following 14 sectors of the Spanish market as being the ones that American companies were most likely to be successful in:

- **pollution control and water resources equipment and services**
- **aircraft and parts**
- **medical equipment**
- **computer software**
- **e-commerce**
- **computers and peripherals**
- **telecommunications equipment**
- **telecommunications systems**
- **electric power systems**

- security
- outbound tourism to the US
- franchising
- industrial controls
- architecture/construction/engineering services

These are just some examples of the sorts of gaps there are in the market in Spain. Some may already have been filled by the time you start your business, so it is vitally important that you look very carefully into the market yourself before embarking on a new venture.

Getting to Know Spain

Climate and Geography 16
Economy 19
The Governmental System 20
The Administrative System 21
Spanish Languages 22

02

Most of us have visited Spain at one time or another – normally for pleasure but sometimes for work – and the country can appear hugely familiar. Spanish stereotypes abound, from bullfights and whitewashed houses to olive groves and flamenco guitars, but such cliches tell only a fraction of the story. In reality, Spain is far more complex and more fascinating. It is a large country with much to explore – many aspects of its diverse culture will be largely unknown to many people.

The country has a greater variety of landscapes than anywhere else in western Europe – from deep-green fjords in Galicia through Alpine mountains to hot deserts in eastern Andalucía – and then there are the subtropical islands of the Canaries. It is more mountainous than any other European country except Switzerland, and Madrid, at 650m, is the continent's highest capital. Four official languages are spoken in different parts of the country. The country's history is unique. It has been occupied by Celts, Phoenicians, Romans and Moors and over its long history has gone from superpower status to decline. The Spanish people have gone their own way in food and customs. Lately, Spain has become one of Europe's fastest changing societies. All this gives life here a special richness.

For a quick snap-shot of Spain, see 'Spain at a Glance', p.218.

Climate and Geography

Geographically speaking, Spain is not one single country. If you have ever taken a flight across the country on a clear day you will have some idea of the contrasts as you move from north to south. However, the view from the air, with its flattened perspective, does little justice to how dramatically the landscape can change as you move about the country.

Broadly speaking, mainland Spain's 492,463 sq km can be divided into three distinct geographical and climatic zones: the Atlantic coast, the continental centre of Spain, and the Mediterranean zone.

Atlantic Spain is formed by the regions of Galicia, Asturias and the Basque Country. To the south of these regions lie the Cantabrian mountains, including the Picos de Europa, which do much to create the un-stereotypically Spanish climate of this Atlantic zone. The rain in Spain does not fall mainly on the plain but in these regions. Santander, for example, has rainfall of 54mm in July, the lowest monthly average, rising to 159mm in December, the highest. Temperatures are also the most British-like in the country with an average high of 23°C in August and 13°C over the winter months in A Coruña. Consequently, this area of Spain is the greenest and has some of the most attractive scenery to be found in the country. Inland from the large coastal towns the combination of climate and relatively sparse population provides habitat for some of western Europe's most exotic wildlife. For those willing to look very hard, the Cantabrian mountains will reveal themselves as home to Spain's main colonies of wolves and the remaining few wild bears. This climate also explains why most of Spain's best dairy produce comes from here. Asturias alone has 28 varieties of cheese, some of them excellent.

Central Spain is characterized by a plateau, the not-so-rainy plain, which is 650m above sea level. This plain land (La Meseta) is separated from coastal Spain by various mountain ranges and also contains smaller mountainous regions of its own. The climate of this region is generally dry, with fierce summers and chilly winters. Microclimatic variations can and do occur within this extensive region. For instance, while Madrid bakes at an average 31°C in August, Toledo, barely an hour's drive south, is often two or three degrees hotter still. Conversely Ávila, just northeast of the capital, is a refreshing summer retreat for frazzled city-dwellers. Variations in temperature and rainfall also crop up in some unexpected ways over the course of the year. In late January and February it might be warm and sunny enough to sit out on a Madrid *terraza* during the day, while March and April could send you scurrying indoors for your umbrella and the central heating thermostat.

Winter snowfall can be heavy in the northern part of central Spain, and in the Sierra de Guadarrama, just north of Madrid, the snow is reliable enough for there to be a winter sports season. However, Spain's most dramatic mountain scenery – and best skiing conditions – is to be found in the Sierra Nevada, just south of Granada, which contains the Pico de Mulhacén (3,482m), the mainland's highest peak.

With general rainfall quite low over the year, it is noticeable how even relatively minor rivers can influence the agriculture and landscape. Higher and drier ground, when it is cultivated, is usually reserved for olive terraces, while in valleys around rivers more demanding crops, such as melons, are widely grown. The most obvious effect of water is the existence of Spain's two great wine regions, Rioja and Ribera del Duero, which cluster respectively around the Ebro and Duero rivers.

Mediterranean Spain is usually taken to mean the eastern and southern coastal areas from the French border to the Portuguese. This may not be literally accurate, as towns like Cadiz and Huelva actually face the Atlantic Ocean, but it is the Mediterranean which exerts its benign influence even here.

Beginning at the most northerly part of this expanse of coast, in Catalonia, the differences in climate from central Spain are already quite noticeable. Barcelona has a much higher average rainfall than Madrid and, while the summers are noticeably milder, the air can be humid in July and August. The Catalan **Costa Brava** also periodically feels the effect of the *tramontana* wind, which can go beyond the level of a refreshing breeze.

Heading south, the stretch of land that runs between Tarragona and Alicante, and that includes the **Costa Blanca**, sees winter temperatures rise noticeably and the average rainfall drop by more than half, to somewhere around 300mm per year. This is the beginning of holidaymaker Spain, and with a winter average of around 18°C in Alicante, rising to the low 30s in the summer months, it is not difficult to see why so many refugees from the British rain choose to make their homes here.

South of Alicante the provinces of **Murcia** and **Almería** get hotter still. Here the terrain inland from the coast is naturally quite barren – it was in Almería's desert-like landscape that many 1960s 'spaghetti westerns' were shot. However, new farming techniques, using subterranean water supplies and cultivation under plastic sheeting, have meant that great areas of Murcia and Almería now produce winter vegetables for northern European supermarkets as well as for their own domestic consumption.

The **Costa del Sol**, stretching either side of Málaga in southern Andalucía, has milder winters and steamy summers. Again there are notoriously strong winds which can blow on this coast for days at a time.

Inland **Andalucía** endures summer temperatures unmitigated by *any* form of coastal breeze. The area between Córdoba and Seville, most notably the town of Écija, is fittingly referred to as the Frying Pan of Andalucía and often sees the thermometer climbing to the very high 40s. The sun may be great for the oranges and lemons which line the streets of the historic Andalucian towns, but the essential water is being piped. Indeed, much of rural Andalucía depends on irrigation canals dating back as far as the days of Moorish Spain in order to be able to produce anything from its sun-baked soil. Winters here can be quite delightful, though, with a morning sharpness to the air followed by pleasantly warm afternoons.

The coast between the Straits of Gibraltar and the Portuguese border, the **Costa de la Luz**, has no significant variation in terms of temperature or rainfall, but the wind is more refreshing, and this is a popular area for windsurfers.

The **Balearic Islands** experience weather broadly similar to the corresponding part of the Mediterranean coast. Ibiza, the most southerly of the three main islands, enjoys the best year-round temperatures but pays for it with a generally brown terrain. Menorca, the most northerly, shares the force of the *tramontana* wind with the Costa Brava – the trees grow at a slant on the north of the island and some say the people, too, have a permanent stoop as if battling against the wind. Mallorca, the largest of Las Islas Baleares, exhibits quite significant micro-climatic variation, with annual rainfall in the north of the island some 1,200mm compared to a mere 300–400mm in the south.

Spain's other main island group, the **Canary Islands**, is in a different climate zone. Heat rising from the Sahara meets winds coming off the Atlantic. Both in summer and winter, average maximum temperatures are in the 20s Centigrade. As a rule the more westerly islands are greener but rainfall is generally low, although much higher in the interior of Gran Canaria or Tenerife than on Lanzarote or Fuerteventura. Las Islas Canarias are volcanic in origin, and the price to be paid for the wonderful weather is that the landscape on Lanzarote or Fuerteventura is almost lunar and barren as soon as you move away from the coastal towns.

Away from the temperate north, Spain's weather patterns are extreme. Two weeks relaxing on the beach every year may not give you a true impression of what it is like to work through a Spanish summer. You will soon realize why Spain has traditionally shut up shop for the month of August. No amount of background reading can explain the difference between a dry and a humid heat until you have actually experienced it. On the other hand, unless you are moving to southern Mediterranean Spain, don't fool yourself that you'll never need a woollen jumper again.

For a comparative rainfall and temperature chart in Spain, *see* **References.** Bear in mind, though, that these figures tell only part of the story. Wind, the amount of shelter or lack of it, altitude, daily variation and many other factors can affect how you actually experience the weather of any location.

Economy

Since its entry into the EU some 17 years ago, Spain has been transformed from the poor cousin in Europe to the fastest growing economy in Europe and one of the EU's top five largest economies. Over this period the economy has radically altered and Spain has gone from being mainly agricultural to a modern industrial nation.

This transformation is partly through the support of the EU. During the period 2000–06, Spain expects to have received over €56 billion in EU support – although with the introduction of the 'new' EU members in 2004, the amount that Spain receives after 2004 is likely to reduce.

The population of Spain was estimated as being 40,280,780 in 2004, making it the fifth largest population in western Europe. It has a population density of 83 people per square kilometre, although it is worth remembering that much of the country is totally uninhabited. Age distribution statistics show that Spain is quite a young country, although this is likely to change as the birth rate has slowed down in recent years, so that now Spain has the lowest rate of child births per couple in western Europe, at 1.3 children per couple. Around 21 per cent of the population is under 19 years old, 62 per cent is between 19 and 65 years old and 17 per cent is over 65 years old.

The local currency in Spain is now the euro, which superseded the peseta in 2002. Economic growth in 2003 was 2.9 per cent, while inflation during the same period was 3.1 per cent. Unemployment of the active population in 2003 was 11.4 per cent, which was the highest in western Europe, although the increase in the number of jobs was also the highest in Europe at 1 per cent. The main industries in Spain are textiles and apparel, including footwear, food and beverages, metals and metal manufacturing, chemicals, shipbuilding, automobiles, machine tools and tourism.

Spain currently has no companies among the 100 largest in the world, but does have four companies among the largest in western Europe. Despite this, it is seen as an attractive country for investment, which is demonstrated by the fact that it ranks within the top 10 countries in the world for foreign direct investment. Two-thirds of outside investment into Spain comes from EU countries. Among the many factors that have attracted foreign investors are Spain's decision to join the euro zone, its broad industrial and technological base, good infrastructure, particularly in transport and telecommunications, a highly skilled workforce, low production costs and its close links with the UK and the US. In addition, the fact that Spanish is one of the most widely spoken languages in the world makes it a good initial access point to other Spanish-speaking countries.

The Governmental System

Spain and its regions has had many different rulers and political structures over the years, ranging from the Iberos in about 2000 BC through to the Romans and Muslims. In more recent history, General Franco was the country's dictator until his death in 1975. Modern Spain is a stable parliamentary democracy, with Juan Carlos I as king and head of state.

The country's constitution was introduced in 1978 and created a two-chamber parliamentary democracy. Elections are held every four years with members elected to the Congress of Deputies (*Congreso de los Diputados*, the lower house) on a system of proportional representation and to the Senate (*Senado*) on a first-past-the-post basis. The constitution also provides for a high degree of devolved power for the 17 autonomous regions. The *autonomías*, or regional governments of Catalonia, the Basque country, Galicia and Andalucía, particularly, exercise a high level of control over how these regions are run – greater, for example, than that enjoyed by either the Scottish or Welsh assemblies.

The base of the pyramid of Spanish government is formed by the municipalities (*ayuntamientos*), a system of elected town councils with mayors. Mayors of even quite small villages exercise considerable powers in comparison with comparable British institutions. A village *ayuntamiento* may, for example, choose to institute a dangerous dog register without reference to national or regional law. EU citizens are entitled to vote in municipal elections, providing they are registered (*empadronado*). As might be expected, relatively small, independent parties and groupings often have a large say in the outcome of municipal elections.

Elections in Spain are held every four years. Each of the provinces on mainland Spain elects four senators, while 16 are elected from the three island provinces. The autonomous cities of Ceuta and Melilla elect two senators each. This gives a total of 208 senators. In addition, each autonomous region appoints one senator plus another senator for each million inhabitants in that region.

For several years it has been possible for foreigners who are resident in Spain to vote in the local elections if their home country has signed a bilateral agreement with Spain. Foreigners must register on the electoral roll in order to be able to vote.

The court system consists of a series of layers with the constitutional tribunal having jurisdiction over constitutional issues and supreme tribunal heading a system comprising territorial, provincial, regional, and municipal courts. For more information on the court structure in Spain, *see* 'Legal Stuff', p.212. Most court cases in Spain are appealed at first instance.

The Administrative System

Anyone starting a business in Spain is certain to come across the Spanish administrative system. Administration and red tape can seem like a way of life and can be very frustrating. It is not unusual to queue for hours to see an official, only to be told that you don't have the correct paperwork. You go away, obtain the correct paperwork, queue for hours again, only to be told that you still don't have the correct paperwork. When you ask what the correct paperwork is you will often be given incorrect or incomplete information. When you go to see an official body take a book to read – you are going to need it. For more detailed information on Spanish administration, *see* **Red Tape**.

Town Halls

If you are starting a business in Spain, then the town hall (*ayuntamiento*) is somewhere you will get to know well. The town hall is where you will need to go to pay certain taxes, apply for planning permission, apply for the business opening licence etc. and is one of the main administrative bodies that you will come into contact with when you run a business. It can be a frustrating place – especially for foreigners. Depending on your location your *ayuntamiento* may have somebody who speaks English or it may not. In the areas which are more popular with foreigners, there is sometimes a foreigners' department.

The mayor is called the *alcalde* and is seen as a powerful force in the area. If you know the *alcalde* and get on well with him this can open many doors for you and your business, and can help to cut through red tape and expenses. There are always stories of corrupt *alcaldes* allowing people to achieve things through bribes or special favours.

If you are not used to dealing with foreign officialdom and cannot speak Spanish – and they cannot speak English – it is well worth taking somebody with you to assist; or you could employ the services of a *gestor, see* **Red Tape**, p.132. This can save you hours, days and possibly months of to-ing and fro-ing.

Provincial Authorities

Provincial authorities (*diputación provincial*) are higher than the town hall in terms of the power they wield. The provincial authority deals with consumer complaints, some roads, tourist promotion, cultural activities, sewerage, urban development and various other activities that affect an area wider than that covered by the administration of the town hall.

Regional Authorities

The regional governments operate everything relating to a region – for example, setting out the general plan for construction in the region. The regional authorities have the power to set the level of various taxes – for example, inheritance tax. You must apply to the regional authority for certain things that are not covered by your local *ayuntamiento* or *diputación provincial* – for example, fishing and hunting licences.

National Authorities

National authorities deal with matters on a national level. For example, if you apply for a residence permit then this is done at national level. Work permits are also dealt with at national level.

National authorities are not just based in Madrid. Each province will have representatives of the national authorities based in their province and it is not always necessary to deal with Madrid for everything.

Spanish Languages

Castilian Spanish

¡Hola! is the greeting used by around 400 million people across the Spanish-speaking world, and Spanish is today, with English and Mandarin Chinese, one of the three foremost global languages. In its homeland it is more often known not as *Español* but *Castellano* (Castilian) in acknowledgement of the place where it originated, in northern Castile. It began life as one of several related Latin-based languages in the Christian 'fringe' north of Muslim territory; the oldest Castilian written texts date from the 970s. From there, it spread southwards with the 'reconquest' of Muslim Spain. Centuries of contact also left behind one of the distinctive features of Spanish: its many words of Arabic origin, such as the great many words beginning with al-, from *alfombra* (carpet) or *almohada* (pillow) to *alcalde* (mayor).

Because the language has a known origin, Spaniards have a clear idea, strange to English-speakers, of where the 'best Castilian' is spoken, and indeed throughout Old Castile people, rich and poor, do still generally speak with remarkable clarity. Valladolid is considered to be the home of the 'most correct' Castilian. Further south, street Spanish tends to come in a variety of accents, some much stronger than others: Andalucíans, above all, are notorious for 'swallowing' the ends of words and missing the 's' off plurals.

English is widely taught in Spain nowadays but, even if only for practical purposes (understanding your own bank account, dealing with shopkeepers, officialdom, etc.), anyone living in Spain requires a certain level of proficiency in Spanish. Spaniards are appreciative when they meet someone who does try to communicate in their own language. Fortunately, several features of Spanish make it an easy language to learn. It is a phonetic language, with (unlike English) a simple, rational spelling system so that, once you've learnt the basic rules, you can tell immediately from how a word is spelt how it should be pronounced. Basic Spanish grammar is also perhaps the simplest in all the Latin languages: in everyday conversation questions, for example, are formed not by changes in word order or use of auxiliary verbs but by tone of voice, so that the difference between *tiene mucho dinero* ('he has a lot of money', as a statement) and *¿tiene mucho dinero?* is just one of intonation, which anyone can understand (this is also why the inverted question and exclamation marks are used in written Spanish).

Other Languages

Castilian Spanish is the only language found in every part of Spain, but three others have co-official status in different autonomous communities – Catalan, Galician and Basque, known to those who speak them as Català, Galego and Euskera. Castilian became dominant with the rise of Castile itself as the hub of the Spanish monarchy, and in 1715 Philip V's *Nova Planta* decree imposed it as the sole language of state business.

Spain's linguistic diversity is an expression of its cultural diversity which makes the country a mosaic and means that, culturally, Catalans, Castilians, Asturians, Basques, Galicians and Andalucíans have as many as or more differences than, say English, Scottish, Welsh or Irish people or Mancunians, Devonians and Londoners. Over the centuries the contradictions and tensions between the regions have been expressed through centrifugal and centripetal swings with, at times, greater or lesser degrees of freedom or autonomy for the 'historical regions' and, at others, a greater emphasis on central – and centralized – rule. Franco and his regime, believing Spain to be *'una, grande y libre'* ('one, great and free') leaned heavily towards the latter, suppressing the political autonomy that had been granted to Catalonia during the Second Republic and wiping out the degrees of freedom that had also been awarded to the Basque Country and Galicia during that period. Apart from in the political sphere, this had its expression in Franco's linguistic policy which, quite simply, meant that Catalan, Galician and Basque were banned from all aspects of public life, were not taught in schools and could not be used in the media, either written or spoken, the field of publishing, or the pulpit. It was Franco's hope that by thus strangling these other languages they would die a natural death and Castilian would impose itself. The fact that they survived is proof of their strength as a symbol of the cultural identity of those who speak them. Franco's regime was all-pervasive but behind closed doors many continued speaking their languages as they had always done. Since the return of civil liberties in the 1970s, each of these languages has enjoyed a renaissance that has, in some cases, been spectacular. All are taught in schools, the autonomous political institutions now use them as their language of administration, there are newspapers, television channels and radio stations that use them, and it is now possible to find literature published in these languages.

Catalan (*Català*)

Catalan is spoken by over six million people in Catalonia, Valencia, the Balearics and one corner of France (Roussillon, around Perpignan) – more than speak Danish or Finnish, both official EU languages. Catalan-speakers form the largest linguistic community in Europe without their own state. Catalan is another Latin-based language but, since the founders of Catalonia were from north of the Pyrenees, in some ways it is closer to French than Castilian – although closer still to Provençal, which still just survives in France. In the Reconquista, as Castilian spread south to Andalucía, Catalan was taken down the Mediterranean coast and to the islands. Again, it is not hard to learn. It has a less 'melodic' sound than most Latin languages, but Catalan phonetics are actually easier for English-speakers than Spanish sounds: the Catalan 'j' has a 'zh' sound like a French 'j', instead of the guttural Castilian *jota* in Juan.

Catalan was the main language of the Crown of Aragon for most of its history; its decline began under the Habsburgs, but even after 1715 it remained the main spoken language in its home areas. Unlike Galician or Basque – or Welsh, for that matter – it has never been relegated to being a 'mountain language', associated only with country people. Catalan's greatest revival came between the mid-19th-century *Renaixença* (rebirth) and the Civil War, which made Franco's subsequent cultural blitzkrieg all the more bitterly resented.

The degree to which Catalan has reasserted itself varies from region to region. In Catalonia itself it has effectively been reinstated as the primary language of public life, including education. In small towns and the countryside it is the main everyday language, too, but Barcelona and its suburbs are still around 50 per cent Spanish-speaking. In the tourist-dominated Balearics, some would say English or German are as common as Catalan or Spanish, but Menorca and inland Mallorca are actually just as Catalan-speaking as rural Catalonia; on Ibiza and the Mallorcan coast, Spanish comes more to the fore. The Valencian region is more bilingual, but still with variations, Castellón being more Catalan-speaking than Alicante. If you move to a Catalan village, learning some Catalan will be as important as learning Castilian is elsewhere; to live and work in Barcelona, you need to be able to understand, and to a lesser extent use, both. Most road and information signs are also in Catalan, as are official forms.

Galician (*Galego*)

This language can sound (and look) like a hybrid of Castilian and Portuguese, but it is a language in its own right, and actually the older parent of modern Portuguese. It is a Latin-based language, and until the 13th century enjoyed comparable status in the northern Christian kingdoms with Castilian, but fell back to second place long before Catalan declined in its territories. However, because Galicia has been poor and rural, producing emigrants rather than drawing in Spanish-speakers, Galego has remained the first language of most of its people, above all in Galicia's countless villages. Galicia too had a cultural revival pre-1936, only with less impact than those of the Catalans and Basques. Since 1980 the regional government has overseen a relatively modest restoration of the language, and many place names have been converted back to Galego from Castilian forms.

Galicians speak Castilian with a musical lilt, due to the influence of their own language, and at times it can be difficult to tell which of the two they are speaking. For anyone with some understanding of Castilian, though, Galego should not be too difficult to grasp in conversation. Galicians are traditionally unassertive nationalists, but, again, if you live in any small community in Galicia you will have closer contact with people if you can handle the local language.

Basque (*Euskera*)

Euskera is spoken by nearly a million people in the three main Basque provinces of Vizcaya, Guipúzcoa and Álava and in neighbouring Navarra, and by some 80,000 more in the French Basque country. No contact with another language prepares you for Basque: decades of study have failed to establish clear links between it and any other living language. It is unquestionably the oldest in Europe. The language – and the Basques themselves – were already described as 'ancient' by the Romans. Basque is a language that combines single words without change of form to express compound ideas (an agglutinating language; other examples are Finnish and Hungarian). This means that instead of prepositions and other parts of speech, it has suffixes that are added on to stem-words: thus, from Bilbo (Bilbao), you can have Bilbon ('in Bilbao'), Bilbo'ko ('from Bilbao') and Bilbo'koa ('to Bilbao'), but there are many more suffixes and combinations, permitting the creation of single words of terrifying complexity. The great Bilbao-born philosopher Unamuno, a Basque-speaker in his youth, later abandoned it, saying that agglutinating languages could not express complex thought, but this has, of course, been hotly contested.

Until the 19th-century nationalist revival, Basque mainly functioned only as an oral language. It was also split into seven dialects, and the form now taught in schools, called Euskera batua, is a deliberately created unified version that some older Basques find artificial. Learning Basque is of a different order of difficulty from learning any of the Latin languages. The Basque government too has programmes to support the language, but they have had less impact on everyday usage than the Catalan equivalents. In Basque towns and villages, though, new arrivals will still find they need to make at least some effort with Euskera if they wish to integrate.

Getting Around

* note that no Galician cities actually have a metro system.

English	Castilian	Catalan	Galician	Basque
Train	Tren	Tren	Trem, Comboio/ *Tren, Convoio*	Tren
Bus	Autobús	Autobús	Bus, Linha/*Liña*	Autobus
Underground	Metro	Metro	Metro*	Metro
Airport	Aeropuerto	Aeroport	Aeroporto	Aireportu
Train station	Estación de tren /de ferrocarril	Estació de tren	Estaçom/ *Estación* do trem/*tren*	Trengeltoki
Bus station	Estación de autobús	Estació de autobusos	Estaçom/ *Estación* dos autobuses	Autobusgeltoki
Underground station	Estación de metro	Estació de metro	Estaçom/ *Estación* do metro*	Metrogeltoki
Departure	Salida	Sortida	Saídas	Irteera
Arrival	Llegada	Arribada	Chegadas	Etorrera
Car rental	Alquiler de coches	Lloguer de cotxes	Agência/*Axencia* de aluguer de autos	Berebilak alokatzeko ajentzia
Parking	Parking/ Aparcamiento	Aparcament	Estacionamento, Aparcadoiro	Aparkalekua
Hotel	Hotel	Hotel	Hotel	Ostatu

General Terms

English	Castilian	Catalan	Galician	Basque
Hello	Hola	Hola	Olá	Kaixo
Good morning	Buenos días	Bon dia	Bom dia/*Bons dias* Bo día/*Bos días*	Egun on
Good afternoon	Buenas tardes	Bona tarda	Boa tarde/*Boas tardes*	Arratsalde on

English	Castilian	Catalan	Galician	Basque
Good evening	Buenas tardes/noches	Bon vespre/ Bona tarda	Boa noite/*Boas noites*	Arratsalde on
Goodbye	Adiós	Adéu	Adeus/*Abur*	Agur
Goodnight	Buenas noches	Bona nit	Boa noite/*Boas noites*	Gau on/Gabon
See you	Hasta Luego/ Hasta la vista	Fins desprès	Até logo/Até mais ver/*Ata logo*/*Ata máis ver*	Gero arte
See you tomorrow	Hasta mañana	Fins demà	Até amanha/ *Ata mañá*	Bihar arte
I am/My name is	Yo soy/Me llamo...	Jo sóc.../Em dic...	Eu sou...	(your name) ... dut izena
What is your name?	¿Cómo se llama?/ ¿Cómo te llamas?	Com et dius?	Cal é o seu nome?	Zein da zuri izena?
How are you?	¿Cómo estás? Or (more formal) ¿Cómo está usted?	Com estàs? Or (more formal) Com està vostè?	Como te encontras? Or (more formal) Como se encontra?	Zer moduz zaude?
Fine/Good, thanks	Muy bien, gracias	Molt bé, graciès	Bem, graças/ *Ben, gracias*	Ederki, eskerrik asko
Not well/Bad	Mal	Malament	Mal	Gaizki
Okay/so-so	Así así	Així-així	Vou indo	Erdipurdl
Please	Por favor	Si us plau	Se fai o favor	Mesedez/Arren
Thank you	Gracias	Gràcies	Graças/*Gracias*	Eskerrik asko
Thank you very much	Muchas/ Muchísimas gracias	Moltes/ Moltíssemes gràcies	Gracinhas/ *Graciñas*	Eskerrik asko
You're welcome	De nada	De res	Nom tem de quê /*Non ten de que*	Ez horregatik
Yes	Sí	Sí	Si	Bai
No	No	No	Nom/Non	Ez
Why...?	¿Por qué?	Perqué...?	Por qué...?	Zergatik?
How...?	¿Cómo...	Com...?	Como...?	Nola?
When...?	¿Cuándo...?	Quan...?	Cando...?	Noiz?
What...?	¿Qué...?	Qué...?	Que...?	Zer?
Where...?	¿Dónde...?	On...?	Onde...?	Non?
How much is...?	¿Cuánto es...?	Quant és...?	Canto é...?	Zenbat?
I don't understand	No entiendo	No ho entenc	Nom entendo/ Non entendo	Ez dut ulertzen
Do you speak English?	¿Hablas/Habla usted inglés?	Parles anglès?	Fala o inglês/inglés?	Hitz egiten al duzu ingelesez?

Numbers

English	Castilian	Catalan	Galician	Basque
1	Uno	U, un (m), una (f)	Un (m), unha (f)	Bat
2	Dos	Dos (m), dues (f)	Dous (m), dúas (f)	Bi
3	Tres	Tres	Tres	Hiru
4	Cuatro	Quatre	Catro	Lau

English	Castilian	Catalan	Galician	Basque
5	Cinco	Cinc	Cinco	Bost
6	Seis	Sis	Seis	Sei
7	Siete	Set	Sete	Zazpi
8	Ocho	Vuit	Oito	Zortzi
9	Nueve	Nou	Nove	Bederatzi
10	Diez	Deu	Dez	Hamar
11	Once	Onze	Onze/*Once*	hamaika
12	Doce	Dotze	Doze/*Doce*	hamabi
13	Trece	Tretze	Treze/*Trece*	hamahiru
14	Catorce	Catorze	Catorze/*Catorce*	hamalau
15	Quince	Quinze	Quinze/*Quince*	hamabost
16	Dieciséis	Setze	Dezasseis/ *Dezaseis*	hamasei
17	Diecisiete	Disset	Dezassete/ *Dezasete*	hamazazpi
18	Dieciocho	Divuit	Dezaoito	hemezortzi
19	Diecinueve	Dinou	Dezanove	hemeretzi
20	Veinte	Vint	Vinte	hogei
21	Veintiuno	Vint-i-un	Vinte e um/ *Vinteún*	hogeita bat
30	Treinta	Trenta	Trinta	hogeita hamar
40	Cuarenta	Cuaranta	Quarenta/*Corenta*	berrogei
50	Cincuenta	Cinquanta	Cinqüenta/ *Cincuenta*	berrogeita hamar
60	Sesenta	Seixanta	Sessenta/*Sesenta*	hirurogei
70	Setenta	Setanta	Setenta	hirurogeita hamar
80	Ochenta	Vuitanta	Oitenta	laurogei
90	Noventa	Noranta	Noventa	laurogeita hamar
100	Cien	Cent	Cem/*Cen*	ehun
1,000	Mil	Mil	Mil	mila
1,000,000	Un millón	Un milió	Um milhom/ *Un millón*	milioi bat

Days of the Week

English	Castilian	Catalan	Galician	Basque
Monday	Lunes	Dilluns	Segunda feira, Luns	Astelehen
Tuesday	Martes	Dimarts	Terça feira, Martes/*Terza feira, Martes*	Astearte
Wednesday	Miércoles	Dimecres	Quarta feira, Mércores/*Corta feira, Mércores*	Asteazken
Thursday	Jueves	Dijous	Quinta feira, Joves/*Quinta feira, Xoves*	Ostegun
Friday	Viernes	Divendres	Sexta feira, Venres	Ostiral
Saturday	Sábado	Dissabte	Sábado	Larunbat
Sunday	Domingo	Diumenge	Domingo	Igande

Business Ideas

The Brilliant Idea – Eureka! 30
Some Common Ideas – the Pros and Cons 31
Will It Work in Spain? 66
Research 70
Legal Advice 71
Talk to People Who Have Already Done It 72
Your Experience 73
Language Skills 74

03

The Brilliant Idea – Eureka!

For my business partner, it started in the bath – his 'think tank'. He spends about half an hour every morning thinking through the problems of the day and coming up with cunning plans to deal with them. He had been thinking for weeks about ways of developing his legal practice, which at that time (1984) was a large practice dealing with criminal, matrimonial, immigration and civil liberties work in the north of England. It was heavily dependent on the legal aid funding, and he recognised that the writing was on the wall for publicly funded legal work. He was looking to diversify into interesting and potentially profitable work.

The practice had become an early pioneer of computerized legal systems (essential for making a profit out of low-paid legal aid work) and he wanted to use this expertise in another context. He also wanted to use his language skills and continue to travel – he had already been doing immigration work in India, Pakistan and Bangladesh.

And there it was. Help people to buy houses in France and Spain. This would involve travel, language, use of computers to reduce drafting problems when preparing documents in a foreign language, and, above all, it would be interesting and challenging legal work in a new field. Upon that basic idea we have, over the last 20 years, built a multi-million pound business.

Lawyers are infamous for not following their own advice when dealing with their personal affairs – just as cobblers wear shoes with holes and mechanics drive clapped-out cars. But, for once, we did it right. My partner discussed the idea with colleagues, subjected it to a 'reality check', carried out a lot of market research (in England, France and Spain), made financial projections, produced a preliminary business plan and then did further research to make sure that the emerging plan was realistic. At the end of all that we launched the product – slowly and quietly at first, so that we could make our mistakes in (relative) privacy.

Of course, it did not turn out exactly as we had envisaged. Things never do. But we had got the general direction right, foreseen at least some of the problems and – eventually – the business worked.

Since then we have dealt with many clients who have had their own 'Eureka!' moment and who are starting their businesses abroad. This book charts their progress – anonymously, of course. Details have been changed so as to spare embarrassment and preserve confidentiality, but the pages that follow draw on our clients' experiences and the solutions adopted to deal with their problems. And the starting point, especially for clients starting small businesses, is almost always the initial idea.

For larger clients it tends to be different. They will have committees exploring possibilities, which they then narrow down to a shortlist from which they choose, by analysis, a project to follow through. This is not as much fun but, generally, it works rather better. The problem with any Eureka! moment is that the person in the bath can get so carried away with the idea they have generated that they lose all sense of objectivity and the brainwave turns out to be a disaster. Yet the best Eureka! ideas tend to be far more original. I do not believe a committee could come up with ideas such as importing English crisps into southern Spain or setting up an OAP's dating agency in France for instance.

The key to any novel idea is letting your imagination run wild and then being ruthlessly controlled in testing whether the idea will actually work. Such analysis may involve running the idea past other people who know the market and the industry concerned. If you can find someone to do that for free, great – provided they don't steal your idea. If you don't know anyone with the knowledge to help, then seek some professional assistance at this stage. It will not cost a lot and could save you from wasting a lot of money.

However, not all successful businesses are based on novel ideas. Money is to be made by establishing more traditional businesses, so long as they are well run and located in the right part of the country. The next section deals with some tried and tested business areas that have worked for foreigners running their own businesses in Spain.

Some Common Ideas – the Pros and Cons

Bars

The aspiration to open a bar in Spain is probably the most common business idea that people come up with. We've all done it! Sitting in a bar while on holiday, we observe the relaxed demeanour of the barman and soak up the sleepy stillness as sun-drunk customers drift in and out during the afternoon. We think too ourselves: I could do this. And from this brief and partial experience it is all too easy to assume that we know what running a bar in Spain is like.

Bars are close to the heart of Spanish culture. Often you will find people go out to talk business over a drink at the local bar and may spend many hours at a table without buying many drinks. The drinking culture is very different to that in the UK. Spanish bars are open longer for one thing and the Spanish tend to linger over their drinks far more than the British. As a result, Spaniards will probably spend much less on a night out in a bar than their UK counterparts.

Competing with Spanish bars can be difficult as most are run by a family and employ few or no outside staff. Obviously a family-run business of this type has a distinct advantage over businesses employing outside staff because they rely heavily on family members working longer hours than paid workers would put up with, and for much less (if any) pay.

Advantages

One advantage of running a bar in Spain is that most people can do it. There is no special training or qualifications needed and most of us will have a good idea of what we want from a bar and therefore believe we know what other people want. A well managed and popular Spanish bar can also be financially rewarding. Owning a bar, or several bars, has made many people very rich over the years.

In addition, running a bar can be socially rewarding as there is a great interaction with the public. This is particularly so when the bar is more relaxed and a bit quieter and you have more time to talk to customers. Hopefully, you will also have plenty of times when the bar is so busy that your feet hardly have time to touch the ground as you serve one customer with a drink and then move on swiftly to serve the next person. You will be amazed how popular you will become when you run a bar in Spain!

Disadvantages

There are obvious downsides to running a bar. Most important perhaps, is to have a good idea of the many costs involved and to have a realistic idea of how much money the bar will make. Talk to other owners and you may discover that owning a bar is not as profitable as you think. Many bars over the years have failed in Spain simply because they ran out of money. A well managed bar should bring in a reasonable profit but there is huge competition in some areas where there is a saturation of bars for the size of the potential market – particularly outside the tourist season. Eventually this will force out the majority of new bars. It has been estimated that in some areas of Spain about 90 per cent of bars close down within the first year of trading and often within a few months of opening their doors to the public.

And make no mistake about it, running a bar in Spain is hard work – or at least it should be if you are to make it as profitable as you can. There are no set opening hours for Spanish bars and owner-managers will have to work late into the night, night after night – or in fact probably more accurately, well into the morning when the last customer goes home.

The popularity of a bar depends entirely on its atmosphere. Get a good atmosphere and your bar is likely to be busy every night. Create a bad atmosphere and you will be twiddling your thumbs waiting for a customer. Bars can also be vulnerable to fashion in the sense that one week it can be 'in' to go to one bar and the next week it can be fashionable to go to another one. Running a bar is therefore to a certain extent dictated by the fickle whims of the public and any bar owner must continue to evolve the business to cater for the customers' shifting requirements. Do not make the classic mistake of believing that what you want from a bar is what everyone else is going to want too. Often, in fact, the reverse can be true.

Running a bar in a tourist area also depends on the seasons. Undoubtedly most people start to think about the idea of setting up a bar because they have been to Spain when the rest of us go on holiday, and never see what the area is like at different times of the year. In the tourist season the bar can be very busy, but at other times of the year you may have long periods where the income you generate may give you only a small profit or may not even cover your costs. It is difficult therefore to budget and plan for this – especially as the tourist season may last only three months of the year. In addition, people tend to overestimate the number of customers that they will attract in the summer and underestimate how quiet the bar will be in the winter.

When deciding to run a bar in Spain, most people think about the nice part of the industry – dealing with pleasant customers. However, you have also got to appreciate the downside of drinking and be prepared to deal with those people who get so drunk that they cause a problem. At best a very drunk person may put off another customer from returning to your bar – at worst they can cause physical damage to you and/or your property and may put off a large percentage of your customers from returning. You will need to have a plan in place and the resources to deal with such problems.

Working conditions in a bar are not necessarily ideal. The hot, smoky atmosphere can be quite hard to endure if you are in it for most of the day. If you are running your bar with a partner or spouse then this sort of working environment, coupled with the pressure to make your business work under intense competition, can put a strain on a relationship to the extent that your dream of running a bar together in a warm country may turn into a nightmare. This in turn can start to reflect on the way that you treat customers, which in turn will affect your profitability. It is therefore very important that you have a frank discussion with your partner before embarking on such a project and that you both understand that there will be some difficult times.

One danger of running a bar in the UK is the temptation to have a quick drink with the locals while you are working. For some reason the temptation is even greater in Spain and some British bar owners in Spain have drunk away most of their profits. This tends to start off slowly and then, as the pressure on the business increases, the drinking also increases. Make sure that you don't fall into this trap, otherwise you will never make any money. You are running the bar as a business – if you want to run a bar because you like drinking, it may be wiser to do something else and use your wages to buy a drink.

Finally, there is an understandable temptation to open a bar that will attract customers of your own nationality. Though there are good reasons why you would do this, it does significantly reduce the number of potential customers out of season. However, even without targeting your own nationality it can be difficult to entice the Spanish into a bar run by a foreigner – especially one who doesn't even speak the language.

Restaurants

Very similar comments apply to restaurants as apply to bars. Again, eating out is part of the Spanish culture and it is very affordable. Competition can be fierce and outside of the tourist season, customers can be thin on the ground.

The Spanish are proud of their food with good reason and tend to go out to restaurants that serve traditional Spanish cuisine. A foreigner will therefore find it difficult to penetrate the Spanish end of the market. Having said that, international cuisine is becoming increasingly popular with Spaniards, especially in the cities, and opportunities for innovative restauranteurs do exist. But if you are providing the sort of basic food that some tourists may want, then it is unlikely that the Spanish will be attracted to your business.

It is also worth remembering that many people who go on holiday to Spain are on all-inclusive package holidays – which means that they will have their food provided for them. In addition, as the property market in Spain has grown, more people are renting out properties to tourists and many people now opt for self-catering holidays. This means that where previously they would have gone out to eat every night, they may now eat out only a couple of times during their holiday and may cook for themselves during the rest of their stay. Maybe a shop aimed at the self-catering crowd would be a good idea?

Restaurants in Spain are graded into five categories, similar to the star system of grading in other countries, with a five-fork restaurant being the best.

Camping and Caravans

An increasing number of people go on camping and caravanning holidays to Spain. Many, having decided to move to Spain, then spend a year travelling around the country by caravan before they commit to a particular area. This is a sensible decision which ensures that they are truly happy with the location before they spend their hard-earned money on property – assuming obviously that they can still afford to buy the property after their travelling, with property prices rising sharply in recent years. With so many people going on holiday to Spain, and so many people looking to cut costs while doing so, there are potential opportunities for running camping and caravan sites.

Owning a camping or caravanning site requires little in the way of stock and, depending on the level of services that you decide to provide, may not require huge amounts of investment. In fact, once you have bought the site, set up some basic amenities and started your advertising you should be pretty much up and running.

The kind of services that you decide to offer will determine what rating you are likely to get for your site and therefore the level of fees that you will be able to charge. The rating system divides sites into one of four categories – luxury (*lujo*), category one (*primera categoria*), category two (*segunda categoria*) and category three (*tercera categoria*). Classifications do change slightly from area to area, so it is important to check with the local authority to make sure that you are providing the correct facilities to achieve the classification that you want. All camp sites, whatever their rating, must provide basic amenities such as safe drinking water, clean toilets and adequate washing facilities. They should also provide a way of sending and receiving letters, and a safety deposit box to store valuables. Beyond that, the difference between the different categories follows general rules.

Luxury camp sites must have at least 90 square metres per plot, one toilet for every 7 plots, a grocery store, swimming pool and a restaurant. They are also likely to have a central lounge area with colour television, a separate bar and games rooms and may have other facilities including a hairdresser and boutique, sports and play areas and even a cinema.

Category One sites must have at least 70 square metres per plot and one toilet for every eight plots. They generally have a restaurant or cafeteria, games room and a grocery store. Many, but not all, have swimming pools. Category Two sites offer 60 square metres per plot, have one toilet for every 10 plots and need only have a bar any grocery store. The lowest rating, Category Three, sites should have 55 square metres per plot and one toilet for every 12 plots. Even Category Three sites will usually have a bar.

The charge for your customers can be per person, per caravan or per tent. You should probably post the method of charging and your prices at the entrance to the site so that people have a good idea before they arrive at reception. You will obviously have to work out what sort of occupancy rate you are likely to achieve and how much you can charge, which in turn will provide you with the income that you are likely to generate. For working out factors such as these, *see* 'Your Business Plan', p.81.

Advantages

One of the advantages of running a camp site is that much of your work will be outdoors, which for many people makes a pleasant change from the humdrum routine of office work. In addition, the opportunity of constantly meeting new people is a side of the business that many people find attractive.

Because running a camping or caravan site is seasonal, this can be an advantage. The off season can be your time to renovate and repair the site and carry out all those little jobs that you meant to do during the peak season. Unless you do this, your site will fall into disrepair and people will stop coming. You could even take the opportunity of improving the camp site in order to encourage new customers and therefore improve your business for the following season. Alternatively, you can use the off season to run a different type of business that will bring in an income when the site is closed.

Disadvantages

The downside of running this sort of business is that it is hard work and very seasonal. I once knew somebody who ran a caravan site in the UK and she had long periods where there was virtually no income coming in – in fact the site closed down for months at a time. You must take this into consideration when drawing up your budget and keep some money back to live on during the 'off' season. Obviously the season in Spain is longer than it is in the UK, but the same principles apply.

In addition, you must be prepared to work hard when everyone around you is relaxing. You are unlikely to be able to take a holiday during the peak holiday season and will be at your most stretched when other people are taking it easy. This is no mean feat and cleaning out a suite of blocked toilets while the rest of the world appears to be relaxing by your swimming pool can play havoc with a camp site owner's peace of mind! As a camp site owner, your job is to make sure that the campers on your site have as stress-free time as possible – this task is likely to mean that your own stress monitor can hit the roof unless you are prepared for the work involved and go about it with a happy heart.

Further details of camping and caravanning can be found on the website of the Spanish Federation of Camping and Caravanning (*Federación Española de Empresarios de Camping y C.V.*); **www.fedcamping.com**.

Advertising

You will have to budget for advertising your site – for more information on advertising, *see* p.127. Registering your camp site with various organisations that draw up lists of approved camp sites is also a good idea. For this, however, you will need to be prepared to deal with inspectors scrutinizing your site. Such inspectors are often retired people and take their jobs very seriously. They will measure the toilets and showers, test the temperature of the pool, pace out the plot size and want to see everything from the kitchens and communal areas to the waste disposal facilities.

Among the Spanish organisations that you can register with are the Federación Española de Empresarios de Camping y C.V. and the Real Automóvil Club de Espana (RACE). The latter is the Spanish equivalent of the RAC or AA and publishes a guide to camping in Spain every year (*Guia Iberica de Campings*). The Spanish National Tourist Office (SNTO) also publishes a map every year showing the location of caravan and camping sites throughout Spain. You may also want to register with foreign organisations or even dedicated websites aimed at providing lists for such things as family-friendly camp sites. In addition to this, advertising in a camping or caravan club can be a good idea, as can advertising in the numerous specialist camping and caravan magazines. Registration with the Spanish Tourist Office (Turespana) is also very worthwhile as they publish free guides with details of all official camp sites.

Location

It is vital that you give some thought to the location of the camping or caravan site – as they say: 'Location, location, location'. This is important for two reasons – marketing and obtaining new customers, and also for any legal requirements.

Where Customers Want You to be Located vs Where You Want to Live

This type of business, like many, is very location-orientated. Most camping and caravan sites are on the coast in the tourist areas – for obvious reasons. It is important to have a location that customers wish to visit and which is in pleasant surroundings – after all that is the main thrust of what people are looking for in choosing a camping or caravan site. It sounds obvious but is worth saying nevertheless – if you set up a camp site in an area where people do not want to stay, then you will have no business. It is likely that you will be living on or near to the site that you are going to be running so you will need to find somewhere not only where the business is going to flourish, but also where you wish to live. These two priorities often do not match up exactly and there will have to be a compromise of some sort. The next question is where the compromise will be. If you compromise on the location that you wish to live in, then you will not enjoy life as much as you would do if you had bought in an area where you wanted to live. If you compromise on the location of the plot, then you are automatically reducing the chances of success. This is a difficult juggling act but is one of the most important decisions that you will make when setting up this type of business as it will have an effect on you for years to come.

Legal Requirements of Location

In addition to the practical implications of location, there may also be legal requirements that have an impact on the location of the site. It is important to investigate the local authority requirements with regard to camp sites as it may not be possible to set up a site anywhere. For example, you may not be allowed to set up a site in an area that is liable to flooding in heavy rain. This actually makes sense (you don't want the customers getting wet feet during high rains), but there are more serious reasons for this – the safety of your customers would be affected if they are sleeping in a tent and there is a sudden flood. The local authorities are also likely to have rules and regulations with regard to the proximity of sites to certain areas such as factories or areas of outstanding beauty.

Permission to run a camp site must be obtained before you open for business. Permission is granted by the local authorities and you will need to have your site inspected before the final go-ahead can be given. The inspectors will have a look at the site to make sure it complies with the relevant regulations. These include health and safety, water and sanitation, waste disposal and any other relevant regulations. Once you have obtained the permission, you have to make sure that you continue to comply with the regulations. You must also keep the authorities informed of changes to the site or to your opening dates.

Bed and Breakfasts

Many people like the idea of moving to Spain and setting up a bed-and-breakfast business. This kind of business is unlikely to make your fortune, but many people enjoy it, despite the hard work.

Bed and breakfasts tend to be located in a more rural setting and are often converted from farms and *fincas* into B&B-type accommodation. For many people, the main advantage of this type of business is that it allows them to live in beautiful surroundings in a property that they might otherwise not be able to afford.

As with restaurants, bars and camp sites, the accommodation market in Spain, including B&Bs, is very seasonal. You will make more money in the peak season and will make very little money in the quieter months. There may be ways of increasing your income during the off season and one way to do this is by doing deals. One B&B, for example, is next to a horse-riding school. The owner of the B&B has come to an arrangement with the owner of the riding school that everybody who goes to the school stays at the B&B at favourable rates. This deal suits the owner of the B&B, as it brings in extra guests during the year, and it also suits the owner of the riding school, as it is an extra he can offer to his customers. It also suits the customers, as they have the accommodation organised at a cheaper rate. Alternatively, some owners run 'schools' out of season, offering anything from writing courses to 'art weeks'. These activities, of course, require the owners to have the necessary skills themselves or be able to employ teachers to run the courses for them.

If you are setting up a B&B in a more rural setting then it is important to look into the local regulations regarding accommodation. Up-to-date information on the different areas can be found at **www.toprural.com**.

Hotels

An increasing number of 'foreigners' are buying or running hotels in Spain. With the large number of foreign visitors this can make sense as the guests can converse with the owner in their own language. More importantly, the owner of the hotel will understand the mentality of his own nationality and is therefore more likely to provide the level and kind of service that his guests require.

There are a surprising number of Spanish hotels available for sale at any one time. When buying a hotel you should try, if possible, to buy both the hotel business and the building, as often these two are separate. If you do not buy the building you are still going to have to make improvements over the years to keep up the standard for the guests and not owning the building means you are effectively renovating a property for somebody else's benefit. In addition, if you own the property and property values go up – as they have over the last few years – you are going to have the benefit of some capital appreciation.

Hotel sizes obviously vary – from those with only a few rooms to those with hundreds of beds. Size is a major factor in the value of a hotel, but there are other factors including the state of repair, reputation, location, distance from airports and so on. Although it can be difficult, it is important that you try to obtain some sort of valuation on the property.

Buying a hotel need not be as expensive as you would imagine, although the bigger and more luxurious they are, the more expensive they become. Whatever the size of a hotel, you are certain to need substantial cash reserves at some point. A hotel that is not well maintained soon becomes an empty hotel with no guests. It is of vital importance that you periodically review the maintenance of the building in order to make sure that you are not falling short of the standards expected. You must also draw up a very careful budget, which should include an annual maintenance cost.

A good way of attracting guests is to enter into a deal with a package holiday company. The contract will guarantee a certain volume of bed nights each year and will give you a degree of financial stability because you will know how much revenue you can count on in advance. However, you do need to be careful. Too many hotel owners have relied on the volume of guests from package holiday companies only to find that one year this source of income unexpectedly dries up leaving them to make up the difference from other introductions.

Running a hotel is one industry where you simply cannot operate without staff. Finding staff is not difficult. However, finding good staff who will look after your clients in a way you would expect can be harder. How often have you been to a hotel where just one member of staff has ruined your stay? A good hotel manager will transform your hotel. Remember that many of the staff at hotels in Spain are temporary and stay only for the peak season.

One of the main things to think about when running a hotel is the degree of competition. If you are in one of the tourist areas of Spain then there is huge competition from other hotels. There is also a huge market. In the summer months you are unlikely to have a problem with unoccupied rooms, but in the quiet season you need to be thinking about what makes you different and why somebody would go to your hotel rather than the one next door. You may need to think what else you can do to supplement income during the off season. One option could be to hold conferences and courses at your hotel.

Having a golf course and leisure facilities is a major bonus for a hotel and means that you are more likely to be able to attract visitors. Golfers wish to play at different times of the year from the rest of us non-golfers, which means that if your hotel is based next to a golf course – or even better has a golf course in its grounds – then it is much more likely to attract visitors outside peak times.

The Hotel Federation of Spain (*Federación de Hosterleria*) is the trade organisation for hotels in Spain and is a useful source of information. Membership of this organisation is not compulsory but is highly recommended. For details, *see* 'Contacts', p.220.

Registering your hotel with tourist and hotel guides is an excellent way of trying to attract guests. Tourist and hotel guides have been traditionally available in leaflets and books, but increasingly there are web-based guides. Turespana publishes a guide each year listing all the hotels in Spain. There are numerous other guides – the most popular being *Hoteles y Restaurantes de España* and the *Michelin Red Guide España y Portugal*.

In order to run a hotel you will need an authorization from the town hall (*ayuntamiento*). The authorization is called the *autorización de centros hoteleros*. The documentation that you will need to present to the *ayuntamiento* to obtain the *autorización de hoteleros* will vary from *ayuntamiento* to *ayuntamiento*. However, the typical requirements are:

- **proof that the property is structurally safe**
- **a fire certificate confirming that the correct fire measures and procedures are in place**
- **title deeds (*escritura*) to the property**
- **floor plan of the building**
- **business plan for the venture (*see* 'Your Business Plan', p.81)**
- **confirmation of the type of accommodation that will be offered by the hotel**
- **confirmation of the prices that you intend to charge**
- **details of waste disposal facilities at the hotel**

The *ayuntamiento* will wish to inspect the hotel to make sure that it is suitable for guests and that it meets certain quality standards.

The quality of hotels is classified through the star (*estrella*) system – with one star (*una estrella*) establishments offering basic accommodation and five star (*cinco estrellas*) hotels offering luxury facilities. There is also a separate five star plus rating known as Five Star GL (*cinco estrellas GL*), where 'GL' stands for '*gran lujo*' or 'high luxury'.

The rates that hotels can charge during different seasons are fixed between a maximum and a minimum according to the quality of the hotel.

A hotel conforms to the standard type of accommodation that you normally associate with a hotel, but a *hotel residencia* is a hotel without a restaurant.

When you have guests staying at your hotel, it is a legal requirement that they produce an official form of identity such as a passport or an identity card. Your guests must also fill out a registration form. As the owner of a hotel you must also have a complaints book available to guests – but of course you won't be needing that, as you will be doing such a good job that you won't have any complaints!

Shops

Holidaymakers to Spain are increasingly opting for self-catering accommodation. On previous visits, these people would have eaten out every night of their holiday but now they have the choice of eating back at their base. One possibility is therefore to open shops that cater specifically for this type of visitor. Certainly if you already have experience of running a shop in the UK, this can seem an obvious business to start in Spain – after all, the business is fundamentally the same but in more congenial surroundings.

As in any area of business, you need to find the type of shop that will have sufficient demand but which will also differentiate you from the big chains, who have the benefit of greater choice and the ability to reduce prices through bulk-buying in a way that the small independent shop has no hope of doing. As a small business, you do not (at least to start with) stand a chance of competing with the larger chains in terms of cost and diversity of products. However, small businesses can outdo the larger shops in a variety of ways and it is important to think about how you are going to do this. Some shops offer a very personal service to their customers – making them feel so special that going to a larger shop simply doesn't feel the same afterwards. Other shops provide goods that are very individual or specialized and therefore cannot be bought from the larger

Things you miss

After 5 years in Madrid I was made redundant and had to consider developing a new career. I had noticed how difficult it was to get traditional British foods and saw an opportunity to provide British expats with items such as Bisto gravy, Branston Pickle, crumpets etc.

A small shop selling Spanish groceries came on the market and I felt that this would be a good vehicle to get started. By Christmas I was ready to introduce the British products, but by then I had a sense of loyalty to my local customers and decided to sell a mixture of both Spanish and British products.

The initial reaction was very positive. Publicity and word of mouth is vital to any new business so I set up a website, placed adverts in the English language magazines and by good fortune my business was featured on a local television channel.

The shop has been going a year now and it has been quite a challenge and my advice for people wanting to start a retail business would be to shop around for suppliers and be flexible. If you are convinced that your idea is a winner, then find yourself a decent accountant to handle your taxes and the local bureaucracy, and go ahead!

Suzanne Chaplin, The Things You Miss, Juan de Austria 11, 28010 Madrid
0034 91 447 0785
www.thethingsyoumiss.com <http://www.thethingsyoumiss.com>

shops. Alternatively, you might try to create an unusual atmosphere, which the customers like and which cannot be recreated on a larger scale. Any prospective shop owner will need to give this careful thought, and the business will need planning around the conclusions that are reached. Find your niche and make it work. It is vital to do some sort of market research – not everybody will appreciate your idea and you may put people off if your shop is *too* different. You need to identify who you are targeting and what exactly they want.

Running a shop means that the opening hours are relatively civilized – or certainly are compared to running a bar. However, the opening hours will be different from the UK. The larger department stores will generally be open 10am–8pm Monday to Saturday, and sometimes open on Sundays. Smaller shops will tend to follow similar hours but unless you have shifts of staff then you are likely to close for a couple of hours during the day (typically 2–4pm) – after all, working 10 hours in a row, six days a week, is a long time (and this doesn't even take into account the time spent buying stock, doing the paper-work, working on advertising and all those other things that need doing). Shop trading hours are fully liberalized, giving you great freedom as to when you wish to open, the only exception being Sundays and national holidays, when opening hours are restricted. Your customers' requirements are likely to dictate the hours that you will work for most of the year. In holiday areas shops are likely to stay open past 10pm.

The Spanish tend to spend a large percentage of their income on food, drink and tobacco compared with other EU countries. There has also been a shift away from the traditional food consumed by the Spaniards in favour of a more international cuisine. Processed and ready-made meals are more in demand as more women go out to work and people's lives become busier. This, together with the buoyant economy, has meant that the Spanish retail market is pros-pering and provides great opportunities for starting up a new business.

Spanish tastes can be quite different from those in the UK and it would be too easy to assume that because something sells well in the UK that it will also be popular in Spain. It is therefore essential that you identify whom you are going to target, and to find out whether the sorts of products you will be selling will be popular in Spain. Bear in mind that the Spanish are very sensitive to quality and will not put up with poor-quality goods, despite the fact that they are quite cost-conscious when it comes to shopping.

IT

As elsewhere in Europe, Spain is increasingly IT literate with 43.3 per cent of households owning a computer and 25.2 per cent of homes having internet access. As a point of comparison, this is some way behind the UK where 54 per cent of households own a computer and 52 per cent of homes have internet access. Spain was one of the first countries to have high-end broadband wireless technology, following France, Ireland and the UK. There are no signs that this area is in decline and the figures are expected to increase further over the next few years – home-computer ownership increased by nearly 50 per cent between 2001 and 2003. In fact, the IT industry is now so progressive in the south of Spain that there are comparisons between the Costa del Sol and California to the extent that it is has been described as the California of Europe.

Assuming you have the relevant knowledge and experience already, there is considerable scope for running a business providing services related to IT. As increasing numbers of people want computers, more people will need to buy computers and the associated peripherals including software, printers, scanners and extra memory. There will also be the need to provide such services as fixing and installing computers and internet access for those people who are less technologically aware than you are.

This is one area where you have to be very clear about whom you are targeting with your business. If you decide to target the expat community then you can safely assume that the computers that they will need or already have will have the operating system and programs in English. However, just targeting the expat community will severely limit your number of potential clients. If you can also target the Spanish-speaking community you will significantly increase your potential client base, but you will need to be able to speak technical Spanish. If anyone has ever changed the language settings on your mobile phone, you will know how frustrating it is to deal with a device that you know well but cannot operate because of lack of language skills.

Programming

Programming can really be done from anywhere in the world and is not necessarily dependent on where the customer is based – although being able to visit the customer and speak to them about what they want is an advantage. However, when it comes to installing specialist programs you will often need to be at the customer's property – although again this can be done remotely. As technology progresses, IT work can increasingly be carried out without having to be 'on site'. It is therefore certainly possible to set up a computer programming business in Spain and deal with customers around the world.

Consultancy

With the rise in computer use there is an expanding market for IT consultancy in Spain. One IT consultancy firm in the south of the country has based itself in the middle of a block of offices, and has filled its client base purely from the different companies surrounding it. Each of the companies effectively has its own IT department next to it without the expense of employing full-time staff.

E-commerce

If you can run your business from anywhere in the world, why not choose somewhere nice? The world of e-commerce is probably the most international type of business there is. Somebody can be in one country, order something on a website that was designed in another country and the goods are despatched from another country entirely. In fact, if you order goods over the internet you often have no idea where the business is based. Because location is less important these days, many people are deciding that when they are running an e-commerce business they might as well be in a country where they can enjoy themselves – and Spain is certainly somewhere where you can do that.

In addition to the upkeep of the website you will also need storage space for the goods that you are going to be sending out. One advantage that Spain has over the UK is that, in general, land is cheaper. This means that storage space for your product is likely to be cheaper as a result – although if you are selling to a particular nationality then paying more for storage may be compensated by the lower cost of delivery.

If you are thinking about setting up an e-commerce business in Spain, you have probably already been involved in a similar business in the UK. Relocating the business is likely to be relatively free of complications and can probably be done in phases.

Because of its international nature, the world of e-commerce is still not particularly regulated. It is absolutely vital that you take professional legal and financial advice to make sure that you are aware of where your business will be based for both legal and tax purposes. Recent changes in the law in Spain have meant that e-commerce is more regulated than it once was. However, these new laws are finding it difficult to keep pace with the way that e-commerce is evolving and certainly technology can move quicker than new laws. Through careful arrangement of your affairs it is possible live in Spain working on the business but still be taxed in the UK (if this is what you wish to do). Such arrangements are a very delicate balancing act and it is imperative that you take advice on this before you relocate.

Farming

Many people dream of escaping the rat race for a simpler life in a different country, carrying out some sort of farming activity. The thought of living in the sun and dealing with almonds, olives, tomatoes, grapes, oranges or lemons is probably very appealing to the majority of us – particularly with the low price of land in Spain compared to the UK.

Agriculture has always been an important part of the Spanish economy and the range of opportunities for different types of farming in Spain is vast. There are also large areas of land that are currently not being used that could be used to grow crops. However, farming has reduced in importance over the last few decades. In 1960 agriculture accounted for 23 per cent of GDP, in 1970 it was 15 per cent of GDP, and in 1980 agriculture accounted for only 5 per cent of GDP. In 2004 the figure had shrunk to 3.6 per cent of GDP.

The type of farming you can go into obviously depends on various circumstances including the local climate, the chemical make-up of the soil, demand for your product and your own expertise. Although Spain has a large land mass, making it one of the biggest countries in western Europe, the percentage of land that can be cultivated is low compared to many European countries. Lack of rainfall and poor-quality soil reduces the amount of land that can be usefully cultivated. Some 40 per cent of the land mass of Spain is suitable for cultivation. Of this, only 10 per cent of the land could be considered very good for cultivation, with the other 30 per cent being poor quality.

The success of a farming venture must, of course, be measured against the initial aspirations. As elsewhere, there are different scales of farming in Spain – from huge farms to modest smallholdings. There is estimated to be 2.3 million farms in Spain with about 62 per cent of these having less than five hectares of land, and 25 per cent less than one hectare of land.

Irrigation is a major factor as much of the country is dry. Only 17 per cent of Spain's cultivated land is irrigated, but that percentage produces 40–45 per cent of the annual value of crop production, and 50 per cent of the value of agricultural exports.

Spain's main agricultural products have traditionally been citrus fruits, vegetables, cereal grains, olive oil and wine, although this has changed over the years with an increase in the consumption of livestock, poultry and dairy products.

The Spanish are very open to foreigners moving to their country to start agricultural businesses, especially if they bring with them agricultural skills and modern techniques. Grants can be available for those starting their first farming project and low interest loans are also available, provided that there is a minimum commitment of five years. On-going grants are also to be found. In fact, one farm managed to get an EU grant to build a reservoir to collect water for the farm. The grant was given, and work on the reservoir was started. Today, this is the nicest reservoir that you have ever seen – it has a lining of blue tiles inside with steps going down into it. This reservoir is so attractive that the family who run the farm even have their barbeques next to the reservoir and regularly go swimming in it – to the extent that it now has a diving board. In fact, this reservoir is so pleasant that if I didn't know better I would say that they had used an EU grant to build a swimming pool!

Even with such grants, no one should go into farming thinking that it is an easy option. The reality is that farming is hard graft, with farmers coming under increasing pressure every year to reduce prices. Farmers are unlikely to make their fortunes or have much time spare. Unless you have been involved in farming previously or have done your research, you will be surprised how long it takes to reap the rewards. Vines, for example, can take four years before they produce grapes that can be used to make wine! The length of time it takes to produce goods that can generate an income will govern the amount of money you will need to live on while the crop or livestock is growing. Farming is a long-term business and should not be entered into by anybody who has to keep a close eye on cash flow.

The alternative to starting from scratch is to buy a business that is already in existence. For the pros and cons of buying a business compared to starting one from scratch, see 'Should You Set Up Your Own Business or Buy Into an Existing Business?', p.86. The main advantage of buying a working farm is that the time it will take to start making money is greatly reduced. However, when buying a farm of any sort it is important to make sure that you know what you are buying. Is the farming equipment included in the price? Is any stock that has already been harvested included in the price? If you are buying a vineyard, is any wine that is in stock included in the price? If you buy the farm or vineyard halfway through a season, will you have to compensate the existing owner for the work that he has done in collecting the crop this year?

Insurance

Nobody likes to take out insurance until they need to rely on it. Crops can fail, fires can destroy years worth of work, there can be drought – anything can happen that would financially cripple a farm. It is therefore worth thinking about some sort of insurance. For a more detailed discussion of the various types of insurance, see 'Insurance', p.203.

Methods

Many of the methods used by farmers in Spain are very different to those in the UK. You only have to look at the vast acres of plastic sheeting that cover crops in the Almeria region, or the stone-wall wind blocks in Lanzarote, to see that somebody who takes up farming in Spain will have much to learn about the local farming methods. The soil, geography, climate and types of crops grown can also be very different. However, coming from a different background may have its advantages, as you may be able to find a more efficient way of growing or harvesting a crop.

Illegal workers

Many illegal workers come from Africa – particularly Morocco – in search of work. The government is aware of the problem of illegal workers and is trying to clamp down on this. It is tempting to use illegal workers when running a farm. Don't – it is simply not worth it. Though they are cheap, plentiful and will work hard you run the risk of heavy fines as well as a variety of other problems such as bogus insurance claims. *See* 'Illegal Working', p.147.

Vineyards

Sitting in the sun, watching your grapes ripen while sampling some of the produce from previous years is an appealing prospect for many people, especially for those of us who enjoy a good glass of wine every so often. Little wonder that vineyards are one of the main types of agriculture that most people think of when they dream of setting up as farmers in Spain. However, the reality is often far removed from the ideal that many people imagine. Like all farming, it is hard work and, unless you are just doing it as a hobby and do not have to rely on the income to live on, may provide only a meagre living. Running a vineyard and making wine as a hobby, or taking it on as a business are two completely different things and it can be all too easy to forget this.

Spain has long been associated with grapes in one way or another – either for eating or for making wine. It has more land given over to vineyards than any other country in the world – in fact, 50 per cent of Europe's vineyards are in Spain, although their output is only about half that of France's. The Spaniards do have a preference for their own wines, but have started to drink more foreign wines in recent years, which has meant that the domestic market has had to work harder to maintain its market share. Spanish vineyards have long had an image of producing low-quality wine, but this is not always the case and there are many excellent wines that come from Spain. Certainly this reputation is changing as more people discover Spanish wines.

Farming has quite a long lead-in time before you can start selling your goods. Vineyards are a good example of this as you can't hurry vines and you certainly can't hurry the production of wine – particularly if you are aiming for the upper end of the market. Making wine is also quite an expensive process in terms of the cost of vines, the cost of equipment and the cost of production. This, coupled with the long-term nature of the business, means that owning a vineyard is not to be entered into by those with limited funds or limited cash flow.

More and more vineyards all over the world have found that one way of easily improving income and cash flow is to open up the vineyards to visitors and turn it into a tourist attraction. Many people are happy to pay to visit a vineyard, to have a tour explaining the wine-making process, and to sample the finished product at the end of the tour. They usually end up buying the odd bottle or two (or even case) that you would not have sold otherwise. Some vineyards also take this one stage further and have some sort of craft shop at the end of the visit, selling not only wine from the vineyard but also a variety of wine-related products (bottle openers, books on wine, etc.) as well as other local products. In addition many areas have wine festivals, which can help to bring publicity to your vineyard.

Cooperatives are big in Spain's wine-making industry and many vineyards will belong to one. The cooperative will collect grapes from all the vineyards that belong to it and produce wine from these vines. The obvious advantage of this is that production costs are shared between the members of the cooperative. The disadvantage is that you have less control over the quality of the production and you lose independence. Be aware that if you buy a vineyard and decide not to carry on with membership of the cooperative, then you may have to compensate the organisation for not fulfilling the agreement they had with the previous owner.

If you are thinking about running a vineyard then your choice of location will be heavily influenced by the different wine-making regions in Spain. There are about 70 different wine-producing areas and there are specific rules governing what you can and cannot do in the production of wine in a particular region. These rules were introduced in order to maintain the quality of the wines and cover such things as what types of grape can be used, the wine-making process, alcohol content, bottling and labelling.

Forestry

Spain produces more cork than any other country in the world other than Portugal, although the production of cork has fallen over the years. Cork is produced in Catalonia, Andalucía and Extremadura. Spain also grows pine trees in the north and northwest, and oak and beech trees in the Pyrenees.

Forestry is obviously a long-term business and therefore it is likely that you will either have to buy an existing forestry business or work for a forestry business. As you know, money doesn't grow on trees, and not many of us can afford to wait for trees to grow before earning an income.

Livestock

Many people think of fish when they think of Spanish food, but the meat that they produce is also very good. Lamb, mutton, beef, veal, poultry, dairy products and pork are all produced in Spain – particularly in the north of the country.

Organic Farming

As the demand for organic goods increases so more farms are turning to organic methods and produce. This is also true in Spain. The European Commissioner for Agriculture and Rural Development has stated that the EU must do all it can to support organic agriculture.

Fishing

When my mother thinks of fish it reminds her of her years living in Spain. Spain has wonderful fish and is one of Europe's leading fishing nations, having the world's fourth largest fishing fleet. The Spanish eat more fish than any other European country apart from the Scandinavians. However, fishing in Spain is now under pressure. In the past, Spanish fishermen have been accused of ignoring fishing quotas and fishing contrary to the European directives. Today, as elsewhere, Spanish fishermen are having an increasingly difficult time as world fish supplies are depleted.

Teaching

Education is a serious business in Spain and I am always amazed at my colleagues' willingness to go on yet another course and get yet another certificate. There are certainly opportunities to teach in Spain. Teaching can incorporate a wide variety of subjects and methods. You may find yourself teaching in Spanish, in English or a combination of the two. You can teach formally in schools, informally in evening classes or 'one on one' as a private tutor. You can teach traditional subjects or something a bit more unusual, such as windsurfing, painting, horse riding – whatever you are good at and feel that you can teach others.

Teaching in Spain can be to either the Spanish or the British. Obviously to teach the Spanish, your command of the language will need to be good enough to get your meaning across. After all, why should a Spaniard wish to learn a subject (other than English) while being taught in English? Teaching native English speakers limits you to working in areas where there are sufficient people in the area willing to learn your subject.

If you decide to teach, a starting point may be one of the many English-based schools in Spain. Teaching in a school of this kind means that your level of Spanish will not need to be as proficient as if you were teaching the same subject to the Spanish – although some knowledge of the Spanish terminology would obviously be of help. Unfortunately, pay at many private schools in Spain is considerably lower than in the state schools. It is also important to investigate the reputation of a school before joining them.

It is possible to teach in state schools in Spain. The pay tends to be better than in private schools and the teachers are generally well treated and respected. However, it is difficult (some would say impossible) to become a teacher in a state school unless you are Spanish. In theory, you would need to validate your UK degree and then take a series of exams called *oposiciones*. The validation process should be easy but some reports indicate otherwise. There is little doubt that the *oposiciones* are difficult both for a Spaniard and for foreigners, with many people spending years trying to pass them after many attempts. For information on foreign qualifications recognition, see the Spanish Ministry of Education webpage, **wwwn.mec.es**.

The *Times Educational Supplement* website (**www.tes.co.uk**) is a good resource for education and has a useful forum dedicated to teaching abroad. This site also has advertisements for jobs available in schools abroad, including Spain.

Teaching English

Probably the most common thing being taught by the British in Spain is 'English as a Foreign Language' or TEFL for short. However, there are a whole range of other acronyms related to teaching English – including TEAL (Teaching English as an Additional Language), TESL (Teaching English as a Second Language) and TESP (Teaching English for Specific Purposes).

The Spanish have long had a thirst to learn English. Initially it was so that they could understand all those American films and songs, but more recently – as the tourist market took off – it was so that they could speak to their customers in their native language and to enhance their job prospects.

Any reasonably intelligent person whose native language is English can be taught to teach English to foreigners. The starting point for teaching English is to take a course specifically aimed at teaching English. If you are going to take such a course it is likely that the course itself will take place in the UK, so you will have to plan this before you move to Spain.

This has been the traditional way of earning a living for people wishing to start off in Spain and is often thought of as a short-term career opportunity – 'until the right job comes along', although some people do intend to do this on a more permanent basis. I had a friend who taught English as a job while studying at university in Spain – it allowed him to pay his way through his degree. He would advertise his services all around the university on notice boards in the canteen and so on, and he would teach the other students. The fact that there were only two native English-speaking students at the university meant that he had little competition – especially as I was the other one.

Details of how to start off in TEFL can be found on a range of websites. A search on the internet will throw up literally thousands of references to TEFL and other associated courses, but one site worth looking at is **www.celta.org.uk**.

Language Schools

You could consider setting up your own private language school in Spain. One of the main considerations here is the location. You obviously need to be in an area that has sufficient demand from students to learn English, but at the same time you want as little competition as possible. Unfortunately, these two factors rarely mix and it can be difficult to find an area that is going to provide you with sufficient students and little competition.

To run your own language school, you will obviously have to think about your staffing and materials requirements. To start with, it may be just you teaching, but as business takes off you will come under increasing pressure to provide courses for different age ranges and levels of proficiency at the same time – meaning that you will need somebody to help you. You will obviously need teaching materials. It will probably be enough to start with books, pens and a whiteboard, but as the school grows you will probably have to provide more materials, and technology will start to become a factor. You may even decide to market yourself as being different from all the other schools by being heavily IT-based while still retaining the personal touch.

The volume of paperwork required for opening a private school is surprisingly little. You will need a licence to open the business (*see* **Red Tape**, p.133) but once you have this, and have satisfied the normal requirements of a new business, then you are on your way. If you are not regulated by an education authority you will have to make this clear in any certificates that you issue to your students.

Translating

Many people who teach English in Spain sometimes supplement their income by taking on translating work. The advantage of translating is that in most cases the work can be done anywhere – meaning that you can sit on the beach working all day if you are so inclined. Translations often have a tight deadline, and are often quite technical, so your understanding of both English and Spanish must be of a high standard.

Often, people who have worked in a particular field may consider specialist translations later on in their working life. For example, you could specialize in translating medical reports or surveys. Specialist translations have to be of the absolute highest standard, as business or legal decisions are often made based on those translations. For high-level translation work you will need to demonstrate that you are experienced and have the relevant qualifications. Details of courses can be found on the internet.

Advertising your skills as a translator can be difficult as there is a great deal of competition out there. A good way is to contact local businesses in your area. A mailshot can generally get the ball rolling although you will have to make your letter stand out from the numerous other ones that the same companies will receive from your rivals. For some further thoughts on this subject, *see* 'Marketing', p.127.

Pilots

Spain needs a wide range of piloting skills – from flying large jets for one of the major commercial airlines running tourists in and out of the country, to teaching people how to paraglide.

If you have a pilot's licence then it is possible to fly in Spain. If you hold a JAR licence then you need no validation to fly in Spain. If you don't hold a JAR licence, then you will have to obtain validation. Having said that, validation is actually a very simple process – you contact the civil aviation (*Aviación Civil*) section of the *Ministerio de Fomento* in Madrid (Ministerio de Fomento, 67 Paseo de la Castellana, Madrid). You fill in some forms and pay a fee of about £100. Your validated licence should be issued to you in about a week.

Details of the different airports in Spain, their layouts and other useful information can be found at **www.ais.aena.es**.

The Spanish national airline is Iberia, which is one of the major world carriers. There are also a number of other small domestic airlines – chief among them being Spanair, Aviaco and Air Europa. All of these often advertise for pilots. In addition to this there are various smaller airlines that concentrate on flying to and from the various islands.

If you have only a licence to fly smaller planes then there can still be odd opportunities for you in Spain. There are companies that specialize in taking tourists on flights around particular tourist areas. Fly Spain (**www.flyspain.co.uk**) is a company that provides paragliding holidays, courses and tuition. There are also companies that specialize in flying up and down the coast towing advertising banners behind the plane. A number of courier companies specialize in delivering packages over distances where a small plane is the best method. One word of warning here: be sure that the deliveries that you carry are legal!

The Tour Business

When most of us think about a holiday to Spain we think about going down to the coast, sitting by the beach, eating, drinking, playing golf and relaxing. However, Spain has much, much more to offer than just the traditional beach or golf holiday. Much of the country's history and culture is often overlooked by the conventional tourist industry.

The country's rich history, which includes invasions by the Romans and Visigoths and, in the 16th century, the emergence of Spain as a global empire, means that there is a potential industry related to the country's past. For the most part, this has largely been ignored by tour companies, who have focussed on the country's coast and stunning beaches. Today, holidaymakers are looking for something more and many want to visit the sites of ancient battles or other historical events as part of a guided tour. A handful of companies already provide such visits, among them Midas Tours (**www.midastours.co.uk**), Holts Tours (**www.holts.co.uk**) and Battle Tours (**www.battletours.co.uk**).

Classic Car Tours

What could be nicer than driving through Spain in a classic sports car? But who wants the hassle of taking their vehicle down to Spain and having to worry about servicing, spare parts and all the paperwork?. The answer is to rent a classic car or go on a classic-car driving holiday. Both of these present good business opportunities.

Obviously there is a whole range of things you will need to think about when setting up such a venture. How are you going to get the cars to Spain? Are you going to be able to source enough left-hand drive classic cars, or are you going to have to rely on some right-hand drive cars? What are you going to do about spare parts and servicing – do you have a source of readily available parts or are you going to have to rely on parts coming from abroad, with the inevitable delay and disruption that this will incur? You obviously need to be thinking about insurance, which is likely to be quite high if you are letting foreign drivers loose on roads that they do not know, driving on the 'wrong' side of the road, in valuable motor vehicles.

Relaxing

In Lubia (about 160km northeast of Madrid) a Spanish company called StopStress has just started to offer a new and rather off-beat service at a junk-yard. For €40 you are provided with sledgehammers and safety equipment (helmets, overalls and goggles) and then you are let loose on all those items that cause stress in many people's lives (cars, computers, phones and photos of the boss). Clients are allowed to vent their anger on the items at the junkyard for up to two hours, although most people apparently do not last more than a quarter of this time. The owner of this business has seen a problem and found a unique way of solving it – and in the process created something much more interesting than just another executive stress ball.

There is a whole range of different types of stress-busting businesses that you can run, which become more and more attractive as the pace of life in many countries gets increasingly hectic. Spain has a multitude of springs and spas and a wonderful climate to go with them, and it is no wonder that the Europeans used to consider Spain to be the 'Spa of Europe'. Spas and the many activities that surround them, such as nature walks, healthy food, sports, art and history appreciation, offer great business opportunities as increasing numbers of people search for different ways of relaxing on holidays, and as 'health tourism' becomes ever more popular.

Property

The market for people buying property in Spain has increased dramatically over the last few years and the market has benefited from a boom. Spain has traditionally been the first choice for most people buying a property abroad. The country has many advantages – it is close to the UK and therefore 'easy to get to'; flights to the tourist areas are plentiful and cheap; the weather is consistently good; we understand the people and the culture; and we feel safe in Spain. These advantages are unlikely to disappear and therefore Spain will probably continue to be one of the major players in overseas property sales even if other countries are catching up. Because of this, many people think about going into business in Spain with an idea that is somehow connected to property.

Sales

As in many parts of Europe, the Spaniards do not require their estate agents to have any special training or education to set up an estate agency. In fact, so many people have set up estate agency businesses in Spain over the years that in some areas of the country it seems like there are more people selling property than buying.

Rental Property

Every year 50 million people visit Spain – a figure second only to France, with 57 million visitors. In the past, the majority of holidaymakers would have gone on holidays organised by tour operators and stayed in hotels. These days the visitor to Spain is getting more sophisticated and doesn't necessarily wish to stay in a hotel. Many more people now opt to rent a property and therefore build greater flexibility into their holiday.

About 70 per cent of the people who buy houses in Spain let them. About half of those people rent out on a 'serious' basis. That is to say, they are trying to make money by letting their property and finding the maximum number of tenants each year. The other half let casually to family, friends and friends of friends. They are looking not so much to make a profit from renting but to defray some or all of the cost of ownership. There are fundamental differences in the way these two groups should approach the task.

The first group should put itself into the mind of the person they want to have renting their property. Which part of the market are they trying to capture? You cannot be all things to all men. The single person or childless couple wanting to enjoy Spanish culture and cuisine will have very different requirements from the family wanting a cheap and quiet holiday in the countryside. Where would they like to rent? What type of property would they prefer? What features do they require? It makes sound business sense to buy a property, convert it and equip it solely for the prospective tenants you have in mind.

The second group should make few concessions to their tenants. After all, their property is first and foremost a holiday home for their own use. The following section relates mainly to the first group. Some comments will be directed specifically at the second group, who may like to pick and choose from the other ideas, depending on how far they are prepared to compromise their wishes to increase letting income.

The Right Area

The choice of the area in which to buy your rental property is by far the most important decision that you will make. There are many parts of Spain where it is fairly easy to let your property regularly enough to make it a commercially viable proposition. There are other areas where this is almost impossible.

The factors to take into consideration when deciding upon the area are slightly different from the factors relevant when you're thinking about buying a home for your own personal use. They will also vary depending upon your target clientele and your preferred way of administering the property.

Letting Agencies?

Strangely, the decision as to how you are going to let your property is one of the first that you should take. This is because if you decide to use a professional management or letting agency it will alter your target market and therefore the area in which you ought to be buying: see 'Property Management', p.67.

If you are going to let your property through a professional management agency then it is worth contacting such agencies before you make a final selection of area to see what they believe they can offer in the way of rental returns. They will also be able to tell you what type of property is likely to be most successful as a letting property in that area.

If you are thinking of finding the tenants yourself then you will have to decide upon your primary market. Most British people organizing their own lettings rent primarily to the British. There are a number of reasons for this. Lack of language skills is probably the most common. The rest of this section is targeted mainly at the person wishing to let to a British market.

Climate

Most people going on holiday hope for decent weather. Fortunately, not everybody has the same idea about what this means. The number of people taking summer holidays in Normandy shows that a higher than average rainfall is not a fatal deterent. Despite this, you are likely to have more success if you are in an area that is known to be warm and dry.

It is particularly important that the area has decent weather during the prime British holiday season. This is normally July, August and September. Apart from this main holiday season, the months of May, June and October offer reasonable letting prospects if you are in an area with a mild climate. There is also a relatively small market for longer-term winter lets in areas with particularly mild climates or which are socially desirable. For more information on climate, see 'Climate Chart', p.228. Information is also available from local tourist offices, in travel publications and on the internet.

Access

Just as important as the climate is a tenant's ability to get to your property. This is true at two levels. The area in which the property is located must offer convenient access from the places where the tenants live, and the property itself must be easy to find.

For most British visitors, convenient access to the area means access from a major local airport. It is worth repeating the results of research conducted by the travel industry, which shows that 25 per cent of all potential visitors will not travel if it involves journeying for more than one hour from a local airport at either end of their trip. If this rises to one and a half hours then the number that will choose not to travel rises to 50 per cent. This research was undertaken in the context of package holidays, but the principles also apply to a certain extent to people renting holiday homes. Of course, if your home is more than one hour's drive from Britain or an airport you will still be able to let it. There are many people who are much more adventurous, and those wanting to rent property in rural Spain will often be in that category. Indeed, they will often view the journey as part of the holiday. It is beyond doubt, however, that if you are within easy travelling distance of the ports or major airports then the number of people likely to rent from you will be increased.

Do not underestimate the importance of being able to find your property. Navigation in the depths of rural Spain can be trying. There are few people to ask for directions (especially if you don't speak Spanish) and there are few signposts of much help when it comes to locating a rural cottage. The situation is not much better if you are trying to locate a villa in Fuengirola. The closer to the main road the better. Providing decent maps and guidance notes is also essential. Nothing is guaranteed to ruin the start of a holiday as much as cruising around for three hours to cover the last 500 yards of a journey.

Tourist Attractions

Governments are keen on tourist attractions because they attract large numbers of holidaymakers! The fact that they are prepared to invest billions of tax-payers' money in marketing and maintaing these attractions should persuade you that having one near to you is a 'good thing' when it comes to letting your property.

'Tourist attraction' is a term that can be applied to a wide variety of attractions. At one extreme it could be a major theme park, attracting millions of visitors each year, all of whom have to find somewhere to sleep. Alernatively, a tourist attraction could be a championship golf course or a famous beach or sailing area. Not all tourist attractions will be found in the guide books and it could simply be a lady in your village who teaches pottery classes or falconry. The point is that there must be something to bring people to your area so that they will need to use your accommodation. The mere fact that the house is located in the middle of the countryside may not, of itself, be enough to attract a significant number of tenants.

In addition, you should bear in mind that many people going on holiday want to eat out. Even those who will probably end up buying food in their local super-market and cooking at home for most of the time may want to eat out during their stay. It will be much easier to let your property if some good Spanish restaurants are within easy reach. Preferably, they should be within walking distance. It is also a good idea if the property is within walking distance (or only a short drive) of shops and other facilities.

The Right Property

The choice of property is almost as important as the choice of area. Not all properties rent to the same extent. My experience suggests that properties that the potential buyer finds attractive will rent up to five times more frequently than properties that do not stand out for any reason. This is such a significant difference that you ignore it at your peril.

New property is generally cheaper to maintain than older property. It is, however, not nearly as likely to be attractive to potential tenants. Most people going on holiday to rural Spain are looking for a 'character' property. Most people going on holiday to coastal Spain are looking for proximity to facilities and a pool.

Make sure that there is no restriction on your ability to let your property. This will normally be the case only in a very small number of apartments or condo-miniums (*comunidades*), where the rules of the community impose restrictions.

To let legally, your property should be registered with the tourist authorities. Many people ignore this rule. There are also significant restrictions in the Canaries and Balearics. If you want to rent in these areas, check your plans care-fully with your lawyer.

Pick a Pretty Home

Most people will decide whether to rent your property after they have seen only a brief description and a photograph. The photograph is by far the more impor-tant. Research carried out for my own buiness showed that 80 per cent of a group shown 32 potential rental properties picked the same three properties. The common factor in these properties was that they were all pretty. If the person was looking at properties in Normandy then they wanted a Norman cottage and not a modern semi-detached house. If they were looking for somewhere by the sea then they wanted a seaside cottage, preferably with either sand or water in view. When buying a house for rental purposes make sure you buy one that 'takes a pretty picture'. At the same time, be sure the external decoration and garden/pool area are kept in good order. These are what will show up in your photographs and create a good first impression. In your marketing it is well worth stressing that your property is clean and well-equipped, and at the same time make the most of the traditional appearance and, if there is one, the pool.

Equipping the Property

If you advertise the property well you will get tenants. But you will only get repeat tenants and recommendations from existing tenants if the property meets or exceeds their expectations in terms of the facilities it offers and its cleanliness.

The facilities required will depend upon the target market you are trying to attract. Think about that market and think about what you would want if you were part of it. For example, if you are trying to attract mountain-walkers or sailors they will appreciate somewhere to dry their clothes quickly so that they can be ready to get wet again the following day. Here are some tips:

Welcome Pack

You should make sure that basic groceries such as bread, milk, coffee, sugar and a bowl of fruit are left in the house to welcome your guests. A bottle of wine goes down well too!

Documents

Make sure that all guests are sent a *pre-visit pack*. The pack should include notes about the area and local attractions (usually available free from your local tourist office), a map showing the immediate vicinity, notes explaining how to get to the property, emergency contact numbers and instructions as to what to do if they are delayed for any reason .

A *house book* should be kept in the property. It should give much more information about local attractions, restaurants, etc., and a comprehensive list of contact numbers for use in case of an emergency. It can also act as a visitors' book. This will be a useful vehicle for obtaining feedback and a means of making future contact direct with visitors who might have been supplied by an agency.

Arrival

It is much better if someone is present either at the property or in a nearby house to welcome guests when they arrive. This helps guests to settle in and allows for any minor problems or particular requirements to be sorted out with minimum fuss.

Cleanliness

The property must be spotlessly clean. This applies in particular to the kitchen and bathroom. This may require some training for your cleaner, as our expectations when going into rented accommodation are generally higher than our expectations in an ordinary home, as many people are likely to be using the property. Again, stress the cleanliness in your marketing. There should be adequate means of cleaning, including a vacuum cleaner.

Kitchen

Even in a period cottage, the kitchen should be modern, though it can be in a traditional style. It goes without saying that everything should work. You should have a microwave, and you should also make sure that there is sufficient cutlery and cooking equipment and that it is all in good condition. A cookbook giving local recipes is a nice touch.

Bathroom

Or rather these days, more usually bathrooms. En-suite bathrooms for each bedroom are ideal. A bidet will be welcomed by Spanish visitors and contribute a local feel for British visitors. Make sure that there is soap in the bathrooms. Guests will much prefer it if you provide towels as part of your service.

Laundry

A washing machine and drier are now commonplace.

Bedrooms

The number of bedrooms you choose is very important. Generally in cities you will get a better return on your investment on properties with fewer (one or two) bedrooms – which will be cheaper to buy – than on larger properties. In rural areas, or by the seaside, where the majority of your guests may well be families, a three-bedroom property is probably your best compromise.

Bedrooms should have adequate storage space. Most importantly, they should have clean and comfortable beds. The only beds that last well in a regularly used property, and where the sleepers will be all sorts of different sizes and weights, are expensive beds such as those used in the hotel industry. Nothing (except dirtiness) generates more complaints than uncomfortable beds.

Beds should be protected from obvious soiling by the use of removable mattress covers which should be changed with each new set of tenants.

Guests will much prefer it if you supply bedding as part of your service rather than expecting them to take their own.

Living Areas

Furniture and upholstery should be in good condition. The style is a matter of personal preference but a 'local' style is often attractive. The furniture must be comfortable.

Heating

Heating is essential – even in Spain. It should be effective and cover the whole house.

Air-conditioning

Air-conditioning is probably best avoided except in the most expensive lettings. It is not yet considered compulsory and can be expensive both to run and to maintain.

Swimming Pool

If you are catering to the British market, a swimming pool is highly desirable. In a rural area it will significantly increase your potential number of tenants. A pool should be of reasonable size, but need not be heated.

The Right Price

When buying a property as a business you will be concerned to pay as little as possible for the property, consistent with getting the right level of rental return. If you are only buying as a business proposition then this price/rental balance (or return on investment), together with your judgement of the extent to which the property will rise in value over the years, is the main criteria in deciding which property to buy.

If you are going to use the property not only as a rental property but also as a holiday home, then there is an additional factor: the amount of time that you will be able to use the property yourself, consistent with getting a certain level of rental return. For example, if you bought a one-bedroom property on the sea-front in Tenerife for £75,000 that property might be let for 45 weeks per year and produce a return, after deduction of all expenses, of, say, 7.5 per cent. If you bought a two-bedroom apartment in the province of Almeria for, say, £50,000, and let that for 20 weeks per year, you might also generate 7.5 per cent on your investment. Both would be performing equally well but the Almeria apartment would allow you and your family to use the property for 30 weeks per year whereas the sea-front apartment would allow you to use it for only five weeks per year. This and the fact that it had one more bedroom could make the old town property the more attractive proposition. These are simply examples to illustrate the point rather than indications as to what is actually obtainable at any particular moment.

Whatever way we look at it, paying the minimum necessary to buy the property is the key to maximizing performance.

Marketing

Properties do not let themselves. You will have to do some marketing. In the early years you will have to do more marketing than in later years because you will have no existing client base. As in any other business, the cheapest type of marketing is catching repeat clients and so some money spent on making sure that the property lives up to or exceeds their expectations (and so secures their return next year) is probably the best spend that you will make.

There seems to be no correlation between the amount spent on marketing and the results achieved. Much money spent appears to be wasted. What are the key points?

- **Choose the method of marketing most appropriate to your property and your circumstances.**

• Follow up all leads generated at once. Contact them again after a couple of weeks to see whether they have made up their minds.

• Send them your details again next year at about the same time, as they are likely to be taking another holiday.

Remember that your marketing is only as good as the quality of the response you give to people making inquiries. You will probably do better spending less money on advertising and paying more attention to following up the leads that you have actually generated.

UK Market

Directories

If your property is pretty then you are likely to get good results from the various directories and magazines focusing on properties to let in Spain. They only work if they are inexpensive because for a private owner with only one property to let you have only one opportunity of letting each week and so a directory that produces, say, 50 inquiries for the first week in September is not particularly helpful. We have had good reports of results from *Brittany Ferries Directory* (for property in northern Spain) and *Private Villas* magazine (for up-market property).

Advertising

The problem with advertising is its scatter-gun approach and, in many cases, its cost. You need only a very small number of responses. You cannot afford to pay a large amount in advertising fees for each let. Except for very expensive properties, traditional advertising is too expensive. We have had good reports of results from the specialist Spanish property press from *Dalton's Weekly*, and even from advertising on your local supermarket notice board! In fact, cheap advertising can often pay dividends. A nicely produced A5 leaflet with a photo and a brief description in local trendy cafés or second-hand bookstores can yield surprisingly good results.

Your Own Contacts

Your own contacts are, without doubt, the best opportunity you have for marketing your property. Remember how few people you need to rent it out for, say, 25 weeks a year. Given that many people will take it for two weeks or more, you will probably be looking for only 10–15 lettings.

The people who find this easiest are those who work for large organisations. If you are lucky enough to work for a major hospital, or BT, or a large factory, you will almost certainly be able to find enough people to keep your property fully occupied within your working environment. You will also have the advantage of knowing the people who are going to rent the property. This reduces the risk that they will damage it or fail to pay you.

Even without people from work most owners will be able to find enough friends, neighbours and relatives to rent a nice property in Spain for 10 weeks per year. This will leave only a relatively small number of tenants to be found by advertising or other marketing means.

When renting to family and friends, or indeed close work colleagues, you will have to learn how to raise the delicate issue of payment. Given that you are not going to be incurring any marketing costs and, probably, very little in the way of property management costs, you should be able to offer them an attractive price and still generate as much income as you would have done by letting through an agency. Make sure that you address the issue when you accept the booking, as doing so later can be very embarrassing.

Spanish Market

Most British people do not speak Spanish well enough to be able to offer the product on the Spanish market other than through a letting agency.

Internet

There are significant English-speaking markets in Scandinavia, Germany, the USA and elsewhere. To an extent these will be covered by the specialist Spanish property press, but they are most successfully addressed via the internet, which offers tremendous opportunities for bringing a specialist niche product to the attention of a vast audience at little cost. The internet also enables people to see pictures and read about your property and the area in which it is located. As such it is ideal for the person wanting to rent out property.

It is worth having your own website designed especially for this purpose. Not only can it be your brochure but it can also act as a way of taking bookings. It is much cheaper to have someone print off a copy of your brochure from their own computer than it is for you to post it. You may already have the expertise to create your own website. If you do not, it's quite fun learning. If you have not got the time or inclination, a simple but very effective site can be put together for around £250.

As well as having your own website you should consider listing your property on one of the many Spanish property websites currently to be found on the internet. These listings are either free or accessible at minimal cost. You will soon find the ones that work and the ones that don't.

You will also have to decide whether you want to use your website only as a brochure or whether you are prepared to take electronic bookings, and whether to price your product only in sterling, in euros or perhaps in multiple currencies including US dollars. You will be able to take payment only by cheque unless you are lucky enough to be a merchant with a credit card account or you are prepared to incur the expense of setting up the facility.

Doing Deals

Two particular forms of deal might appeal.

If your property is in a rural area where there is somebody offering a very local tourist service it can be sensible to make contact with them and to try to arrange for the people visiting that facility or attending that course to be introduced to your property. This can significantly increase your lettings, particularly off peak. If you pay the person concerned, say, 20 per cent commission, you will be well ahead.

The second type of deal is worth considering if you know some other people in the area who have properties to let. One of the frustrations of marketing your property is when you find four lots of people who want to rent the property for the same week. Getting together with others in a mutual assistance group will allow you to pass excess lettings to each other.

Property Maintenance

All properties need a certain amount of maintenance. This is especially the case in hot, dry climates. People who own properties often do not have the inclination or the ability to maintain their properties themselves. This is where the maintenance man comes in. Obviously, your handyman skills need to be up to scratch. The Spanish love their gossip as much as anybody and stories of bad workmanship will soon get around and you will have no customers.

There are several different types of people that you could carry out maintenance for – individuals, rental agencies, communities, holiday-home owners and companies.

Think of every home-owner living in your area as a potential customer. You are likely to start off carrying out work for your friends and neighbours. Soon word gets around that you do a good job and the number of jobs that you have increases. Another way of getting clients is to advertise in the local paper, on notice boards, mail shots and the like. This is going to be a very local business – you don't want to be travelling long distances in order to fix a window that won't shut!

Rental agencies need a network of people who can carry out maintenance for their clients. The maintenance man may be employed in-house, but it is more likely that they are an outside contractor. If you can get a contract with an agency to look after the houses that they rent out, then you will have an in-built source of work. If you can persuade the agency to employ you rather than contract you, then you will have the security of being employed rather than having the uncertainty of being a contractor.

Some properties share facilities with others. In Spain the ownership of items such as pools, parking areas, tennis courts, stairways, the structure of the building (in the case of an apartment), maintenance facilities, services, etc.

is shared between the various owners who have the right to use them. The body that facilitates this is the 'community of owners'. It is the community of owners that decides the maintenance budget and also who is to carry out the maintenance. Each year, communities look at the options regarding maintenance contracts. You will need to persuade the community of owners that you can do the job and that you can do it at a reasonable cost.

There are thousands of people who own properties as holiday homes in Spain. Many of these people either use it themselves only every so often or rent it out themselves. Those who do not use an agency still need somebody who can do maintenance for them.

It is not just individuals who need maintenance on their properties – companies do too. In fact, all but the smallest of companies will normally need a friendly maintenance man. The smaller companies will try to do the work themselves in order to minimize costs. In most other businesses the owners and staff of the business simply won't have the time or skills to carry out maintenance themselves.

Property Management

Recent statistics estimate some 82.6 million tourists visit Spain every year. Of these it is estimated that 30 million visit Spain for shopping or weekend trips from Portugal or France, leaving over 50 million holidaymakers coming from further afield and staying for longer periods. Statistics also show that many people stay in more than one hotel during their stay because they often travel around the country. Therefore, logically, the number of visitors staying at hotels should be over 50 million per year. However, hotel statistics in Spain show only 23.6 million guests per year. This leaves 26.4 million people who are staying in accommodation other than hotels – meaning that they are renting property. The upshot of this is that there is a huge number of people who are currently renting a property out in Spain. Many of these people need to rely on a management company to rent the property out for them as they do not have either the time, inclination or know-how to do it themselves. In addition to this, many of the owners of properties that are rented out do not have the contacts, or are too far away (often in a different country), to deal with the day-to-day care that a property needs, such as organizing a plumber to fix a leaking tap and a cleaner to visit the property between lettings. A good management company can be worth its weight in gold and often property owners find it very difficult to locate one. If you can manage property well for clients then word will soon get around and in theory you will have people queuing up to use your services.

Unfortunately, quite a few management companies do not do things properly – they often do the minimum necessary to rent the property out and do not look into all those extra services that are so useful for an owner. In extreme cases some management companies have rented the property out and have kept the rental income themselves rather than passing it on to the owner.

Running a management company well is hard work. First of all you will have to find clients who wish you to manage the properties for them. Then you have to find people who wish to rent the property. You should be constantly advertising for properties to rent out and for people to rent them. You should also have a good network of tradesmen who can carry out the sort of services that your clients (both owners and their visitors) require. You will need to be thinking about what services you can provide.

If the business is going well, you should have a continuous cycle of work that will need to be done for each property. The cycle will be something like this:

- **Advertise the property for rent.**

- **Take inquiries about the property by telephone, in person, by post or e-mail and answer the potential clients' questions regarding the property and the rental process.**

- **Check that the property is available for the time that the visitors require.**

- **Make the booking for the visitors and make sure that there are no double bookings.**

- **Inspect the property to make sure that everything works, is in order and is present and correct, and agree an inventory with the people renting the property.**

- **Arrange for somebody to be at the property to let the visitors in and to explain how the appliances work and any other relevant details about the property.**

- **At the end of the visitors' stay somebody needs to go and collect the keys and inspect the property to make sure that it has not been damaged, and that everything is still in place and nothing is missing.**

- **Arrange for the property to be cleaned and prepared in readiness for the next visitors.**

- **Keep the owner of the property up to date with details of the number of visitors, income and expenditure and any other information that is necessary.**

This list is quite long and if you are managing many properties you will have to have a slick organisation to make sure that all the steps are carried out. The worst thing that you can do is double-book a property or not have a property ready for the visitors when they arrive after a long journey. The above list also assumes that nothing has gone wrong with the property. If there is a leaking tap, a broken window, the air-conditioning fails or any other problem arises then it is obviously important that this is resolved. Otherwise you will find it more difficult to rent that property out and your business will obtain a reputation for renting out properties of a low standard. This is why arranging for the repair of such problems through a network of reliable plumbers, electricians, and handymen is so essential.

The best management companies will go one stage further – arranging car hire for visitors, ensuring a 'welcome pack' is available at the property when visitors first arrive, assisting with arranging insurance for owners and a whole range of other services that clients may need.

Formalising the Letting

You will need a contract with the clients for whom you rent properties out. The contract is required so that it is very clear what you are expected to do for the owners of the properties and what extra services you can provide at an extra cost. Without this the temptation for clients is to ask you to do certain things at no cost. You will draw up a standard rental contract – one between you and the property owner and one between you and the people renting the properties.

The Letting Agreement

A properly drafted tenancy agreement will protect you and your clients in the event of a dispute with the tenants and, in particular, if any of them wish to stay on at the end of the tenancy. If the property forms part of a community of owners (*communidad de propietarios*) then the tenants will have to abide by the rules of the community, and this should be indicated in the rental agreement. Tenants should be given a copy of these rules, or at least the part that is relevant. In the rental contract you should also stipulate what is going to be covered by insurance and what is excluded – typically, for example, tenants' personal possessions would not be covered under the policy.

There are two types of rental agreement in Spain – long-term and short-term – and each of these will require a different type of contract. Short-term rentals are called *por temporada* and long-term rentals are known as *viviendas*. It is possible to obtain standard rental contracts from street kiosks, but it is still imperative that you get a lawyer involved in making sure that these contracts are suitable for you, or even better that they draft a contract that is tailor-made for your business, as you will be relying on this over and over again and it is important that it is correct from the start.

Will It Work in Spain?

Some people have brilliant ideas for a business that will work in their own country, but forget to ask themselves whether the idea is appropriate for Spain. Similarly, many people attempt to start a business in Spain and each year many of them fail. Make sure that you do your homework and get some advice before you get in too deep. It is vital that, when you get your idea, you give some thought as to whether the idea will 'translate' well to a different country.

Different countries have different cultures – also in terms of business. Different nationalities have different expectations from a business in terms of what they think that business should provide and how they should work and treat their customers. It is important that you give some thought to how your business will work in Spain.

If you have found a business that nobody has started previously, does this mean that you have struck gold with a wonderful opportunity, or does it in fact mean that people have tried this type of business in the past but have not been able to make it pay?

You may be able to make a certain type of business work in one country in terms of the economics of the business, but different countries have different costs and pricing, so it is important to investigate whether the sums still add up when you move a particular business idea to Spain. Luckily in many areas the cost of labour and materials is likely to be cheaper in Spain than in the UK, but this is not necessarily the case and it is important to do some research to make sure that you can still make a profit.

It may be that the type of business that you are thinking about setting up is not particularly desirable in Spain for any number of reasons. There was a television programme not long ago which followed the fortunes of different people who started up businesses in Spain. One of those filmed had opened an Indian restaurant. The logic behind this was that Indian food was very popular in the UK, there are many British people in Spain but there are few Indian restaurants. Logically, this seemed to be a good case of the owner finding a niche that had not been tapped into. Unfortunately, it seemed that what worked in one country did not work in another – the owner of the restaurant had overestimated how popular his restaurant was going to be, as many of the British people in the area did not seem enthused by Indian food while they were in Spain, despite liking Indian food when they were in Britain.

You also can't assume that a business will work in Spain in the same way that it does back in the UK in terms of staff. Over the years, the British have visited Spain in such great numbers and with such frequency that we think that we have become accustomed to the way that the Spanish think and work. However, dealing with the Spanish on a day-to-day basis for many years can still throw up surprises in the way that they react in different circumstances. All Spaniards are individuals and have their own personalities, but the Spanish mentality – although reasonably close to the British – can be surprisingly different in many ways. This is more pronounced as you move around the country, and the Spanish themselves will happily recount the stereotypes of different areas of Spain. Because the people are different it means that the way that you treat staff and how they treat you is going to differ from UK practice. This could mean that your business may actually stand more chance of success in Spain (after all, the Spanish can be very hard working), but it may equally well mean that you stand less chance of success. What is important to you as the head of a business may simply mean nothing to a Spanish member of staff who may struggle to understand why you wish to do things in a certain way.

Business Names

It is also important to think of the name of the business and the product or service that you are selling. A name that seems ideal in the UK may be totally inappropriate or even insulting when put into a Spanish context. The most famous example of this is the Vauxhall Nova. Vauxhall are known as Opel in Spain and the Nova was known as the Corsa for many years before the Nova became the Corsa in the UK. The reason for this was simple – Nova could easily be seen as being *no va* which translated into Spanish means 'doesn't go' – a totally inappropriate name for a car!

You may have a fantastic business selling a brilliant product or service, but if the name is off-putting to your market, then you might as well pack up and go home as you will not get the customers. This is obviously assuming that you are trying to aim your business either partly or fully at the Spanish market, although even if you are not, word will still get around that your business name or product name means something strange in Spanish, which is bound to affect how many customers you get. It is therefore important that you run any names that you intend to use – either for your business or for any product or service – past somebody who understand both the language and the culture of Spain to make sure that you are not inadvertently making a mistake. It is also important to make sure that the person who checks this for you is somebody whom you can trust!

Remember, too, that working hours and opening hours in Spain are different from those in the UK. If your business has an element of time-sensitivity then you need to be thinking about this in the context of Spain and whether the plan can still be made to work. For example, some Spanish bars only open in the evenings, while others will be open all day; others may open for part of the afternoon and then again in the evening.

For these reasons, and many others, it is very important that you do some further reading to find out as much as you can about setting up a business before you embark on your project. For many people, such research is part of the fun and will pay dividends in the end.

Business Information

It is relatively easy to obtain basic information on setting up a business in Spain. Every year there is an increasing number of magazines dedicated to Spain – from buying property there to magazines aimed at the culture for people intending to move there. For details of other books and magazines available, *see* 'Further Reading', p.219.

As well as reading up on the subject, take time to go and speak to people who have already set up their own businesses. Many people have done this over the years and the combination of their experience is great – it would be a shame for this to go to waste. It is important, if possible, that you speak to people who have been successful in their business – to find out what they have done to make the business successful. It is equally important to speak to people who have not been as successful – to find out what they have done wrong so that you can avoid the same mistakes! In an ideal world you would speak to any potential competitors in the area to find out what they are doing, but in reality they are unlikely to give away their secrets or wish to assist somebody to set up in competition against them.

Local knowledge is crucial to a business that relies on local trade, and therefore you should not only speak to people about setting up a business, but also to people who have set up a business in that particular area. If you find out that local authorities are difficult to deal with, or that the local mayor does not wish to encourage businesses of your type, then you may decide to reassess where you are going to base your business or take the opportunity of redrafting your business model to accommodate any information that you have gathered.

The culture of Spain is such that relationships are Important and this is reflected in the way that business is carried out. For more discussion on this point, see 'Business Practices', p.138. In order for your business to be successful you will need to build up a network of contacts. These contacts will assist you getting around some of the challenges that you will face during the lifetime of your business. If you have a personal contact at the town hall, at the tax office, at the local suppliers, etc. you will find that the business will work much better. The Spanish have a word for such contacts – *enchufes* (which means a plug – the analogy being that you plug in your contact to make something work). These *enchufes* will be formed much quicker and will be much more useful if they are made personally rather than by telephone or e-mail.

The internet has dramatically increased in popularity in the last few years and most people in the UK and Spain now have some form of internet access. There are many internet sites with basic information about setting up businesses. While there are some very good sites, there are also some that are not as good and even some that are factually inaccurate. It is difficult to sort out which is a good site and which is not worth looking at, and therefore it is prudent to treat internet sites with a degree of scepticism.

All these sources of information are a good starting point, but are no substitute for taking professional advice early, as this can often save you a fortune later on in terms of expenses, administration and taxes. Professional advice will also be able to tell you whether what you are trying to do is possible or not. It is much better to find out that a business idea will not work in Spain at the beginning, before you have invested huge amounts of money and time, than going down a particular route only to find yourself in a cul-de-sac that is difficult to back out of. Talk to a specialist lawyer who understands business in Spain and business in the UK to establish whether your idea is likely to work.

Research

The need for research cannot be overstated. Without research you are doomed to failure. Even if you think that you already know the business or the market, it is important to carry out as much research as you can – you may be surprised by the results. Research can tell you whether the business really does stand a chance of success. Among the many items to research are:

- **Area where the business will be located.**
- **Area where you are going to be setting up the business.**
- **The market in the area.**
- **Your competition. What are their strengths and weaknesses compared to your own business?**
- **Potential customers.**
- **Analysis of your competitors' pricing structure.**
- **Type of business that you are going to be running.**
- **Attitudes towards products and service.**
- **Who are your potential customers? What are they like?**
- **What do your potential customers want from you?**
- **How many potential customers will you have?**
- **Are there any businesses that you could work with in the area?**
- **Market and sector analysis.**
- **What sorts of advertising are usual in the sector that you are entering? What could make you different from the competition?**
- **Who are the suppliers to your business and are there better suppliers?**
- **What are the legal requirements of your business?**
- **Are you affected by restrictions on importation and exportation?**
- **Are there any peculiarities of the sector you are entering that you need to be aware of?**

Obviously the type of business that you will be running will affect the type and extent of the research that you need to be doing. Different types of business are going to be served by research companies in different ways. You may find that some companies have already carried out market research that would be suitable. It may be that you need to employ a market-research company to carry out the specific research for you. Your local chamber of commerce is probably a good starting point as they will probably have access to market research that may be suitable for you and your business.

Again, the internet is a remarkable tool and it is possible to obtain a huge amount of information. Simply typing in the phrase 'starting a business in Spain' on Google shows well over 2 million listings. Not all will be relevant of course and it is important to stick to official websites or websites of good standing in order to avoid unreliable, out-of-date or irrelevant information. Many good quality market reports require you to subscribe or pay for information, although they may provide a taster of what the report says without the need to pay.

There is also a wealth of information out there to be read and it is important that you carry on reading. The more reading you do before you embark on your business, the more likely it will be that you will succeed. You need to know about Spain, about the type of business that you will be running, about your customers, about the changes around the corner in your industry – the list goes on. Many industries have their own trade magazine or newspaper. These publications often have useful articles, which may help you when starting and also during the continuation of your business. Obviously there will come a time when you have to stop reading and start acting, but start off with the reading.

Legal Advice

I have a friend who is always convinced that he is right. No matter how much you reason with him he is always certain that his latest scheme is foolproof and cannot fail. He simply won't see anything wrong with his logic and cannot understand how anybody (including his wife) can see any faults in his idea. He steamrollers over the point of view of others in his pursuit of his goals. Even when the idea fails he still manages to persuade himself that his thought-process was correct and that the idea should not have failed. He spends his life being amazed when things don't work out the way that he had envisaged and leaves in his wake a trail of family members and friends thinking 'I told you so'.

While my friend's belief in himself and his ideas is to be applauded, it is also his downfall. When starting a business it is easy to get wrapped up in your idea. Too many people over the years have managed to persuade themselves and others that a business idea will make their fortune only to be astounded when they end up either not doing as well as they thought or losing everything that they had. Certainly you need optimism and the drive to make your idea work, but it is important that you go into any new venture with your eyes wide open. Think about all the different possible scenarios and try and work out plans for each one.

It is vital, however, that you talk to a lawyer at the outset. You cannot foresee every eventuality yourself and, though there is no harm in taking advice from friends, family and people who have done similar things, consulting a lawyer may save you a fortune. You may think to yourself that lawyers are expensive and talking to a lawyer will *cost* you a fortune rather than *saving* you one. However, the advice a good lawyer can give is likely to save you far more than it costs over the many years that your business will trade. An example: I had a meeting with a client that cost them £200. While this may seem expensive, in that meeting I saved my client over £50,000. Suddenly the meeting seems cheap!

When you see your lawyer, take your business and life plan with you (for more discussion on these plans, *see* 'Your Business Plan', p.81 and 'Writing a "Life Plan"', p.83). Also, go armed with statistics and ideas. A lawyer should be able to look at them, point out any obvious problem areas and suggest ways forward. If any work is required to clarify your plans your lawyer should, if you wish, be able to help or to do it for you.

If you deal with all of the key points before you get in too deep, you will know that you are ready to go ahead and you will not have to deal with the issues in a hurry when surprises come out of the woodwork or when you are running out of money. The lawyer will also be able to tell you whether what you are trying to do is legal in Spain and what issues are important for such a business.

Only UK lawyers who specialize in dealing with Spain will be able to help you fully. Your average English solicitor will know little or nothing of the issues of Spanish law and a Spanish lawyer is likely to know little or nothing about the British tax system or the issues of English or Scots law that will affect the way the transaction should be arranged. A specialist lawyer may also be able to recommend estate agents, architects, surveyors, banks, mortgage lenders and other contacts in the area where you are looking.

A physical meeting is still the best way to start an important relationship. It has a number of advantages. It allows you to show and be shown documents and to wander off more easily into related topics. Most importantly, it is usually easier to make certain that you have understood each other in a face-to-face meeting. But, these days, 'seeing' your lawyer does not need to involve an actual meeting. If it is more convenient for you, it could be done by a telephone conference call, by video conference or even over the internet.

A good lawyer will go further than just telling you what the law says – they will also be able to go into the more practical sides of the business and almost act as a partner in your new venture.

Talk to People Who Have Already Done It

Why not learn from other people's experiences? After all, it is much better that somebody else has tried something and made the mistakes rather than you. There is no point in your trying things that have failed in the past unless you are going to do them differently. Similarly, if something has already been successful then it is likely (although not guaranteed) that the same thing can be successful in the future.

There is certainly no shortage of people to talk to. Some of these have been very successful, others have lost everything they had. There are many people in between these two extremes. Go and speak to people who have started businesses in Spain and get their input – you will be amazed at how friendly most of them are.

If somebody has been successful then they must be doing something right. Learn from what they have done and then go and do the same sort of thing in your own way. Don't just copy what other people have done – if you do this then you are just as likely to fail, as you won't really understand why they were successful in the first place. It is also important to get both sides of the story. Don't just talk to people who have been successful. Try and find out why businesses have failed and what mistakes were made. When you start a business you should at least try and make your mistakes (and there will be some) your own mistakes rather than ones that other people have made in the past.

Your Experience

How much experience do you have? I regularly see clients who are selling up in the UK to move to Spain and start a business and am often surprised at how many of them have never worked in the industry that they intend to go into – or even have never run a business before.

The classic example is a couple who were setting up a bar in Spain. They had never worked in a bar before but had decided that they would sell up everything in the UK, move to Spain, buy a bar and make their fortune. They had no idea that the opening hours in Spain go on for longer than they do in the UK and that in all probability they would have to be working long hours serving customers until they reached the level of turnover where they could afford to take a back seat and let their staff do more of the work! They had clearly never worked in or run a pub in the UK and had no idea how things actually happen.

In any industry, the more experience you have, the more successful you are going to be. In the majority of cases the experience that you have will be useful in Spain. However, it is also important to gain experience in Spain as the way things are done can be very different to the way you would expect things to be done in Britain. If the type of business that you are thinking about setting up in Spain already exists, try and find a job working in the industry before you start up your own business. In this way you can gain valuable experience in the industry before setting up on your own.

Language Skills

Running a business is hard enough work without making life unnecessarily difficult for yourself. If you cannot speak Spanish, undoubtedly running a business in Spain will be more difficult for you.

One of the many advantages of setting up a business in Spain compared to many other 'foreign' countries is the large percentage of people who speak English. This means that many people have been able to set up businesses despite not being able to speak Spanish that well at the outset. While this is possible, it is not advisable.

You are going to find it much easier to make the all-important personal relationships and contacts if you can speak the language, as the person that you are trying to form the relationship with will appreciate the effort that you are making. If you can't speak Spanish then you will also be at a considerable disadvantage when it comes to dealing with suppliers. Yes, there are English suppliers with whom you can deal, but these are generally few and far between and you may find that you are paying a premium for dealing with such businesses. Dealing with authorities and official bodies – particularly the tax office – is difficult enough when you can speak the language. If you cannot speak Spanish then dealing with officialdom is at best more difficult, and potentially a complete disaster.

If you are intending to live in a country it also makes sense to learn the language in order to make the most of the people and culture on offer. You will miss a great deal of the vibrancy of Spanish life and culture if you speak nothing but English and associate only with other English-speakers. Without a good knowledge of Spanish you will miss the true meaning of certain words or phrases. Language is a fascinating subject and history is littered with misunderstandings between people who thought that they understood what the other person was saying. If you can avoid these potential problems it will again make your life easier and therefore improve your chances of success. For information on how to learn the language *see* 'Learning Spanish', p.158.

Remember, too, that in Spain they don't just speak Spanish. Spanish as we think of it is actually *Castellano* (Castilian). In addition to this there are several other regional languages spoken around the country. Most people speak *Castellano* and may speak one of the other regional languages, but occasionally you come across somebody who can speak only – or wants to speak only – their regional language. For more information on the various regional languages, *see* 'Spanish languages', p.26.

Setting Up a Business in Spain

First Steps 76
Finding Business Opportunities 76
Your Business Plan 77
Working from Home 80
Relating to Your 'Parent' Business 81
Should You Set Up Your Own Business or Buy Into an
  Existing Business? 82
Business Structures 90
Licences and Registrations 97
Raising Finance 98
Getting Finance into Spain 101
Spanish Banks 103
Business and Personal Taxes 105
Acquiring Business Premises 109
Employing Staff 118
Marketing 123
Final Plan Checklist 124

04

First Steps

Lawyers and accountants are needed at the beginning of your new venture, during its running and at the end, should you decide to stop or sell the business. They are needed no matter how small your business is – don't assume that only large companies need this sort of specialist advice. It is advisable that you employ both a lawyer and an accountant. Ideally, your lawyer and accountant should not only speak English and Spanish but also have an understanding of both the Spanish system and the system in your own country. By understanding both systems, your lawyer or accountant will be able to advise you how to do things in a way that does not cause a problem either in Spain or in the UK. In addition, having somebody who understands both systems will enable you to use both systems to your advantage.

Further Research and Action Required

The easiest way of getting rid of any of your money is to start a business in a country that you do not know without carrying out research. Acting in this way is like throwing bank notes out of the window of a moving car.

You will have carried out some research to start with. Now that you have decided to proceed with the business it is time to carry out more detailed research. You will need to investigate every single aspect of your business. You will be spending a lot of your money on getting the venture up and running – you should not do so without carrying out further research. Having initially discussed the idea with you, your advisers will also have to carry out some research and report back to you on whether your idea will work, whether it is legal, what the requirements are for your industry and so on.

Finding Business Opportunities

There are no end of business opportunities in Spain and it is not hard to find them. Many seem too good to be true. They are. It is important to keep your wits about you and to use only legitimate sources of business opportunities. It is also important to do your homework and take legal advice before parting with any money. Chambers of commerce often have lists of business opportunities published on their websites. Both the Spanish Chamber of Commerce in Great Britain and the British Chamber of Commerce in Spain offer this facility. In addition to this, local chambers of commerce in Spain should have lists of business opportunities.

A number of other avenues are open for enquiries. Chapters 1 and 3 of this book may help you with some of your ideas. Trade shows can be a great source of inspiration. There are many trade shows both in Spain and in the UK. Obviously the trade shows in Spain are more likely to have business opportunities in Spain than the UK ones, unless a UK show has a specific Spanish connection. Trade organisations often have publications and websites that advertise job opportunities. It is worth joining the relevant trade organisation for your industry. Magazines and newspapers will often have business opportunities advertised. Local newspapers can either be in English (for example, the *Costa Blanca News*) or in Spanish. The internet comes into play yet again and it is possible to find many business opportunities with just a few minutes searching. Another good way of finding business opportunities is through personal contacts and word of mouth, or just by keeping your eyes and ears open. Although this may sound easy, you must be very wary of such an introduction – even if it is through a friend. A person mentioning that he is looking to invest in a business opportunity in Spain is rich pickings for a 'con' artist. You need to be absolutely sure that you can trust the people involved and do your research well. Too many people are introduced to a wonderful opportunity only to find that they end up losing everything because they are too trusting. It is also worth remembering that the majority of frauds committed on the British in Spain are carried out by other Britons. Dealing with your own nationality gives no protection in itself. Another route is to employ one of the consultants who specialize in finding business opportunities for people wishing to invest. Before using such consultants you need to ask yourself several questions. What is this costing me? What is in it for them? Do they have an interest in the deal that I am not aware of? Whom are they really acting for?

Your Business Plan

Once you have a business idea, you'll also need a plan. This is a vital part of your preparation. You obviously have a plan of what you intend to do with your business. This is crucial as otherwise your business will not succeed – but have you written it down? It is amazing how many people have all their business plans in their head but never take the trouble to sit down and commit their ideas to paper. By making a proper written business plan it is much easier to identify potential problems, which are unlikely to be spotted when they are just in your head. It is also much easier to share your plan with others and get their opinion. You are much more likely to succeed if you have a written plan than if you don't have a plan at all. If you are not prepared to sit down and write out a business plan then you might almost say that you don't deserve to succeed.

You will need a written business plan for a variety of reasons. The most obvious one is when you go and borrow money. The bank or mortgage lender will need to see your plan before they lend you money. Without a business plan you are unlikely to be able to obtain finance.

It is also useful to refer back to your written business plan from time to time. It is too easy to get sucked into running a business on a day-to-day basis and forget what you are trying to achieve. By looking at the plan you can see whether you are still on the right track. Sometimes you will get your business plan badly wrong. You might have under or over estimated how successful your business may be. It may actually be quite amusing to have a look back at your business plan and see how your business has changed over the years. Time and markets change and you cannot rigidly stick to the business plan that you first thought of – you will probably need to evolve your business as time goes on.

There is a whole range of items that you need to think about when you are writing a business plan. You need to be thinking about what type of business you wish to run and what area the business will succeed in; the formalities for setting up the business and taxes; who your customers are going to be and who your competition is. Is the business seasonal and how is your cash flow going to be affected? You need to be thinking about premises and staff and a whole range of other items. In short, you need to be thinking about every aspect of your business and write down how you are going to be dealing with each aspect. Once you have done this you will be able to identify whether or not the business is likely to work.

Do not forget that many of the businesses in Spain are affected by the seasonal nature of the tourist market. If the seasons affect your business, it is important that you factor this into the budget so that you don't get caught out in the 'off' season. Depending on the sort of business you are running you will need to work out how many months you expect to have regular income and how many months you are likely to have to live on no or a reduced income. Do not be tempted to spend the money while you have it – you will need something to live on for the rest of the year.

If you have run a business in the UK you are probably used to the business-plan format that is common in the UK. This type of plan is still likely to work in Spain, but it is much more advisable that you draw up a business plan in the Spanish format, which is different from the typical UK plan. A Spanish-format business plan will be useful when you need to go and borrow money. You may wish to go into business with local people or bring in partners – they will expect to see a Spanish-format business plan. You may wish to discuss your plans with your lawyer or accountant – they will also need to see a plan in a Spanish format.

There can be all sorts of different reasons why you would need to present a business plan and if you are going to somebody who is used to Spanish business plans then this is what they will expect to see. In addition, you are going to be running a business in Spain – you might as well get used to doing things in the Spanish way from the start.

See **Appendix 3**, p.257, for an outline of how to go about producing a Spanish-style business plan. The more work you can do on this at the beginning of your venture, the better.

Writing a 'Life Plan'

In addition to a business plan, you should think about your 'life plan'. Your decision to move to Spain to start a business may partly have been made because of a need to change your life in some way. However, moving abroad brings with it many changes to the way you are used to doing things. Take time to think about where your life is heading and whether you are happy to go in that direction. Just like a business plan, it is worth putting a life plan into a written document as this helps you focus on all the different aspects of your move abroad. Do this before you make the big leap to running your own business abroad and before you commit too much money to the project. To make a life plan you might like to think about the following questions. Of course there are many other points that you could add to your life plan. These will depend on your personal circumstances and what you are trying to achieve.

- What is your timescale?
- Why are you thinking about setting up a business?
- Why are you thinking about moving to Spain?
- Where are you going to live? Are you going to buy or rent?
- Why are you considering this type of business?
- What is your Spanish like?
- What experience do you have?
- How much money are you going to need to set up the business?
- How much money are you going to need to live on until the business is up and running?
- How long will it take for the business to become profitable?
- How much time are you going to need to invest in the business?
- Do you wish to go into business with other people?
- What are you going to do about schools?
- What are you going to do about health care?
- What are you going to do about pensions?
- What are you going to do about your existing investments?
- What do you wish to be doing in 5 or 10 years' time?
- Do you wish to live on or next to the business premises or do you need separation between work and home?
- If your family is going to work with you, how are you going to cope in times of stress?
- Have you got a back-up plan or an exit strategy?

Working from Home

In some countries there are strict laws regulating the use of your home for business activities. Thankfully, the laws in Spain regarding running a business from your own home are surprisingly relaxed and many people choose to do so. In fact, the majority of small businesses in Spain are probably run from home.

The main advantage is that you do not have to worry about separate premises – there is only one lot of rent or mortgage, one lot of insurance and so on. The paperwork is much less as a consequence. In addition, part of your home expenses can be set off against the business taxation – therefore making the cost of living cheaper. Furthermore, if the business fails for some reason it is a lot easier to contract out than it would be if you had separate business premises as you would not have to find somebody else to take them over.

On the down side, it can be difficult to motivate yourself to work from home and it certainly takes a lot more discipline than if you are in a dedicated work environment. There are always things that need to be done around the house and it is surprising how even the most mundane of tasks looks inviting compared to work. Another factor is that the business is always present – even when you have stopped work or at weekends. There is always the temptation to just go back and check on something when you should be focusing on life outside work.

If you are planning to run your business from home then you need to ask yourself some questions. Is your home big enough to run a business? It might be to start with, but hopefully you will soon be so successful that you will need to have your own premises. You will need somewhere that is big enough for your staff and any stock that you have. I visited somebody recently who ran a business from home making food hampers – their house was full of tins, jars and bottles, hampers, packaging and paperwork.

If you have customers visiting your business premises at home, does it give the right impression? Having a dedicated business premises gives a more professional image, whereas running a business from a home can look as though your are an amateur or just starting out.

Assuming you have decided that running a business from home is for you then you need to check to make sure that you are allowed to do this. As discussed above, this rarely causes a problem with the authorities, but different types of business have different restrictions. The landlord or the community of owners (if there is one) will probably have restrictions on the use of your home as a business premises if you have customers visiting regularly, as this will cause a disruption to your neighbours and in addition will cause more wear and tear to the premises. If in doubt, get your lawyer to go through the rules with you. If you intend to have customers or goods delivered regularly to your business and your business is based at home, then you will need permission from the local authorities.

Obviously, running a bar, restaurant or shop from home is not going to be practical and most businesses that are run from homes are paper-based or mail order. However, it is possible to do this if your home is suitable, although it is likely that this would be considered a change of use of the building and therefore permission from the local authority would be needed. In order to do this you will need to discuss it with your lawyer and your architect, and liaise with the town hall for the application for change of use of the building or part of the building. Once you have obtained this then you should be able to apply for the opening licence. Unfortunately, you will not be able to apply for the opening licence until the change of use has been granted and therefore you will have to put a certain amount of faith into the project.

Relating to Your 'Parent' Business

Assuming that the business you are setting up in Spain is not completely stand-alone, you will have to decide how it is going to relate to the 'parent' business. You may have a business in the UK that you intend to keep going and open a similar business in Spain. The relationship between these two businesses is important as this will have an effect on the administration and running of the business as well as other issues – taxation, for example.

There are basically three different ways that a new business can relate to its parent business – it can be a branch office, a representative office or a self-contained business.

Branch Office

A branch office (*sucursal*) is an organisation that depends on the head office for its existence – it is not a separate legal entity. The branch office is therefore subject to the same rules and regulations as the head office. The head office is often in a different country from the branch office, but may be in the same country. You may consider setting up a branch office if you already have a business in the UK and are thinking about expanding that business to Spain. A branch office will act as a separate entity when dealing with third parties, but will be controlled by the parent company. The formalities for setting up a branch office are very similar to setting up any other type of business. There is no minimum assigned capital, but the liability of the parent company is also unlimited.

In order to register as a branch office it is necessary to execute a public deed before a notary public (*notario*) and then register the branch office at the equivalent of Companies House in Spain – the *Registro de Sociedades*. The same documents will be required for setting up a branch office as for setting up a new company, but in addition to this you will need to produce certain papers relating to the parent business – the certificate of incorporation, memorandum and articles of association, minutes of the decision to open a branch office in Spain and a certificate from a Spanish bank proving that the capital of the business has been deposited into a Spanish bank.

If the parent company is not Spanish then the documents that you have to provide are probably not in Spanish either. If this is the case then you will have to get these documents translated, get them certified as a true translation and then legalized. Once the public deed is signed then the branch office will have to register for tax and VAT and obtain a tax identification number, pay transfer tax, pay opening licence tax and register for social security. Taxation of the branch office will be in Spain, as will the taxation of the parent business unless there is a double taxation treaty between the country in which the parent business is located in and Spain.

Local Representative Office

A representative office (*oficina representativa*) is similar to a branch office. The main difference between the two is that the branch office carries out business transactions in Spain. The formalities for opening a local representative office are very similar to setting up a branch office.

Should You Set Up Your Own Business or Buy Into an Existing Business?

This is a very important personal decision and one you will have to live with once made. There are many factors to consider and the answer may not be clear cut. It is worth taking legal advice on this point on an individual basis.

Setting Up a New Business

Setting up a business from scratch and making it successful is hugely rewarding but incredibly hard work. Setting up a new business means that everything you achieve is yours. You had the idea and put everything into place. And if the business works out you will have the ultimate satisfaction of knowing that you have done everything. Setting up a new business also means that you have total control over how the business is formed and run. There will still be compromises that you have to make, but at least you have made them.

A further important advantage of setting up your own business from scratch is that there are no surprises about the business – you know everything that has ever happened in the business and therefore know the whole history, both good and bad.

However, starting your own business is hard work. Most businesses fail within the first couple of years. They do not fail because they are a bad idea. They do not fail because the products or services are bad. They fail because they run out of money before they start to make a profit.

Buying an Existing Business

Buying an existing business means that the business is, in theory, up and running and you can (again in theory) begin to make some money straight away. This takes away a certain amount of doubt over the running of the business. It also means that you have let somebody else take the initial risks in terms of location, products, advertising and so on. Somebody else has had to suffer the cash-flow problems associated with setting up the business. Somebody else has had to attract the initial customers and build up the reputation. In theory, buying an existing business should be easier than starting up a business from scratch.

However, there are downsides to buying a business from somebody else. For a start you are taking over somebody else's ideas. Over time you can adapt and change the business to suit your taste and to incorporate your ideas, but the basic structure of the business was started by somebody else and you will have to live with this for some time. You don't have the satisfaction of doing everything yourself, although you do have the satisfaction of being up and running a lot quicker than if you were starting the business from the beginning.

One question you need to ask yourself when thinking about buying an existing business is: why is that person selling? If the business is profitable, why are they leaving it? Of course there can be very good reasons why somebody would wish to sell a profitable business – they may have got to an age where they wish to retire, their family circumstances may have changed, they may have got bored and decided to start another venture. On the other hand, there could be more sinister reasons for wishing to sell an apparently profitable business. For a start, the business may not be as profitable as it first appears. It can often be difficult to gauge this – especially when you consider that many businesses will have several sets of accounts – one for themselves (the true accounts), one for the tax man showing a lower profit than they are really making, and one set for the prospective buyer showing an inflated profit. It could be that the business has a problem on the horizon that the existing owners cannot see a solution to and therefore wish to off-load the problem onto somebody else. It is important that you carry out some investigation into why the business is being sold. Speak to other people in the area to see whether the reason that you are being told stacks up; don't just take the seller's word. The last thing that you want is to pay somebody else to take a problem off their hands!

One of the main advantages of buying an existing business is that it will already have built up a reputation. Assuming that the reputation is a good one, this makes it easier for you, as building up a good reputation takes time. However, just because the business has a good reputation doesn't mean that this good reputation will carry on when you take over. A good reputation may take years to build up, but can be lost in a very short time. How many times have you seen a bar or a restaurant in the UK taken over by new owners only for the whole character to be changed and for people to stop going? Exactly the same happens in Spain. The reputation of the business is only as good as the current owner makes it, although maintaining a good reputation is a lot easier than building one up from scratch.

If you are buying an existing business from somebody it is important to find out what the selling owner intends to do in the future. Many people have been caught out in the past by buying a thriving business from somebody, only for the previous owner to set up in competition close by and take all his previous customers from you. This may seem unfair to you, but unless you have put in place measures to avoid this, there is little you can do. It is therefore important that when you are negotiating the purchase of the business that your lawyer should include clauses that prevent the existing owner from setting up in direct competition within a certain period. Such clauses are not always effective and may be seen as anti-competitive, but this doesn't mean that this is something that either you or your advisers should overlook.

In some cases you may wish the existing owner of the business to assist you with the business for a certain period of time in a consultation capacity. You can negotiate for the existing owner to help you run the business for some time, to teach you the ins and outs of the day-to-day running of the business, to intro-duce you to suppliers and so on. This is a very attractive proposition as it has the advantage that you are learning from somebody who knowns what they are doing and you are not having to re-invent the wheel. It also has the advantage that existing customers see a gradual change in ownership and therefore do not feel as threatened by a new owner. However, this is only worth doing if the existing owner has a genuine interest in assisting you. If he or she is selling to retire then there is a temptation for them to slow down and not actually be as useful as you thought they would be. In fact, in some cases you may find that you have paid somebody only to find they are a hindrance to your getting on with the running of the business.

If you need a licence to run a business (a bar, for example), look into this before you buy. Many people over the years have been told that when they buy the business they automatically take over the licence from the previous owner. Remember that the person selling you the business is doing exactly that – selling you the business. If you need to hear that you will take over the licence then that is what you will be told – whether it is true or not. Most licences are personal to the individual and will not automatically be issued to the new owner, so it is important to look into this. In fact, sometimes prospective buyers are told anything to make sure that a sale goes through.

Staff

When you buy a business you will also take on the responsibilities of the previous owner – including the responsibilities towards staff if there were any. You may therefore find yourself responsible for their salary, social security payments and pension commitments.

The staff are entitled to receive advanced notice of the date for change of owner for the business, reason for the change and any consequences to the employees. The employees or their representatives are entitled to a consultation period should there be changes to their employment conditions.

The seller of the business will also be responsible for employment disputes that arose prior to the sale for a period of three years after the sale, as will the new owner.

Finding a Business to Buy

Finding a business to buy in Spain is not difficult – just go into any bar in Spain and start to make inquiries and you will be amazed at the number of people who are happy to part you from your cash in return for a business that is 'guaranteed' to make your fortune. Of course, no business is guaranteed to make your fortune, and many businesses in Spain need to be sold as the owner has not been able to make any money from it, but it does show how many businesses are for sale at any one time.

Estate agencies in the area will often have details of businesses for sale and there are specialist estate agencies dealing with the sale of businesses. Commercial estate agents will often go further than just the traditional role of advertising businesses for sale and putting buyers in contact with the sellers – they may offer to assist with opening licences, advice on business practices, due diligence on the business and a whole range of other activities both before you buy and after you have bought. While these services are useful, and in most cases are given with a genuine desire to help their clients, it must not be forgotten that the agency gets its commission only if the sale goes through. Any advice given by an agency, no matter how good it is, is no substitute for independent advice from lawyers, tax advisers and business consultants.

Buying from a commercial agency is no guarantee that the business is sound and that what the seller is telling you is correct. Their primary job is to sell the property and you must not forget this. If, after you buy a property, the business turns out not to be as much of a bargain as you initially thought, or there are major problems with, for example, staff, then it is pointless complaining to the agency that acted in the sale – it is simply not their job to look into these things for you and they will not compensate you for any losses that you have incurred.

There are also numerous publications and internet sites with details of businesses for sale. In the UK, *Daltons Weekly* has a whole section dedicated to businesses abroad for sale. Various other newspapers and magazines, including *Exchange and Mart*, the *Daily Telegraph* and the *Mail* also advertise foreign businesses for sale. Spanish publications obviously have a wider selection. There are specific newspapers for the English-speaking communities in Spain. These tend to be aimed at a particular geographical area – for example, the *Costa Blanca News* and the *Costa del Sol News* both concentrate on their geographical areas. *Sur In English* is a newspaper in the Málaga area targeted at the English-speaking community. All of these newspapers have classified sections listing businesses for sale. There is also a range of other English-language newspapers and publications in different areas of Spain. And don't forget the internet, which has pages and pages of links either to businesses for sale or to people who can help you find one.

Franchises

If we look at the retail sector in Spain over the last few years, we can see a major change in the market just as in many other countries. The number of businesses has reduced, with smaller retailers closing down as they struggle to compete with the larger chains and supermarkets – particularly with major foreign chains entering the market. However, over the same period the number of franchises has increased dramatically – nearly 400 per cent in the last 10 years, and more and more people who start a business think about doing so as a franchise. Starting a business does not necessarily mean that you have to continue as a franchise – although the advantages of the franchise mean that 80 per cent of franchises continue under the same branding.

A franchise (*franquicia*) is a way in which a small business can appear to be larger than it really is and allows it to compete with larger organisations. The franchisee buys the right to use the franchisor's name and business system. A franchise agreement can cover many different types of activities. Unsurprisingly, perhaps, the first franchises in Spain were the top American fast-food chains, but since then the number and variety of franchises has increased dramatically.

Franchises are big business in Spain with their number growing year upon year despite the difficult world economic climate. In fact, some sources estimate that franchises account for about 10 per cent of all retails sales in the Spanish economy (up from 5 per cent in 1997) with an expected growth of about 10 per cent over the next year. The most popular franchises in Spain are fast-food and restaurants (14 per cent), supermarkets (11 per cent), vending (9 per cent) and clothing and footwear (8 per cent).

However, not all franchises are successful. Before embarking on a franchise agreement it is important that you look carefully at the franchise itself. Have other people using the franchise system been successful? Do they enjoy working under the system? If possible, go and talk to other people running similar franchises and find out what they like and, more importantly, what they do not like about the system. Only when you have done this will you be able to determine whether or not you can make a success of it.

The downside of a franchise is that you are effectively regulated by the franchisor in that you have to have common images, common systems and procedures and you must look like you are the same company. This leaves very little scope for your own business ideas to flourish. There are several points that you need to take into consideration when thinking about taking on a franchise in addition to the points that you would normally consider when starting your own business. Are you happy to follow somebody else's system of working? One of the joys of working for yourself is the ability to make your own procedures and set up your own systems. You will not be able to do this with a franchise – it is a bit like running your own business under somebody else's rules. If you are too independent for this then franchising is not right for you. It is better to find this out before you take on the franchise rather than after you have paid out good money for it.

You should get your legal adviser to look at the franchise agreement or contract. This is the document that will determine how you are to be running the business and you need to know that you can work within the rules of the franchise. You must understand what your obligations are as otherwise you could end up losing the right to the franchise.

Many franchises fail. The reason for this is that the person taking it on often believes that by being a franchise a lot of the hard work is taken away from the business, as the name and reputation is set up right from the beginning. They forget that they need to maintain the reputation and still need to work hard to make the franchise work.

Often people who go into a franchise are those who have already run their own business and who wish to use the franchise system to allow them to compete with bigger firms, or those who have come into some money either by an inheritance, a redundancy or some other means and see this as a quick and simple way of establishing their own business.

Further information on franchises can be obtained from the International Franchise Organisation. There are also numerous websites selling franchises in Spain and several large franchise trade shows that run throughout the year in various parts of the country.

Joint Ventures

A joint venture (*empresa conjunta*) is one where two or more parties get together and carry out a specific economic activity through a business arrangement. It is basically a contract with other parties to work together for common benefit and profit.

Joint ventures can be a good way of starting to work in Spain without going to the expense of starting a completely new business from scratch. Both parties will contribute something to the venture and hopefully the sum of the parts will be greater than the individual pieces. Joint ventures can also be a very good way of expanding your business.

However, joint ventures in Spain can be difficult to establish successfully. In trying to set one up you will often find that you spend hours in meetings trying to reach some common goal. Just when you think that you have made a break-through, you may find that there is one sticking point that sends you back to the beginning. It is absolutely crucial to know and understand the people with whom you are trying to enter into the joint venture. If you do not, then at best you will spend hours deciding what the venture is to be called. At worst you may lose your reputation, time and money. Joint ventures come in two broad types.

Temporary Business Association

A temporary business association (*Unión Temporal de Empresas* – UTE) is where two parties or more get together for a joint venture for a specific project. Once the project is finished the joint venture also finishes. This type of venture tends to work well in the construction, engineering and IT industries. UTEs are created by a notarial deed and must be registered at the Spanish Ministry of Economy in their special register for such joint ventures.

Economic Interest Group or European Economic Interest Grouping

The Economic Interest Group – EIG (*Agrupación de Interés Economicos*) – and its European equivalent, European Economic Interest Grouping – EEIG (*Agrupación Europeo de Interés Economicos*) – is where two or more parties enter into a joint venture not for profit but for the general benefit of its members. The joint venture itself will not make a profit, but will help its members to make one. The EIG is created by a notarial deed. The EIG must not interfere with the members' decisions relating to staff, finance or investment. The activities of the members must not be managed or controlled by the EIG. The EIG must not own part of another company. Each member of the EIG will contribute to the costs and expenses of the joint venture. If the joint venture has any debts then each member is liable for the whole of the debt of the joint venture.

Due Diligence

When you go into a joint venture with somebody it is essential that you carry out due diligence. Due diligence is nothing more complicated than carrying out some background checks – in short, doing your homework. Every business has its little secrets that they would rather you didn't find out about. It is much better that you discover all you can about these before you go into business with them. You need to gather as much information as possible. You need to make sure that what you are being told is correct. The following checklist is not exhaustive and may not be suitable for your particular case, but it gives an example of the sorts of things you need to be looking into. The checklist is in no particular order.

Due Diligence Checklist

A due diligence checklist is never something that should be rushed. Allow plenty of time to carry out these checks – it can take much longer than you think. Do not just concentrate on the financial side – there is much more to due diligence than money.

In fact, due diligence is so important that some companies actually specialise in carrying out this sort of work investigating other companies. This shows how much work needs to be done. It is important that you do not go into a joint venture with somebody that you don't fully understand – the joint venture is much more likely to fail if you do.

If in doubt, walk away. If you are being pressured not to carry out due diligence, walk away. If you are being given only a short time to carry out due diligence, walk away.

- Licences and permits – are there any and are any needed?
- Is the person or body who they say they are?
- What do the other person's accounts look like?
- What are the other person's accounting and audit procedures like?
- Does the other person or body have employees?
- What is the current situation regarding these employees?
- What about the other party's liabilities?
- What are the existing contracts, agreements and obligations of the other party?
- What assets does the other party own?
- What is the condition of any assets owned by the other party?
- What is the situation regarding insurance of the other party?
- Are there any pending claims?
- What are the sales and marketing strategies of the other party?
- Have you seen any statutes or company documents for the other party?
- Does the other party have any pending litigation against them or against other people?
- What is the other party's cash flow like?
- What are the other party's operating procedures like?
- Does the other party have the same business ethos as you do?
- Can you work together?

Business Structures

When you are setting up your business it is important that you take advice on which is the best structure for it. Each business entity has its advantages and disadvantages in terms of ease of administration, taxation and, most importantly, the liability of the owners.

As time passes and hopefully the business grows and expands, the structure of the business may have to change to reflect any changes but also to take advantage of some of the features of other business structures.

Sole Traders

The definition of a sole trader (*empresario individual*) according to the Spanish ministry of industry, tourism and commerce is 'a physical person who carries out in their own name, or through a business, an activity which is commercial, industrial or professional'. From this you can see that a sole trader does not necessarily mean that the business is just one person, but can have employees.

Advantages

Because a sole trader is not bound by any company rules and regulations, they can be very flexible and make decisions quickly and efficiently. The sole trader is not covered by any specific laws, but has to observe the general laws and comply with their rights and obligations under the *Código de Comercio* (commerce code) and also the *Código Civil* (civil code). It is the sole trader who has control over the business and who decides how that business is going to work and perform.

Setting up as a sole trader is easy – there are no special documents that need to be completed nor any minimum capital that must be invested in the business. In fact, the amount of capital invested is entirely governed by the needs of the business and the resources of the sole trader or his lending institution.

Running a business as the sole trader is relatively devoid of red tape – certainly compared to running a company. This means that the person running the business can concentrate on the business rather than getting tied down in administration, but it also means that they have greater flexibility. The flexibility and lower administration costs mean that working as a sole trader is a good structure for small businesses, particularly those just starting up.

Disadvantages

The owner of the business has no protection, as the business debts are also his own debts. If the business gets into financial difficulties, then it is the owner's responsibility to deal with these problems. This, in turn, means that his creditors can try to recover their debts from whatever the business owner owns – including his house, car and bank account. Running a business as a sole trader is not the most tax-efficient way of running a business, as you will find that the rates of tax that you pay are often much higher than if you were running a business in some other form – particularly if the business is doing well. The taxation of a sole trader is done on a personal income tax basis.

A sole trader is not entitled to unemployment benefit. It is therefore vital that you have an exit plan just in case things don't work out in the way that you had originally planned.

Partnerships

The definition of a partnership according to the Spanish ministry of industry, tourism and commerce is 'a contract by which the ownership of a thing or right belongs jointly to several people'. Running a business as a partnership (*asociación de bienes*) means that several individuals own the business together without the structure of a company. There needs to be a minimum of two partners to form a partnership. Obviously going into partnership with other people means that you must have complete faith and trust in them, as they will be running the business with you. You must share the same vision for the business and have the same desires and ambitions. Too many partnerships have failed because the people who went into business together did not share the same ideas and aspirations.

Advantages

A partnership can be very flexible in what it can do because it is not bound by any company rules and regulations, which means that decisions can be made quickly and efficiently. Just as with a sole trader, the partnership is not covered by any specific laws, but has to observe the general laws and comply with its rights and obligations under the *Código de Comercio* and also the *Código Civil*. It is the partners who have control over the business and who decide how that business is going to work and perform.

Setting up as a partnership is very easy. Again, no minimum capital is required and very little paperwork is needed. The only thing you will need is a partnership agreement setting out the relationship between the parties and how the partnership is to be run, the percentage shares between the partners and how any profit and loss will be treated. The partnership deed should be done before a notary public if it deals with real estate or rights.

Disadvantages

There is no protection for the partners of the business, as the debts of the business are also the partners' debts. If the business gets into financial difficulties, then it is the responsibility of the partners to deal with these problems. This in turn means that its creditors can try to recover their debts from whatever the business partners own.

'PYME' (Small and Medium-Sized Enterprise)

A small and medium-sized enterprise in Spain is referred to as a PYME (*Pequeña y Mediana Empresa*). The vast majority of companies in Spain are PYMEs. In fact, in 2003, 99.87 per cent of all companies in Spain were classified as PYMEs. There are various reasons for this:

- **It is relatively easy to set up a small business in Spain.** *See* 'Types of Spanish Business Structure', p.263.
- **The level of share capital required for a small business is low.**
- **Subsidies and grants are available for setting up small businesses.** *See* 'Grants and Subsidies', p.104.
- **Small businesses are flexible and can adapt quickly to the market.**
- **Small businesses do not have the red tape that larger firms do.**
- **The Spanish prefer to work for themselves rather than for others.**
- **Many business owners do not like the responsibility of employing staff.**
- **The Spanish like the personal touch. Small businesses are much more able to provide this.**

Limited Companies/Corporations

Sociedad Limitada (S.L.)

The definition of a *Sociedad Limitada* according to the Spanish ministry of industry, tourism and commerce is 'a company in which the shares are divided in participation units which are indivisible and where the shareholders are not personally responsible for debts'. An S.L. is the Spanish equivalent of the British limited company (ltd).

The transfer of the participation units must be done by public deed. It is possible to have one person running an S.L., but this requires special regulations. The participation units can be transferred only to other unit holders. The participation units cannot be certificates and cannot be held as security.

An S.L. is regulated by *Ley de Sociedades Limitadas* law 2/1995 of 23 March 1995, which reformed the previous laws on S.L.s. The formation of the company requires a formal constitution registered by public deed and then registered in the company register. The company name must include the words *Sociedad Limitada, Sociedad de Responsabilidad Limitada* or the abbreviations 'S.L.' or 'S.R.L.' at the end. The deed incorporating the company must be signed by all the founding shareholders and this must also be registered in the company register. The deed of incorporation has to include a range of information including the following: full names and ages of the person or companies forming the new company, the objects of the company, the length of duration of the company, the number of shares and their nominal value and class.

In order to set up an S.L., a minimum amount of capital must be invested into the business – currently €3,005.06. (You will often find that such amounts in Spain appear to be curiously specific. When Spain joined the euro zone they simply converted the round figures in pesetas to euros at a fixed rate, resulting in some rather strange figures. Over time, these rates will change and we will once again have round figures.) All the shares subscribed must be paid for at the time of incorporation. Shareholders can be either private individuals or other companies.

The company administrators have the right to carry out the running of the business. The company administrators must also approve the company's annual accounts and comply with the regulations expected of an S.L. The administrators can also name new administrators, modify the statutes of the company, increase or reduce the share capital, transform, merge or dissolve the company and many other activities set out in the statutes.

The rules regarding the annual accounts are set out in the law relating to *Sociedades Anonimas*. Dividends in the company must be paid out, subject to the company statutes, in proportion to the percentages owned by the shareholders. A minimum of 5 per cent of the shareholders' stake is needed in order to examine, at the registered office of the company, the documents that support the annual accounts (unless the statutes of the company state otherwise).

Sociedad Unipersonal de Responsabilidad Limitada

This is a limited company with only one entity running it, or, effectively, this is a limited company where there is only one director and shareholder.

There are two types of *sociedad unipersonal de responsabilidad limitada*. The first is where there is only one entity who sets up the business – either an individual or a legal entity. The second is where there are two or more entities setting up the company but where all the shares have passed to only one of them. The *sociedad unipersonal de responsabilidad limitada* has to be registered in the company register.

Sociaded Anónima (S.A.)

The definition of a *sociedad anónima* according to the Spanish ministry of industry, tourism and commerce is 'a company in which the capital, which is divided into shares, is provided by the shareholders, who do not have responsibility for the debts of the company'. An S.A. is the Spanish equivalent of the British public limited company (plc).

The running of a *sociedad anónima* is regulated by law 1564/1998 issued on 22 December 1998, which is referred to as the law of *Sociedades Anónimas*. The formation of the company requires a formal constitution registered by public deed and then registered in the company register. The company name must include the words '*Sociedad Anónima*' or the abbreviation 'S.A.' at the end. The deed incorporating the company must be registered in the company register and must include a range of information including the following: full names and ages of the person or companies forming the new company, the objects of the company, the length of duration of the company, the number of shares and their nominal value and class.

In order to set up an S.A., a minimum amount of capital must be invested in the business – currently €60,101.21. All the shares must be subscribed and at least 25 per cent of them must be paid for from the time of incorporation. Shareholders can be either private individuals or other companies.

An S.A. must hold certain meetings of the shareholders and directors, and every year there must be an annual general meeting (AGM) and sometimes an extraordinary general meeting (EGM). At the AGM various resolutions can be passed, providing that there are the appropriate numbers of votes. Different resolutions will require different numbers of votes to pass them. An EGM can be called when it is deemed necessary by the company or when a minimum of five per cent of the shareholders request one.

The administrators of the company run the business and are responsible for calling general meetings, informing shareholders of important news, keeping and signing off the annual accounts, and registering the annual accounts in the company register. The administrators can be individuals from other companies, providing that there is nothing in the company statutes to preclude that. The administrators must also be shareholders.

The shareholders have the right to attend and vote at general meetings. They have the right to preferential purchase of subsequent share issues and also the right to share in the profits of the company.

The annual accounts of an S.A. have to be clear and reflect the reality of the business. It is the responsibility of the administrators to provide these and to have them approved at the AGM. The annual accounts must be signed by all the administrators and must be audited.

Running a business as an S.A. is convenient when there is a large investment in the company and where there are many shareholders. The main advantage of an S.A. is that the shareholders do not have any responsibility for the debts of the company over and above the amount that they have already invested. Running a business of this kind can be tax advantageous as companies are taxed on the basis of company tax (*impuesto de sociedades*) at a rate of 35 per cent of profits.

A *sociedad anónima laboral* is a kind of *sociedad anónima* formed by workers who own the company's share capital and are employed by the company.

Sociedad Colectiva

This is a commercial company but the shareholders are liable for company debts. It is normally used for joint ventures and therefore partners are companies.

Cooperatives

A cooperative (*sociedad cooperativa*) is a group of people who voluntarily get together to carry out joint economic activities. The structure and the running of the cooperative is conducted on a democratic basis between its members – although different members may be given different levels of votes within the cooperative. The voting rights may be divided equally or in some other way – for example, proportionally according to the economic size of the members.

Any economic activity may be carried out within a cooperative and a cooperative can also enter into economic activities with outside entities (such as trading). The name of the cooperative must contain the words *Sociedad Cooperativa* or its abbreviation *S.Coop.* The cooperative must have its registered office within Spain in the place where the principal activity is carried out. There are different types and classes of cooperatives, depending on the activity or industry sector. For example, class one cooperatives include:

- **cooperative of associated work**
- **cooperative of consumers and users**
- **housing cooperative**
- **farming cooperative**
- **cooperative for the common exploitation of the land**
- **cooperative for services**
- **cooperative of the sea**
- **truckers cooperative**
- **insurance cooperative**
- **sanitation cooperative**
- **teaching cooperative**
- **credit cooperative**

Each of the many different types of cooperative has slightly different rules as to how they can operate. In addition, the rules will also vary between autonomous regions.

First-grade cooperatives must have at least three members, while second-grade cooperatives must have at least two members. Members can join or leave the cooperative over the years. The cooperative will have an assembly of members to decide how the cooperative is going to be run.

Which Is Best For You?

Comparison Between Different Types of Company Structure

There are major differences between the various company structures, so it is important to look at your business and decide which is the best for you. If you are just starting out it is unlikely you will want (or be able) to form a *sociedad anónima* but your legal and financial advisers should help you decide which is the best structure for your business. You cannot assume that the way that you would do things in the UK will necessarily be suitable for Spain. *See* **Appendix 4**, p.263, for a table of the various company structures in Spain.

Limits on Liability

One of the main differences between the different business structures is the liability of the owners of the business. This is very important because in personal and partnership structures you will be personally liable for the debts of the business. The company structures tend to have liability limited to the amount of capital put into the business. The advantage of this is that if the company becomes bankrupt for whatever reason then the owners of the business can distance themselves from the debts of the company.

Amount of Capital Required

Different business structures require different amounts of investment capital. This can range from no minimum capital for a sole trader or a partnership, right up to a minimum of €1,803,036.30 for a company of reciprocal guarantee. These different requirements are often a major factor in deciding which business structure to select.

Taxation

Another major difference is how the business is taxed. Sole traders and partnerships will be taxed as private individuals and pay IRPF, whereas the company structures will be taxed differently and on the basis of company tax (*impuesto de sociedades*). For a discussion of the rates of tax for the different business structures, *see* 'Business and Personal Taxes', p.109.

Red Tape

As the business structure gets more complex, the amount of red tape associated with running the business increases. Setting up a business as a sole trader or a partnership involves minimal red tape and regulations. A company, on the other hand, not only has to follow the laws associated with that type of business but also the statutes of the business. In addition, the simpler forms of structure are easier and quicker to set up than the more corporate forms of business.

Credibility

A limited company has to file its accounts in the company register. This means that clients and suppliers can carry out searches into the company's credibility to see whether the company is in good financial shape, whereas this is much more difficult with a sole trader or a partnership.

Licences and Registrations

It is highly likely that you will need one or more licences to open and run a business in Spain. The wait for some of this paperwork can be lengthy. It can, for example, take several months to obtain an opening licence in some areas. It is therefore sensible to apply for such licences and registrations as soon as possible – do not wait until the last minute.

Of course, Spain being Spain, many people open and run a business before they receive the relevant paperwork, or even without applying for it in the first place. They have done this for many years and got away with it. This does not mean that you will get away with it. It also does not mean that this is what should happen. Do not do this – if you do and you get caught your business will be closed down and any chances of having a licence issued in the future will be ruined.

When you apply for a licence – for example, the opening licence – the authority will rubber-stamp your application to show that you have applied for the relevant licence. This is basically a receipt to show that you have applied for a licence – it is not an authority to open or run the business. However, because licences can take so long to obtain, many businesses start to operate in antici-pation of the licence being issued and simply have the rubber stamp on the application form. You should not do this, although it is common. This is like a half-way house between having the licence and running a business with no licence at all. The authorities in some areas know that there is great delay in issuing licences and therefore tend to turn a blind eye to people operating in this way – particularly if you are discrete and keep out of trouble. However, there is no guarantee that the authorities will turn a blind eye – nor is there a guar-antee that they will issue the licence at all! There is also no guarantee that one of your competitors will not find out and complain to the authorities.

Because the process of applying for, and the issuing of, licences can take so long, it is advisable to get a lawyer or *gestor* to assist you with the application as this can avoid unnecessary rejections and re-applications for the paperwork. For more information about the role of the *gestor* and licences, *see* **Red Tape**, p.132.

Raising Finance

Few people can afford to set up and run a business using just their own funds. Even if you can afford to do this you may not wish to put all your savings into the business at this stage. It is therefore likely that you will wish to raise some finance in order to set up the business. You will need to borrow money for two main reasons.

Firstly, though you are setting up your own business to make money you will, initially at least, be poorer than you were before you started the business. Any business needs money in its start-up phase. There is going to be a huge list of things that you will need to pay for and the amount of money that you will need is usually far more than you initially imagined. Then, once you have set up your business, it is going to take some time before you break even, and even longer to make a profit. You will need something to live on until the business is up and running profitably and therefore in addition to the cost of setting up the business you will also have the cost of living to take into consideration. Many people opt to borrow money to cover the start-up costs of their business and use their savings to live on until the business goes into profit.

Spanish Lenders

The most obvious way of raising finance is through a Spanish lender. The business is based in Spain, you are living in Spain, your clients are in Spain and therefore it can make sense to use Spanish lenders.

If you own your own home in Spain you may be able to re-mortgage that property in order to release some of the equity, which can then be put into the business. If you do decide to take out a mortgage you may wish to give serious consideration to a fixed-rate mortgage so that you know what your commitment will be over, say, 5, 10 or 15 years. In this way you can more easily work out your monthly payments, which in turn makes budgeting for the business easier. There are obviously advantages and disadvantages to a fixed-rate mortgage and you should take advice on this point from your mortgage lender or broker. For further information about Spanish mortgages, *see* **Living in Spain**, p.167.

Using Your Own Cash – Tax Efficiency

You may have saved up money that you now wish to use for the business, or you may have come into some money – either from the sale of a house, an inheritance or a redundancy payout. By financing your business through your own funds means that you do not have to pay interest on money that you have borrowed. It therefore seems sensible not to borrow money for the business. However, borrowing money – particularly in Spain, where the interest rates are lower than they are in the UK – can have advantages. For a start you can put your own money to other uses. Secondly, you can use your own money to make your plans bigger than you originally envisaged. There is however another reason for borrowing money which many people do not think about – tax efficiency. If you borrow funds to run your business, you can often offset the interest payments that you have to make against any profits, meaning that the tax you have to pay is lower.

Friends and Family

The majority of Spanish businesses are set up using money that has been provided in part or in full from friends and family of the owners of the business. If you have this opportunity available, it is a great low- or no-cost way of borrowing. The people that you will be borrowing from – friends and family – are likely to be more flexible in their attitudes to lending than the banks.

However, one major consideration is the effect the loan will have on your relationship with the person lending you the money. What happens if it takes you much longer to pay the money back than you initially envisaged? What happens if you cannot pay the money back? What happens if your business fails or if you fall out with the person? It is important to think about these matters before entering into such an arrangement with your friends and family. It is also important to talk to the person lending you the money to make them realise that nothing is guaranteed and they may lose their loan. Advise them to take independent legal advice before entering into the agreement, even if they are close to you. If necessary, have a written agreement drawn up that sets out the terms of the loan.

I know of one person who lent a family member some money to help them out of a difficult financial situation. The person who had borrowed the money never repaid the money despite various vague promises to do so. The relationship between the person lending the money and the person borrowing the money deteriorated to the extent that a court case was brought for the recovery of the money due. An amicable relationship ended up in court with the two people vowing never to speak to one another again.

Business Partners

Another way of injecting some much-needed capital into a business is to join forces with somebody else. This means that not only can you put your money into the business, but so can they. Taking on a partner is not something to enter into lightly. You should go into business only with somebody that you have full confidence in and whom you know well.

Another case I once heard of involved the purchase of a property in Spain. The idea was that two business partners would pay for half of the property each.

Then they would rent out the property and keep half of the profits each. In this way they could achieve something that they could not do individually. Unfortunately, as soon as the property transaction was finished, one of the partners went out to Spain and continued to live there. Effectively one business partner had paid for half of the property but was using it as if he owned the whole thing. The other partner could not rent the property out as the co-owner was living there, and the co-owner refused to pay rent for their time in the property. Again, the relationship degenerated to the extent that correspondence had to be done through their lawyers and court action was discussed.

If you do go into business with a partner, make sure you discuss how you are going to run the business. Is your business partner going to be a silent partner – allowing you to run the business and simply injecting capital and taking their share of the profits – or are they going to wish to have a say in its running? If they are going to have a say in how the business is run, you need to discuss how this is going to work right at the beginning.

Grants and Subsidies

There is a bewildering number of grants, subsidies and incentive schemes for businesses in Spain. These forms of financial assistance come from a range of sources – from the EU, the Spanish government, the autonomous regions of Spain and even the local authorities. There can also be a whole range of financial subsidies and grants available for specific types of business or businesses employing specific types of people. It can be difficult to find out what is available, what you are entitled to, and how to apply for these. For this reason many people give up before they manage to find the grant or subsidy that they are entitled to.

It is best to think of a grant or subsidy as a bonus to your business rather than an integral part of the business finance, unless of course you have already secured the money. The reason for this is that the application process for such financial assistance is often very bureaucratic (even by Spanish standards) and you can be waiting months, if not years, for the money actually to arrive.

The local chamber of commerce is a good starting point for information on financial assistance, not just regarding grants and subsidies, but about a whole range of other information. The chamber of commerce will often be able to point you in the right direction regarding what is available and may even be able to assist you with the application process.

The Spanish body that deals with small businesses (*Dirección General de Política de la PYME*) is also a good source of information on financial assistance. Their website (**www.ipyme.org**) has a whole section on European aid.

The European Union will also give you information on financial assistance. A good starting point is their website (**www.europa.eu.int**), where there is a section dedicated to grants and financial assistance.

Websites for Grants in Spain

www.ipyme.org	*Dirección General de Política de la PYME* Body for small and medium-sized businesses. There is a section on Europe that details grants and subsidies available in Europe.
www.europa.eu.int	*European Union* There is a section under 'Enterprise' for grants and loans.
www.vue.es	*Ventanilla Unica Empresarial* There is a section on *Ayudas* and *Subvenciones*, which is for grants and subsidies.
www.enisa.es	*Empresa Nacional de Innovación S.A.* National company for innovation. State business-creation grants.
www.inem.es	*Instituto Nacional de Empleo* National employment agency. Has details of grants and subsidies that are based on job creation.
www.ico.es	*Instituto Oficial de Credito* Official Institute of Credit. Has details of subsidized credit and finance available to PYMEs.

Getting Finance into Spain

Electronic Transfer

The most practical way is to send it electronically by SWIFT transfer from a UK bank direct to the recipient's bank in Spain. This costs £20–£35, depending on your bank. It is safer to allow two or three days for the money to arrive in a rural bank, despite everyone's protestations that it will be there the same day.

Europe has now introduced unique account numbers for all bank accounts. These incorporate a code for the identity of the bank and branch as well as the account number of the individual customer. These are known as IBAN numbers. They should be quoted, if possible, on all international currency transfers.

For the sums you are likely to be sending you should receive a better exchange rate than the 'tourist rate' you see in the press. There is no such thing as a fixed exchange rate in these transactions. The bank's official inter-bank rate changes by the second, and the job of the bank's currency dealers is to make a profit by selling to you at the lowest rate they can get away with! Thus, if you do a lot of business with a bank and they know you are alert, you are likely to be offered a better rate than a one-off customer. For this reason it is often better to send money through your UK lawyers, who will be dealing with large numbers of such transactions. This also has the advantage that their bank, which deals with international payments all the time, is less likely to make a mistake – which could delay the payment – than your bank, for which such a payment might be a rarity.

You or your lawyers might use a specialist currency dealer to make the transfer of funds instead of a main UK bank. These dealers often offer a better exchange rate than an ordinary bank. Sometimes the difference can be significant, especially compared to your local high street bank. Although these dealers use major banks to transfer the funds, you need to make sure that the dealer who is acting for you is reputable. Your money is paid to them, not to the major bank, so you could be at risk if the dealer was not bonded or otherwise protected.

However you make the payment, be sure you understand whether you or the recipient is going to pick up the receiving bank's charges. If you need a clear amount in Spain you will have to make allowance for this, either by sending a bit extra or by asking your UK bank to pay all the charges. Make sure you have got the details of the recipient bank, its customer's name, the account codes and the recipient's reference precisely right. Any error and the payment is likely to come bank to you undeliverable – and may involve you in bearing the cost of it being converted back into sterling.

The bank in Spain will make a charge – which can be substantial – for receiving your money into your account.

Banker's Drafts

You can arrange for your UK bank to issue you with a banker's draft (bank certified cheque), which you can take to Spain and pay into your bank account. Make sure that the bank knows that the draft is to be used overseas and issues you with an international draft. Generally, this is not a good way to transfer the money. It can take a considerable time – sometimes weeks – for the funds deposited to be made available for your use; the recipient bank's charges can be surprisingly high; and the exchange rate offered against a sterling draft may be uncompetitive as you are a captive customer.

Cash

This is not recommended. You will need to declare the money on departure from the UK and on arrival in Spain. You must by law do this if the sum involved is over €8,000. You are well advised to do so for smaller amounts. Even then, if you declare £200,000 or so the risk is they might think you are a terrorist or drugs dealer. That suspicion can have far-reaching consequences as you could then be listed in police files as suspicious and could be put under surveillance. To add insult to injury the exchange rate you will be offered for cash (whether you take sterling and convert there, or buy the euros here) is usually very uncompetitive and the notary may refuse to accept the money in his account. Just don't do it.

Exchange Control and Other Restrictions on Moving Money

For EU nationals there is no longer any exchange control when taking money to or from Spain. Some statistical records are kept to show the flow of funds and the purpose of the transfers. When you sell your business or property in Spain you will be able to bring the money back to England if you wish to do so.

Spanish Banks

Who Can Open a Bank Account?

There is no reason why you should not retain your UK bank account when you move to Spain. It will probably be convenient to do so. You are also likely to want to open a Spanish bank account. To do this, you will have to prove that you are over 18 and provide the bank with proof of your identity, your civil status (*estado civil*), your address in Spain, etc. The type of bank account that you open will depend upon whether you are resident on non-resident. However, for most practical purposes, there is little difference between the two types of account.

Which Bank Should You Use?

Banking needs vary dramatically from person to person. If you are retiring to Spain or running a business there you may need a complete and fairly sophisti-cated banking service. If, however, you are a tourist with a holiday home, your banking needs will probably be very simple. Most British people fall into the latter category. For them there is virtually no difference between the service offered by any of the major Spanish banks. The two major considerations when choosing between Spanish banks will be the convenience factor – whether the bank is located near your property and if staff at the bank speak English. If you do not speak Spanish, you may prefer, at least initially, to deal with a bank where the staff speaks your own language. However, in many small towns you will have no choice of bank.

If at all possible, it is important to deal with your local bank. It will make you feel part of a local community and, more importantly, will make the local community feel that you want to be part of them. Who knows, your bank manager might even take you for lunch! When you have the luxury of a choice between various convenient banks that speak English, perhaps the most significant factor to take into account would be the bank's charging structure for receiving money. Spanish banks charge for absolutely everything. Some charge a lot more than others for the simple task of receiving money that is sent from the UK. There is no real advantage to choosing Barclays or another 'British' bank as they are a separate Spanish entity and you will probably receive exactly the same service from any other Spanish bank. Most Spanish banks offer excellent – and, for non-residents, really useful – internet banking facilities.

Which Type of Account?

Most people will operate a simple current account (*cuenta corriente*) and will ask the bank to pay the electricity, water and other bills directly from that account. There are no cheque guarantee cards in Spain, yet cheques are still widely accepted – if reluctantly. There are severe penalties resulting from cheque abuse. Do not even think about writing a cheque on your Spanish bank account if there are insufficient funds in that account to cover the value of the cheque. This is a criminal offence. Bounced cheques also lead to substantial bank charges and later problems with your own bank and others.

Spanish banks generally pay very low interest on current accounts, say around 0.1 per cent. It is therefore sensible to have a deposit account as well. Most banks will arrange for the balance on the current account over a certain sum to be transferred automatically into an interest-bearing account. Interest rates in euroland are low. If your needs are more sophisticated, study carefully the various types of account available to you. These, and the terms and conditions of use, differ substantially from the accounts you may be familiar with in the UK.

'Offshore' Accounts

These are the subject of considerable mystique. Many people resident in Spain think if they have an offshore bank account they do not have to pay tax in Spain. This is not true. They only don't pay the tax if they illegally hide the existence of the bank account from the Spanish tax authorities; *see* 'Business and Personal Taxes'. There is no reason why you should not have an offshore bank account either as the owner of a holiday home in Spain or as a person resident in Spain, but you should only do so for good reason. If you are thinking of taking up residence in Spain, take financial advice.

Key Points

Whichever bank you use, and whichever account you open, the most important messages are:

• **Learn to write the date in Spanish and use the Spanish 7 rather than the English 7 when writing cheques.**

• **Remember that in Spain (and other European countries) numbers are written differently: €5,500.00 is written €5.500,00.**

• **Keep a close eye on your bank statements and reconcile them with the payments you send to Spain and the items you paid out in Spain.**

• **Make sure that you do not write cheques when there are insufficient funds in the account to cover those cheques.**

Differences from UK/US Banks

Banks are generally open Monday–Friday, 9.00am–2.00pm and Saturday 9.00am–1.00pm. In summer they may close slightly earlier. Spanish banks can be just as good as UK banks and provide an excellent service. We often forget that most banks are owned internationally and therefore have global objectives. However, a bank is only as good as its employees and therefore it comes down to individual branches as to whether you are going to get a good service. You must understand the bank charges. These can be surprisingly high. It is worth negotiating with your bank over the charges as they are often willing to compromise.

Business and Personal Taxes

As an individual, or a business that is taxed as an individual (sole trader or partnership), there are a number of potential tax liabilities to take into account in Spain. The basis and extent of those liabilities depend upon whether you are classified as resident or non-resident for tax purposes. This is determined by applying a number of rules to your situation.

1. The 183-day rule. If you spend more than 183 days in Spain during the tax year (1 January–31 December) you will be classified as tax resident in Spain, whether that time is spent in one block or in several separate chunks.

2. If your main home is in Spain you will be classified as tax resident in Spain.

3. If your 'centre of economic interests' is in Spain you will be classified as tax resident in Spain.

4. If your spouse is tax resident in Spain you will also be assumed to be, but you can prove the contrary to be true.

If you fall into any of these categories you will be classified as a Spanish tax resident and you will be under a duty to pay all of your taxes on your worldwide income and assets in Spain. You will then normally stop paying taxes in the UK. In certain circumstances, you may still have to pay some tax in the UK; *see* 'Income Tax', p.111.

In certain cases you can be caught as tax resident in more than one country. For example, if you spend 200 days in Spain and 100 days in the UK, both governments could claim you as tax resident. In this case there are a series of 'tie-breaking' rules set out in the UK–Spanish double taxation treaty. These determine to which country you must pay each category of tax.

If you are running a business in Spain then it is highly likely that you are going to be a Spanish tax resident. The rest of this section is based on that premise. It is a very general introduction to the subject and further professional advice should be sought before you commit yourself to the move. Tax law is complicated in every country and Spain is no exception. There is enormous scope for saving tax when you move to Spain but the best opportunities are available to you only if you make your plans before you move there.

As in many European countries, the tax year in Spain corresponds to the calendar year. The tax authorities are the *Hacienda*, a historical name although the correct name is the *Agencia Estatal de Administración Tributaria* – often referred to as the *Agencia Tributaria*. They are surprisingly helpful should you need assistance.

Dealing with tax at home is often difficult. Dealing with tax in a country where you do not know the system and often don't even know the terminology is even more difficult. It therefore makes sense to get a good accountant (*contable* or *asesor fiscal*) to assist you. The *contable* is roughly equivalent to the accountant we are used to in the UK; the *asesor fiscal* is comparable to a chartered accountant.

Taxes and Fees on Buying a Property

Fees and taxes associated with buying a property in Spain generally amount to about 10–11 per cent of the value of the property. The tax element typically consists of IVA (VAT) tax at 7 per cent on a new property or ITP (transfer tax) of 6 or 7 per cent on a resale property, although this can vary.

Local Property Taxes (IBI)

They are generally low by UK standards. Typical amounts would be €140 a year for a rural property and, perhaps, €420 a year for a two-bedroom apartment in the Costa Blanca.

Income Tax (IRPF)

You will have to pay income tax to the Spanish government in respect of all the income you receive, wherever it comes from. Various deductions can be set against that income. Each individual is entitled to a personal allowance. For example, a single person under 65 will receive €3,400 tax free. A married couple will receive €6,800. The rate of tax payable on sums over this amount will depend upon how much is involved. In certain cases there may be special deductions allowed against the tax otherwise payable.

If you have income from a UK government pension, or from renting out property in the UK, this will still be taxed in the UK. You will also have to declare the income on your Spanish tax return as part of your worldwide income. The Spanish tax department will assess the income tax due, allowing you all the appropriate Spanish deductions, and will then give you full credit for any tax that you have already paid in the UK.

Capital Gains Tax

When you sell your property you should make a profit that will then be subject to capital gains tax in Spain. You will be taxed on the difference between the value declared to the tax authorities when you bought the property and the value declared when you sold it, less various allowances. These include acquisition and disposal costs and the cost of any major improvements to the property. The acquisition cost will also be adjusted by applying a coefficient to take account of inflation since the date you bought the property. Tax is paid on the resulting amount. The taxable gain is added to your income and tax is therefore paid at your top tax rate. In some cases the gain from selling property can be rolled over into a new property and the payment of tax thus deferred.

Residents over 65 who have lived in their house for at least three years before selling will not be liable for CGT on the profit made. If you are not a UK tax resident, there will be no UK capital gains tax liability.

Wealth and Inheritance Tax

Most people will pay wealth tax at either 0.11 or 0.2 per cent of the value of their property in Spain, depending upon when it was last re-valued. Higher-value properties will attract tax at higher rates of tax.

The inheritance tax payable in Spain will be calculated by assessing your worldwide assets. The tax is calculated individually for each person who inherits. The amount payable depends on the amount inherited and the relationship of the beneficiary to the deceased. There are various tax bands. *See* **Appendix 5**, p.265 for the 2004 rates of inheritance and wealth tax.

Company Taxes

If you are running your business as one of the company structures which is taxed as a business, you will have to pay corporation tax (*Impuesto Sobre Sociedades*). Sole traders or partnerships do not pay corporation tax but the individuals involved are taxed on the business income.

Corporation tax is normally 35 per cent. Small businesses pay only 30 per cent on the first €90,151.82 of income and 35 per cent on anything above that figure. Certain other types of business also pay different rates of tax. Cooperatives, for example, pay tax at 20 per cent. Holding companies pay tax at 40 per cent.

For many years it was common to own a property in the name of an offshore company (Isle of Man, Jersey, Guernsey, Gibraltar, etc.). If you do this then there is a special tax for the privilege. The tax is based on the rateable value of the property and will be taxed at 3 per cent per annum. For a property with a rateable value of £100,000 this equates to an additional tax of about £3,000 every year.

VAT

If you run a business in Spain you will have to register for VAT (*Impuesto de Valor Anadido* – IVA). This is a requirement no matter how low or high your level of turnover. The only difference that your turnover will make to the IVA is the frequency in making your IVA returns.

If the goods or services that you supply are liable for IVA you will charge IVA to your clients (most prices include IVA) and then make an IVA return to the tax authorities. If your business has a turnover of less than €6 million then your business will have to make their IVA return every quarter (and pay the tax within 20 days of the end of that quarter). If the turnover of the business is greater than €6 million then the IVA return has to be made every month (and the tax must be paid within 20 days of the end of that month).

There is not just one rate of IVA in Spain – there are several. The standard rate is 16 per cent, which applies to most goods and services. Some goods and services carry reduced IVA rates, such as restaurants, cinemas and theatres which charge 7 per cent IVA. IVA is charged at 4 per cent on food items and books and newspapers. Cars, alcohol, petrol and tobacco have special taxes on them in addition to IVA. The Canary Islands, Ceuta and Melilla do not have IVA – although they have an equivalent. The Canary Islands have the Canarian indirect general tax (*Impuesto General Indirecto Canario* – IGIC) at 5 per cent. Ceuta and Melilla also have their own similar taxes.

The Black Economy

There is a huge black economy in Spain. Many businesses only manage to compete or even survive because they do not do things properly. Some pay neither taxes nor social security and get away with it for years. Some people may try to persuade you that it is easy to get away without paying taxes and that the authorities do not have the resources to investigate everybody.

In some instances this is true. The tax authorities have only a fixed period of five years in which to claim any tax due to them. If the authorities do not collect the taxes due after this period they lose the right to claim the tax. Some people use this as a 'tax planning' exercise. They try to avoid having to pay the taxes until after this limitation period has expired. This is not to be recommended. If you get caught you will end up paying not only the tax that you should have paid in the first place, but also fines for late payment and interest on the amount originally due.

The Spanish authorities are fully aware that many people do not declare everything and that many things are paid for in cash. However, following the events of 11 September 2001, there is a far greater need to trace exchanges of money and the Spanish government has begun to clamp down on black economies. One way in which the authorities can find out that you are doing something wrong is if somebody has told them. Spain, like many countries, has a culture of shopping people to the authorities. You can even download an official form to shop somebody from the *Agencia Tributaria* at **www.aeat.es**! Apart from the fact that you are breaking the law if you avoid taxes, you also risk heavy fines and in some cases imprisonment.

Acquiring Business Premises

If you do not wish to run a business from home then it is important to give some thought to what type of business premises you are going to need. There are two options – renting and buying. Each has its advantages and disadvantages. Sit down and work out what is important to you before committing one way or another.

Of course you may not have a choice – in which case you will have to go along with what is available.

Renting

If you are just starting a business there is a lot to be said for temporarily renting a place in the area where you are thinking of running the business. If you rent you are less likely to commit yourself to a purchase in an area you turn out not to like or where the business does not work. It allows you to retreat from a business far more quickly and cheaply than if you buy a property. It also avoids the expensive process of having to sell the property and buy another, either in Spain or back in the UK. The overall cost of moving within Spain is likely to be about 15 per cent of the price of your new property, 10 per cent being the fees on the purchase of the new property and 5 per cent being the estate agent's fee for selling the old one. A move back to the UK would (depending on the value of the property bought) be likely to cost about 8 per cent: 5 per cent sales expenses in Spain and 3 per cent purchase expenses in the UK.

Disadvantages

In the recent past, property prices in many areas have risen rapidly. For example, if two years ago you had been buying in Marbella then delaying 18 months would probably have cost you about 15–20 per cent in increased property cost. This is a lot more than your money would have made if invested, so the delay would have cost you money.

Another disadvantage is that the rent you pay out is dead money. Rent would probably amount to about 5 per cent of the value of a property per year. On the other hand, by renting a property rather than buying, you can use your capital for other things that the business needs until it is on its feet – for example, set-up costs, stock, advertising or living costs.

Moving is stressful and disruptive for a business. If you decide to buy premises later, this will involve the business changing location. This will mean that all your stationery, advertising and anything else carrying your address will have to be changed. You will also have to inform all your customers of the move. If you miss any of them you may lose existing customers. If the new location is not as convenient for some of your customers then again you stand the chance of losing business.

Finally, and perhaps most importantly in some respects, moving into temporary accommodation can prevent you from getting fully involved in the area in which you are living; you don't commit to it and you don't give it a fair try as a result. There is the risk that you are always looking back over your shoulder at the UK rather than forward to Spain.

Buying

Most people, given a choice, would prefer to own a property that they use, but this is not always the best decision when starting a business.

One advantage of owning your own business premises is that it gives you more freedom than if you rent. A rented property will normally come with restrictions on what you can and cannot do. If you can afford to pay for your property with cash this has the advantage that your monthly outgoings will be reduced, as there is no rent or mortgage to pay. On a month-to-month basis your business will stand a greater chance of success during those times when business is slow.

Few people can afford to buy property these days without some sort of finance, however, and should you wish to buy a property, you will probably need a mortgage. Unfortunately raising a mortgage on a business that is only just starting is likely to be difficult if not impossible because the bank will not be able to see a trading history. A personal mortgage rather than a mortgage taken out by the business is the most probable route you will have to go down. For further details on raising finance, see 'Raising Finance', p.102.

One advantage of buying premises is that if the business doesn't work out, you are still left with an asset (assuming that the business hasn't gone so far down that your creditors are trying to acquire the premises). You can close the business, rent it out to somebody else to run as a business and at least receive some sort of monthly income from then on. This will be in addition to any potential capital growth.

Who Should Own the Property?

There are many ways of structuring the purchase of a property. Each has significant advantages and disadvantages. The right structure could save you a great deal of money during your lifetime and on your death. In Spain, you do not have the total freedom that we have in the UK to deal with your assets as you please. On your death an innappropriate choice of ownership can also result in the wrong people being entitled to your inheritance. This is a particular problem for people in second marriages, and for unmarried couples. There are various simple ways to own a business property, such as sole ownership and joint ownership or, for tax reasons, you may decide to give your business premises to your children. In all instances, it is best to check with a lawyer on the most suitable way of setting up ownership of the property.

Limited Company

Larger companies are likely to own a property through a limited company. This can be a very attractive option for some people as you own the shares in a company, not a property in Spain. There are various types of company.

Spanish Commercial Company

Ownership through a company will mean that the income from the property is taxed in the way usual for companies – basically, you pay tax only on the profit made – rather than at the flat rate applicable in the case of an individual owner who is not tax resident in Spain. This can reduce your tax bill. Ownership in the form of a company also gives rise to certain expenses, such as accountancy, filing tax returns, etc.

Buying through a Spanish company gives rise to a host of potential problems as well as benefits. The plan needs to be studied closely so that you can decide whether it makes sense in the short, medium *and* long term.

UK Company

It is rare for a purchase through a UK company to make sense for a single investment property or business in Spain. This is despite the fact that the ability to pay for the property with the company's money without drawing it out of the company and paying UK tax on the dividend is attractive. Once again you need expert advice from someone familiar with the law of both countries.

Offshore (Tax Haven) Company

This has the added disincentive that you will have to pay a special tax of three per cent of the value of the property *every year*. This is to compensate the Spanish for all the inheritance and transfer taxes that they will not receive when the owners of these companies sell them or die. This tax treatment has more or less killed off ownership through such companies, yet they still have a limited role to play. A 93-year-old buying a £10 million property, or someone who wishes to be discrete about the ownership of the property, might think that three per cent is a small price to pay for the avoidance of inheritance tax or for privacy.

The Use of Trusts

As a vehicle for owning a property, trusts are of little direct use. Spanish law does not fully recognise trusts and so the trustees who are named on the title as the owners of the property would be treated as private individual owners, having to pay all of the income, wealth and inheritance taxes applicable in their case. In a few cases this could still give some benefit but there are probably better ways of getting the same result. This does not mean that trusts have no place for the owner of property in Spain. A trust could still, for example, own the property through a limited company if this fitted the 'owner's' overall tax and inheritance planning objectives.

Which is Right for You?

The choice is of fundamental importance. If you get it wrong you will pay much more tax than you need to, both during your lifetime and on your death. The tax consequences arise not only in Spain but also in your own country. For each buyer of business premises or a home investment one option may suit you perfectly. Another might just about make sense. The rest would be an expensive waste of money.

The trouble is, it is not obvious which is the right choice! You need to take advice. If your case is simple, so will be the advice. If it is complex, the time and money spent will be repaid many times over.

In summary, there are two main drawbacks to buying:

1. You have tied up a large amount of your capital in the property. This capital is precious when you are starting a business and could have been used for a variety of other uses.
2. It can be difficult to find suitable business properties that are available to buy. Many of the properties have been owned by the current owners for many years. They will enjoy the rental from the property and will watch the value of the property go up until they retire, when they are likely to sell the property and live on the proceeds.
3. Choosing the right kind of ownership can be complicated.

The Process of Buying a Property in Spain

The Law

The law relating to the purchase of a property in Spain is, as you would expect, complicated, but there are basic principles which are helpful to understand.

1. The main legal provisions relating to property law are found in the civil code, which was introduced in 1864 but has been modified since. The analysis of rights reflects the essentially agrarian society of late 18th-century Spain and pays limited attention to some of the issues that would seem more pressing today. That has only partly been remedied by the later additions to the code.

2. The civil code declares that foreigners are to be treated in the same way as Spanish people as far as the law is concerned.

3. Spanish law divides property into two classes – moveable property (*bienes muebles*) and immovable property (*bienes inmuebles*). The whole basis of ownership and transfer of ownership depends on which classification property belongs to. The distinction is similar to the English concept of real and personal property but it is not exactly the same. Immovable property includes land and buildings, but not the shares in a company that owns land and buildings.

4. The sale of *inmuebles* located in Spain must always be governed by Spanish law.

5. The form of ownership of land is always absolute ownership. This is similar to what we would call freehold ownership.

6. It is possible to own the buildings – or even parts of a building – on a piece of land separately from the land itself. This is of particular relevance in the case of flats, which are owned 'freehold'.

7. Where two or more people jointly own a piece of land or other property they will generally own it in undivided shares (*pro indiviso*) – the piece of land is not physically divided between them. Each owner may, in theory, mortgage or sell his share without the consent of the others – though the others might have certain rights of pre-emption (the right to buy the property in preference to any outsider).

8. Where a building or piece of land is physically divided between a number of people, a condominium (*comunidad de propietarios*) is created. The land is divided into privately owned parts – such as an individual flat – and communally owned areas. The management of the communally held areas is the responsibility of the owners of the privately held area, but can be delegated to someone else.

9. In the case of a sale of land, certain people may have a right of pre-emption. One is the co-owner mentioned above. Others are (in each case only in certain circumstances) the municipality or a sitting tenant and certain statutory bodies.

10. Transfer of ownership of *inmuebles* is usually by simple agreement. This need not be, but is usually, in writing. That agreement binds both parties but is not effective as far as the rest of the world is concerned. They can rely on the land register (*registro de la propiedad*). Thus, ownership of land can be transferred between buyer and seller, for example, by signing a sale contract (*contrato privado de compraventa*) even if the seller remains in possession and some of the price remains unpaid. But that ownership would not damage the interests of someone other than the buyer or seller (such as someone owed money by the seller), who is entitled to take action against the person named as owner in the land register. Ownership can also be acquired by possession, usually for 30 years.

11. Other rights – short of ownership – can exist over land. These include rights of way, tenancies, life interests, mortgages and option contracts. Most require some sort of formality to be valid against third parties but are always binding between the people who made the agreements.

12. There are two land registers. Each commune maintains a tax register (*registro catastral*) where all the land in the district is divided into plots and assessed for tax purposes. The second register is the deed and mortgage register (*registro de la propiedad*). Not all land is registered here. The entries (size, boundaries, etc.) do not necessarily correspond in the two registers.

General Procedure

At first glance, the general procedure when buying a property in Spain seems similar to purchasing a property in England. Sign a contract. Do some checks. Sign a deed of title. This is deceptive. The procedure is very different and even the use of the familiar English vocabulary to describe the very different steps in Spain can produce a dangerous sense of familiarity with the procedure. This can lead to assumptions that things that have not been discussed will be the same as they would be in England. This is a dangerous assumption. Work on the basis that the system is totally different.

Choosing a Lawyer
The Notary Public (*Notario*)

The notary is a special type of lawyer. He is in part a public official but he is also in business, making his living from the fees he charges for his services. Notaries also exist in England but they are seldom used in day-to-day transactions.

Under Spanish law only deeds of sale (*escrituras de compraventa*) approved and witnessed by a notary can be registered at the land registry. Although it is possible to transfer legal ownership of property (such as a house or apartment) by a private agreement not witnessed by the notary, and although that agreement will be fully binding on the people who made it, it will not be binding on third parties. Third parties – including people who want to make a claim against the property, or banks wanting to lend money on the strength of the property – are entitled to rely upon the details of ownership recorded at the land registry (*registro de la propiedad*). So if you are not registered as the owner of the property, you are at risk. Thus, in practice, all property sales in Spain must be witnessed by a notary.

The notary also carries out certain checks on property sold and has some duties as tax enforcer and validator of documents to be presented for registration. His fee is fixed by law. For an average property the fee will be about 0.4 per cent of the price, although there can sometimes be extras.

In theory, the notary is appointed by the buyer but, in many cases – particularly with new property – the seller (*agrupación*) will stipulate the notary to be used. This is a practical time- and cost-saving measure. The notary has already drafted the documents, gathering together all the bits of land bought by the seller and then split off the various individual plots to be sold (*segregación*). It makes sense for him to deal with all the resultant sales. Otherwise all of the powers of attorney etc. would need to be produced before lots of different notaries, potentially all over the country.

The notary is strictly neutral. He is more a referee than someone fighting on your behalf. He is someone who checks the papers to make sure that they comply with the strict rules and so will be accepted by the land registry for registration.

Many Spanish notaries, particularly in rural areas, do not speak English – or, at least, do not speak it well enough to give advice on complex issues. Very few will know anything about English law and so will be unable to advise you about the tax and other consequences in England of your plans to buy a property in Spain. In any case, the buyer will seldom meet the notary before the signing ceremony and so there is little scope for seeking detailed advice. Moreover, it is rare for notaries to offer any comprehensive advice or explanation, least of all in writing, to the buyer.

For the English buyer, the notary is no substitute for using the services of a UK lawyer familiar with Spanish law and international property transactions. This is the clear advice of every guidebook, of the Spanish and British governments and of the Federation of Overseas Property Developers, Agents and Consultants (FOPDAC).

Lawyers (*abogados*)

Most Spanish people buying property in Spain will not use the services of a lawyer (as opposed to the notary public [*notario*]) unless there is something unusual or contentious about the transaction.

The services the notary can provide are unlikely to provide people from the UK with all the information or help they need to buy a home in Spain. They will often require advice about inheritance issues, the UK tax implications of their purchase, how to save taxes, surveys, mortgages, currency exchange, etc., all of which is outside the scope of the service of the notary. They should retain the services of a specialist UK lawyer familiar with dealing with these issues. The buyer's usual solicitor is unlikely to be able to help as there are only a handful of English law firms with the necessary expertise.

The Price

This can be freely agreed between the parties. Depending on the economic climate there may be ample or very little room for negotiating a reduction in the asking price. At the moment, negotiating scope is limited for popularly priced properties in the main cities and tourist areas, where property is in short supply.

How Much Should be Declared in the Deed of Sale?

For many years there was a tradition in Spain (and other Latin countries) of under-declaring the price actually paid for a property when signing the deed of sale (*escritura*). This was because the taxes and notaries fees due were calculated on the basis of the price declared and a lower price meant less property transfer taxes for the buyer and less capital gains tax for the seller. Often the price declared was only one quarter of the price actually paid. The days of major under-declarations have now largely gone. In rural areas you can still sometimes come under pressure to under-declare to a significant extent, but it is rare. In many areas the seller will still suggest some more modest form of under-declaration. Under-declaration is illegal and foolish. There are severe penalties. In the worst case the state can buy the property for the price declared. In the best case there are fines and penalties for late payment. In addition, unless your buyer under-declares when you sell, you create an entirely artificial capital gain – taxed at 35 per cent.

Nevertheless, you may find that you have little choice but to under-declare. The seller will often refuse to sell unless you do. Fortunately, there is a semi-legitimate 'grey area' for manoeuvre over declared price, rather like doing 40mph in a 30mph limit. It is wrong but you will not get into serious trouble.

Where Must the Money be Paid?

The price, together with the taxes and fees payable, is usually paid by the buyer to the seller in front of the notary. This is the best and safest way. You can, in fact, agree to pay in whatever way and wherever you please. So, for example, in the case of a British seller and a British buyer the payment could be made in sterling by bank transfer. In the case of a seller who is not tax resident in Spain the buyer is obliged to retain 5 per cent of the price and pay it to the tax authorities (*agencia tributaria*) on account of the seller's potential tax liabilities.

Try to avoid arrangements, usually as part of an under-declaration, where part of the money is handed over in cash in brown-paper parcels. Apart from being illegal, it is dangerous at a practical level. Buyers have lost the bundle – or been robbed on the way to the notary's office. Sometimes there is a suspicion that the seller, who knew where you were going to be and when, could be involved.

General and Special Inquiries

Certain inquiries are made routinely in the course of the purchase of a property. These include a check on the planning situation (*informe urbanistico*) of the property. This will reveal the position of the property itself but it will not directly tell you about its neighbours and it will not reveal general plans for the area. If you want to know whether the authorities are going to put a prison in the village or run a new AVE line through your back garden (both, presumably, bad things) or build a motorway access point or railway station 3km away (both, presumably, good things) you will need to ask. There are various organisations you can approach but, just as in the UK, there is no single point of contact for such inquiries. If you are concerned about what might happen in the area then you will need to discuss the position with your lawyers at an early stage. There may be a considerable amount of work (and therefore cost) involved in making full inquiries, the results of which can never be guaranteed.

Normal inquiries also include a check that the seller is the registered owner of the property and that it is sold (if this has been agreed) free of mortgages or other charges.

In order to advise you what special inquiries might be appropriate, your lawyer will need to be told of your plans for the property. Do you intend to rent it out? If so, is it on a commercial basis? Do you intend to use it for your business or are you going to live there? Do you want to extend or modify the exterior of the property? Do you intend to make interior structural alterations?

Agree in advance the additional inquiries you would like to make and get an estimate of the cost.

Your Civil State (*Estado Civil*)

This is something you will have given no thought to. For most of the time it is a matter of unimportance in the UK, but it is something the Spanish get very worked up about.

When preparing documents to purchase a property in Spain you will be asked to specify your civil state. This comprises a full set of information about you. They will not only ask for your full name and address but also, potentially, for your occupation, nationality, passport number, maiden name and sometimes the names of your parents, your date and place of birth, date and place of marriage and, most importantly, your matrimonial 'regime' (*regimen matrimonial*). What is a *regimen matrimonial*? It is something we do not have in England. In Spain, when you marry you will specify the *regimen matrimonial* that will apply to your relationship. There are two main options for a Spanish person: a regime of common ownership of assets (*comunidad de bienes*), or a regime of separate ownership of assets (*separación de bienes*). Under the first all assets acquired after the marriage, even if put into just one party's name, belong to both. Under the second each spouse is entitled to own assets in his or her own name, over which the other spouse has no automatic claim. The effect of marriage under English law is generally closer to the second than the first. If possible, the notary, when specifying your matrimonial regime, should state that you are married under English law and, in the absence of a marriage contract, there is no 'regime' but your situation is similar to a 'regime' of *separación de bienes*.

This is no idle point. The declaration in your *escritura* is a public declaration. It is treated in Spain with great reverence and is of great importance. It will be hard in later years to go against what you have declared. If appropriate you will declare that you are single, separated, divorced, widowed, etc. at this point.

The authorities are entitled to ask for proof of all of these points by birth certificates, marriage certificates, etc. If the documents are needed, official translations into Spanish may be required. The notary may often take a slightly more relaxed view and ask you for only the key elements of your *estado civil*. It is worth checking in advance what is required, as it is embarrassing to turn up to sign the *escritura* only to find the ceremony cannot go ahead because you do not have one of the necessary documents. In the worst case, that could put you in breach of contract and you could lose your deposit.

Employing Staff

Offering somebody a job can be one of the joys of running your own business. However, when you employ staff there is a whole range of new challenges to face and a completely new level of administration and taxation to get involved in. Do not be tempted to cut corners when dealing with the paperwork and administration of employing staff – it is likely to haunt you later on.

If you are starting a business that is seasonal (for example, running a bed and breakfast, a bar in a tourist area, or, in fact, any business that relies on tourists for trade) you will need to think about how to arrange your staffing requirements. There is no point in employing huge numbers of staff during the winter months when little is likely to be happening and you have a low income.

Employment law is a huge subject. It is recommended that before you take on staff you speak to your lawyer about any issues that may arise in your particular circumstances.

The first thing that you need to do when taking on staff is decide what sort of person or people you wish to employ. Think about what characteristics and skills you are looking for in your staff and write them down. This will make it much easier when it comes to interviews and decision time.

Remember that children under the age of 16 are not allowed to work. Between the ages of 16 and 18 the parents of the child must give their consent for the child to work. There are limits on children's working hours; they are not allowed to work between 10pm and 6am.

What is the best way of advertising your job vacancy?

Where to Find Staff

You could list your job vacancy with the government employment agency (*Insituto Nacional de Empleo* – INEM). In fact, it is a legal obligation for employers to register any job vacancies with INEM (**www.inem.es**) and provide them with the details (full or part-time, salary, etc.). INEM has both national and regional offices and has details of jobs available both nationally and regionally.

Private Agencies

As in most countries there are private employment agencies where you can register your vacancies. Unlike most countries, however, Spain's private employment agencies are still highly regulated by the government and are really secondary to the INEM. Unlike similar agencies in the UK, Spanish agencies do not charge fees (other than perhaps the cost of providing the service) and are non-profit making organisations.

Private employment agencies come in two varieties – private placement agencies (*agencia privada de colocación*) and temporary work companies (*empresa de trabajo temporal* – ETT). The first of these acts as an intermediary between employers and potential employees. They will charge a fee. The ETT works in a slightly different way. They will employ staff themselves and then effectively contract them out to other companies.

Agencies often specialise in specific areas of employment. For example, they may specialise in finding jobs for those people in the IT business.

HR Consultants

HR consultants in Spain are more akin to the employment agencies that we are used to in the UK, in that they will search for people who are suitable for the post that you have available and will charge you a finding fee. The fees work in a similar way to the UK, and they will often charge a percentage of the final salary of the person employed.

The body that deals with this is the *Asociación Espanola de Dirección y Desarrollo de Personas* (AEDIPE) (**www.aedipe.es**).

European Employment Service

The European Employment Service (EURES) is an organisation that brings together the European Commission and the public employment services of the EU countries. It helps people to find work across Europe. If the person that you are looking to fill your vacancy does not have a local connection then you can register your vacancy with EURES and get the benefit of having applications from different parts of Europe.

The function of the EURES is threefold – information, advice and recruitment and placement of workers. It helps to overcome problems with qualifications. Details can be seen at **www.europa.eu.int**.

UK Employment Agencies

If none of the other methods of finding staff has proved fruitful you may end up advertising for staff back home with UK employment agencies. Some agencies are general, while most specialise in some particular area of work. Agencies are likely to charge either a fixed fee for finding staff or, more likely, a percentage of the salary offered. Rates paid as commission will vary and it is probably worth trying to negotiate the rates down – particularly if you employ staff regularly. A list of UK employment agencies can be found from the Recruitment and Employment Confederation (**www.rec.uk.com**), although there is a small charge for the list.

Internet

When you run your own business you will probably have your own website. A no-cost option would be to add a page to your own site listing job vacancies. If your business has a good reputation and is well known then people will regularly visit your website for job vacancies, or they might come across your site while searching for employment. Unfortunately, unless you are very well known, advertising your job vacancies on your own website is unlikely to generate huge numbers of inquiries as there are so many websites.

An alternative way of advertising job vacancies on the internet is to list the job with a web-based agency.

Advertisements

Advertisements can be an effective way of advertising job vacancies and can be placed in a wide variety of places. The easiest and most cost-effective way of advertising a job vacancy is the 'situation vacant' sign in the window of your own business. If your business is in a popular area, many people will pass your window and it is possible that the right person will walk past at the right time. However, a sign in the window may not necessarily project the right image for your business and you may decide not to advertise in this way.

Where you advertise will depend on what type of business you run, your budget and the sort of person you are looking for. National newspapers have the advantage of a large circulation with millions of people reading them each day. You can therefore reach a wider audience and the chances of finding the right person are greatly increased. Unfortunately, advertising in a national newspaper can be expensive. Regional newspapers have a lower circulation but have the advantage that a greater percentage of the readers are in your business area. Their advertising rates will also probably be cheaper. Local papers have a smaller circulation still, but have the advantage that everyone reading the newspaper either lives in or is interested in the area. Someone looking for a job is much more likely to go to their local paper first before branching out to the national press – particularly if they do not wish to relocate.

If your business has its own trade newspaper or magazine, then this might be a good place to advertise your vacancy as the readership will either already be in the industry or interested in joining the industry. Advertising in the trade press will help to eliminate speculative job applications.

Contract and Employment Law

Contract and employment law is a book in itself – and one that is almost guaranteed to solve the problem of sleepless nights that you may have when starting a business. Although not the most exciting subject to most people it is a very important subject as the rules can be very different from those you are used to back home. If you are not careful, this area can cause you more trouble than running the business itself. In addition, many industries are likely to have specific rules that you should be aware of. Do take professional legal advice when contemplating contracts and employment law.

This area is also discussed from the employee's point of view in **Working in Spain**, *see* 'Terms and Conditions of Employment', p.149.

Part-time Contracts

In some countries, part-time employment contracts are illegal. Spain is not one of them and it is therefore possible to employ people on a part-time basis as long as you follow the part-time workers' rules. Part-time workers are entitled to similar benefits to full-time employees.

Fixed-term Contracts

It is possible in Spain to employ staff under fixed-term contracts – i.e. where the length of the contract is fixed for a certain time or project. This is particularly relevant when you are starting up a small business and your business may be affected by the tourist season. Taking on staff on a fixed-term contract basis means you are not obliged to keep them on during the 'off season' – thereby reducing your staff wages during the months of reduced turnover.

Unfortunately, some employers try to use the fixed-term contract as a way of reducing their responsibilities to staff and to try to avoid making redundancy payments in the event of staff cut-backs. Employees on fixed-term contracts are permanent workers in all but name, but do not have the full protection of full-time workers. The Spanish law has put in place measures to counteract this practice and you are allowed to take on staff on a fixed-term basis for a maximum period of 12 months only. You are not allowed to employ staff on a series of connected fixed-term contracts.

Probation Periods

A probation period, although not compulsory, is a sensible option to include in the employment contract. The maximum probation period is six months for people with a degree, and two months for all other workers – unless the company has fewer than 25 workers, in which case this is increased to a maximum of three months. During the probation period the employee is entitled to the same benefits as if he had finished or did not have a probation period.

The employment contract can be terminated either by the employer or employee within the probation period without needing to give a reason and without prior notice – unless this is varied in the contract.

Spain has a minimum annual wage of €6,447 although if you are an apprentice and a first-time worker this is reduced to 0.85 per cent, or €5479.95 per year.

Taxation of Staff Earnings

Staff earnings are taxed as income tax. For more discussion of income tax, *see* 'Business and Personal Taxes', p.109.

Social Security Payments for Staff

As an employer you must not only register your staff for social security but make social security contributions for them to the National Institute of Social Security (*Instituto Nacional de la Seguridad Social*). The amount paid in social security covers your employees for a range of benefits including healthcare, sickness benefits, maternity leave, unemployment insurance and pensions.

The level of social security payments is high – very high in fact. This is why employers are tempted to take on illegal workers, as the difference between making these payments or not can significantly affect the profitability of a business.

Social security payments (*cuotas*) are paid by both the employer and the employee. The employer pays a greater percentage. The level of payments is calculated according to the occupation and the salary for that occupation; it is a complicated calculation. Each profession has a maximum and a minimum contribution for social security, which is based on the official salary (*nomina*) for that job. For example, one occupation may have a minimum amount of €537.50 per month and a maximum of €2,731.60 per month.

If you receive the minimum salary then 37.2 per cent of your salary is paid in social security contributions. The majority of this is paid by the employer and only 6.4 per cent is paid by the employee.

Employees' Entitlements

All employees are entitled to certain minimum conditions. According to the law, workers are entitled to: effective occupation during the work day (that is that they should be kept busy and have enough to do); promotion prospects; proper training to do the work they are employed for; no discrimination; physical integrity and privacy; receive the agreed remuneration in their employment contract, and any other entitlements set out in their contract of employment. For more details on employment contracts and employee benefits, *see* 'Terms and Conditions of Employment', p.149.

Marketing

You can have the best product in the world, backed up by the best customer service and the most inviting premises, but unless people know that you exist then you are not going to be a success. Marketing therefore plays a major part in any business and you must decide how you are going to do this. Marketing in Spain takes many forms.

Personal Contacts

Spain is still very much a country where personal contacts make a huge difference. Therefore, get to know anyone who may be able to point some new work in your direction. Obviously this comes at a cost too – either by referring clients back, paying an 'introduction' fee or supplying cheap or free goods or services.

Advertising

There is a whole range of different ways to advertise. Many of these you will have thought about already as they also exist in the UK. The type of business or product will dictate your advertising, as will your budget.

The more personal contacts you have the more your business will be advertised – through word of mouth and recommendation. Although this is not an official form of advertising, it is very effective and cheap.

The following are some useful advertising avenues to pursue: local newspapers, national newspapers, specialist newspapers for the expat community, magazines, trade magazines, advertising hoardings, handing out flyers in the street, television and radio. Many newspapers and magazines are crying out for news stories. Think of ways of dressing up an advertisement so it can be turned into an article.

There are some more interesting forms of advertising. If you have ever sat on a beach in southern Spain you will have seen planes flying up and down the coast trailing banners advertising local businesses. You may have also seen some companies advertising on the side of buses. Even your car can be turned into a mobile advertisement.

There are only three limitations on your advertising – your imagination, your budget and any professional, trade or legal restrictions. For example, until recently, lawyers in Spain were not allowed to advertise at all. If in doubt check with your trade organisation to see what – if any – restrictions on advertising are in place. The law sets out certain guidelines on decency in advertising.

Final Plan Checklist

Now that you have carried out more research and taken more advice, it is time to make the final plan. This is not the same as your business plan (*see* 'Your Business Plan', p.81) or your life plan (*see* 'Writing a "Life Plan"', p.83) but is rather more like a checklist of things that you need to consider when setting up your business. Think of everything that you might need to get your business up and running. You will forget things off the list. Things that you never thought about will crop up and have to be dealt with. No matter how much planning you do, there is always something else. This doesn't mean that you shouldn't make a plan. An incomplete plan is better than no plan at all.

Your plan needs to consider each aspect of your business, from this moment until you open, and then beyond. You need to be thinking about stationery, stock, staff, telephones, advertising, the grand opening, cash tins – the list will go on and on. You might like to make a list with columns. Column one could have the thing you need to get or do, column two the person who is in charge of that job, column three the date that task was completed, and save a fourth column for any comments.

As deadlines approach you also will also find yourself updating the list. As you think of new items, add them to the list. By doing this you will be sure that there are no nasty surprises just as you are about to open. At least that is the theory!

Red Tape

Permits and Paperwork 126
NIE 127
Using a *Gestor* 128
Social Security 129
Licences 129
Taxes 130
IAE 130
Ministry of Labour and Social Affairs 131
Professional and Other Qualifications 131
Registration with a Consulate 132

Red tape in Spain is often excessive and is characterised by long queues, unhelpful officials, snail's-pace processing and a strong urge to bang your head against a wall – even if you get there in the end. All residents interviewed for this book mentioned time-consuming, Kafka-esque bureaucracy as one of the downsides of living in Spain. Whether you are dealing with the employment authorities, the tax office, the legal system, the health service or the traffic police, the general advice is to expect the worst and imagine that whatever you aim to do will take longer than you thought. Learn to live with it; it is as much a part of life as constant drizzle and grey skies in Britain. You might be pleasantly surprised when it does not take as long as you expect.

This chapter looks principally at red tape in so far as it affects becoming a resident and working. It should be stated that, for EU citizens at least, things are not nearly as onerous as before, as they now no longer need a work permit or even a residency card in order to work as employees, ply their trade as freelancers, set up in business or study. Non-EU citizens, on the other hand, can expect rather a rougher ride.

Permits and Paperwork

EU citizens

A Spanish person living in Spain needs paperwork in order to do so. So does a foreigner. Any foreigner staying in Spain for more than 90 days at a time needs the appropriate paperwork to justify their extended stay. Any children under the age of 18 are entitled to be included on your residence paperwork unless they are working. What sort of paperwork you require depends on what you are doing in the country.

Many people confuse the issue of residence permits with the issue of citizenship. As a UK national (or any other nationality) you are entitled to retain your nationality for as long as you like, even though you are living in Spain. Most British people who have settled in Spain will, 40 years later, still have their British passport and British nationality.

The granting of a residence permit of whatever type makes no difference whatsoever to your nationality. Nor does it generally make any difference to your tax residence status; for further discussion on this topic, see 'Business and Personal Taxes', p.109.

For a British person seeking a residence permit in Spain the procedure is relatively simple and the authorities are generally helpful. The first step is to go to your local foreigners' office or police station that deals with 'foreign' matters and get the application form (*solicitud de tarjeta en régimen comunitario*). Return the completed form together with your passport, three recent passport-sized colour photographs and, if requested, a health certificate. The residence permit is usually issued within a relatively short time, although it can take several weeks in larger cities, such as Madrid or Barcelona.

Do not be tempted to live in Spain as an 'illegal'. Many British people went to live in Spain many years ago and never quite got round to applying for a residence card or permit. Sometimes this was in the quaint belief that they would somehow not have to pay taxes if they never applied for a permit, or else the paperwork seemed too much trouble. Many of them have never been challenged and, indeed, have never paid any tax in Spain. There are severe penalties for living in Spain without a permit and there are also severe penalties for non-payment of tax. Times have changed greatly in the last 20 years and the odds of being able to get away with all of this in the future are slender.

Non-EU citizens

Subject to any special arrangements between Spain and your home country you will need permission to visit, stay and work in Spain. This is outside the scope of this book.

NIE

If you live in Spain and undertake any form of work or business activity, want to buy a car or pay your taxes, you will need a *numero de identidad de extranjeros* (NIE). This is basically a foreigner's identity number.

The process of obtaining an NIE is straightforward. You go down to the local foreigners' office or police station with your passport. You fill in a form and in due time an NIE is issued. Simple? Well yes, in theory. Although applying for an NIE should be one of the easiest parts of moving to work in Spain, in practice it can be just as frustrating as anything else and is an excellent introduction to Spanish bureaucracy!

Sometimes the authorities will insist that you obtain your NIE yourself – other times they will allow you to do it through somebody else who has been granted a Power of Attorney to apply on your behalf. Sometimes you can apply for an NIE without a need to explain why – other times the authorities will need to see some proof as to why you want an NIE. In some instances you can apply for an NIE outside the area that you are going to live in – at other times you will need to be local. Unfortunately, as is often the case in Spain, the rules seem to be interpreted differently in different areas and therefore it is a bit hit and miss as to how the process works.

If you wish to save time, the application form for the NIE can be found at **www.europelaw.com**. The form is obviously in Spanish but is fairly straightforward if you have a basic level of fluency.

Using a *Gestor*

When you first move to a new country, there are so many new things to come to terms with that, on a bad day, you can feel you've taken on a mountain to climb. In Spain, this is compounded by local officialdom's inordinate love of form-filling, certificates, official stamps and all forms of paperwork in general. Apparently straightforward procedures require three or four different pieces of paper, all with lots of small print, and fees that have to be paid at separate counters – many bureaucratic procedures can only be done over the counter at the relevant department, not by phone, post or, even less, on-line. Many departments will only have one office in each province, in the capital, so if, for example, your new home is in Ronda, having to travel to Málaga to spend a whole morning waiting in line can be seriously annoying.

Left to themselves to face the baffling demands of bureaucracy, foreign residents often wonder whether Spaniards go mad at having to deal with such a system all the time. The answer is, they don't. Instead, they turn to the very Spanish institution of the *gestor*, a word with no English translation since the job doesn't exist, although it could be rendered as 'administrative services'. The fundamental role of the *gestor* is to take away the burden of bureaucracy by handling things for you. You can go to *gestores* with anything and everything that might involve permits, licences, insurance or similar issues, and they will be able to explain what procedures you need to follow, and point out time- and money-saving shortcuts that you would never discover on your own. They will also have blank copies of many forms. Armed with a letter of authorisation signed by you, they can also go to present the papers at the relevant departments in your place. One standard procedure for which many foreign house-buyers use *gestores* is that of applying for Spanish residency. They can do many other useful things for you as well, such as acting as accountant, bookkeeper and small business adviser. Many Spaniards routinely use a *gestor* in all small-scale dealings with the state – such as renewing a passport – in a way that would be completely unheard of in English-speaking countries.

A good *gestor* can be an invaluable asset, and is near-indispensable if you are working or, above all, setting up any kind of business in Spain. Regarding them as a luxury and insisting on doing everything yourself, as some expats do, is a recipe for spending much of your time feeling angry and frustrated rather than enjoying what brought you here in the first place. It is worth building up a good, ongoing relationship with a *gestor*, to whom you can turn whenever you need a problem solved. *Gestores* are far less qualified than lawyers, but should still have an official licence; there will be a choice of small *gestorías* (the offices of *gestores*) in any town. In areas with significant foreign communities, there will probably be several who speak English. *Gestores* are, of course, paid for their services, but fees are generally reasonable and, once you realise how much stress you've avoided, you won't begrudge the expense.

Social Security

Anyone working in Spain or starting their own business must have a social security card (*tarjeta de seguridad social*). You obtain this either by filling in the form given to you by your employer or, if you are the employer or are self-employed, by going to your local social security office.

In order to apply for your social security card you will need to present various documents – birth certificates and marriage certificates for you and any of your dependants, and proof of residence (property deed or rental contract). If any of the documents are not in Spanish then they will need to be translated.

If you are the owner of a business then it is also your responsibility to register your employees for social security. You must register with the social security treasury prior to opening the business. The business will be given a social security number. In order to register your business for a social security number you will need to fill in a form and present various documents – your NIE and passport, a copy of your insurance policies for accident and health cover, deed of incorporation of the company and copy of your application to register for tax.

Licences

Opening Licence

All businesses need an opening licence (*licencia de apertura*), which is obtained from the town hall (*ayuntamiento*). The calculation of the fees is complicated and it is often hard to tell if you are being charged the correct amount. The cost of the *licencia de apertura* will vary depending on the type of business that you are opening and also from region to region. For example, in Marbella the cost of the *licencia de apertura* depends on:

1. The business activity.
2. The location of the business premises. Different streets are classified as different categories and different categories have different rates.
3. The size of the business property by area.

After this calculation is done, the figure is adjusted depending on a number of factors. These include whether the business has changed its activity or just its owner.

Before a *licencia de apertura* is issued, there may have to be an official inspection of the business. This could be to ensure that you are complying with health and safety regulations. In addition, you may have to have the structure of the building inspected if you have made alterations or if you are running certain types of business, such as a hotel.

The *licencia de apertura* can be transferred to the new owner of a business if the business is sold. However, it is important to check this in advance. The licence is based on the business premises and not the business or the people running it. If the type of business that you are going to be running is substantially different from the one that was there before you will probably have to apply for a new *licencia*.

Licences for Construction and Alterations to Premises

If you are going to carry out any building work on the premises you will need a building licence (*licencia de obra* or *permiso de obra*). This is obtained from the town hall and the cost will vary but is usually a percentage of the cost of the construction works. The length of time to obtain the building licence also varies from area to area with considerable delays in some areas. In certain areas there is a stop on the issue of new building licences in order to try to control the massive construction that is taking place.

Many people will undertake the work or construction without having the building licence approved, or even worse – without applying for it in the first place. This is a risky strategy as you could be ordered to pull the property down if it is built illegally.

Once work has been completed you will need a certificate of end of works (*licencia de fin de obras*). This is issued by the architect who oversees the project and confirms that the works have been done in accordance with the building licence. Once you have the *licencia de fin de obras* you can register the new work officially through a declaration of new works (*declaración de obra nueva*).

Taxes

You must register your business with the tax authorities (*agencia tributaria*) so that they know of your existence and can tax you appropriately. The registration must be done at one of the offices of the *agencia tributaria*.

IAE

You must also register to pay the tax on economic activities – known as the *Impuestos Sobre Actividades Economicas* (sometimes know as *licencia fiscal*). For further information on this, see 'Business and Personal Taxes', p.109.

The tax rate will depend on the type of business that you will be running, as different types of business have different tax codes.

The government is trying to encourage small businesses to start up. One way of doing this is to reduce the IAE that is payable by small businesses. In fact, you may find that there is no IAE payable at all if your turnover is below a certain amount.

Ministry of Labour and Social Affairs

Once you start to run the business you must register it with the ministry of labour and social affairs (*Ministerio de Trabajo y Asuntos Sociales*). This must be done within 30 days of starting the business. Again you have to fill in a form. You must register at the local provincial office. Details of the nearest office can be found at **www.mtas.es/infgral/provin/espana.htm**.

Professional and Other Qualifications

If you have a qualification from another EU country then, in theory, this should be recognised in Spain. However, the reality can be somewhat different. Some professions by law require certain qualifications. Some professions do not require qualifications but it is customary to obtain them. Other professions do not need qualifications at all. Sometimes employers will refuse to accept foreign qualifications. Some organisations require a convalidation of the foreign qualification. Check with the relevant body whether your qualifications will be acceptable. If they are not then ask what will make them acceptable.

Even if your qualifications are recognised by the relevant Spanish authority there may be certain professional codes or limitations that may apply. Again, it is important to find out whether there are any special professional codes or limitations which may apply within your profession.

In order to have your qualification accepted you must apply to the local office of the ministry of education and science (*Ministerio de Educación y Ciencias*). There is a fee payable – for a degree the fee is €81.60, while lower qualifications carry a fee of €40.80. You will have to provide copies of your certificates – with translations as necessary – and also details of any other courses and examinations that you may have completed.

Getting a qualification recognised and accepted can take time – just like many things in Spain. In fact, it can take up to 18 months for a degree, and about half that time for a lesser qualification. The education department of the Spanish embassies should be able to advise you, otherwise bodies that can assist with the validation of qualifications include:

Ministerio de Educación y Ciencias
Ministry of Education and Sciences
c/ Alcala, 36, 28071 Madrid
t (0034) 90 2218500
f (0034) 91 7018648
www.mec.es

Subdirección General de General Subdirección
Paseo del Prado, 28-2ª Planta, 28071 Madrid
t (0034) 91 506 5600
f (0034) 91 506 5704
www.sgci.mec.es

National Academic Recognition Centre
Oriel House,Oriel Road, Cheltenham, Glos GL50 1XP
t 0870 990 4088
f 0870 990 1560
www.naric.co.uk

Centro NARIC
National Academic Recognition Centre in Spain
Subdirección General de Titulos Convalidaciones y Homologaciones
Paseo del Prado, 28, 28014 Madrid
t (0034) 91 5065 593
f (0034) 91 5066 706
www.enic-naric.net

Registration with a Consulate

When you arrive in Spain you ought to register with your local consulate. This allows the authorities to keep a track of who is in the country. The consulate like to know this so that if there is any information that they need to pass to you they will be able to contact you. This information could either affect all emigrants or could be personal. The information could be of a routine nature (changes in tax regulations, etc.) or could be used at times of emergencies (the Tsunami disaster at the end of 2004 was a good example of why the consulate needs to know which emigrants are living in a country).

For a list of consulates and embassies, *see* 'Contacts', p.220

Working in Spain

Business Practices 134
How to Find a Job 138
Terms and Conditions of Employment 145
Dismissal and Redundancy 147
Benefits 149
Unions 151

06

For many people, the first step to starting a business in Spain is to relocate and work for a period. This has two main advantages. It allows you to get to know the country without the added pressure of running your own business and, if you obtain the right job, may help in gaining a deeper understanding of the kind of business you intend to start up. Anybody planning to go to Spain to live and work should expect to earn less than they might be used to at home and you may even have to work for nothing at the beginning. Unemployment can also be a factor that contributes to difficulties, although there are areas in which expats may enjoy better opportunities than locals.

Having an understanding of such things as etiquette, Spanish job interviews and contracts will also be invaluable once you start your own business as a misunderstanding of the business culture and practice in a different country can be the difference between your business succeeding and failing.

Business Practices

Relationships

Personal relationships are very important in Spanish business. In order to succeed you will have to build up a network of contacts within your industry and within your community. These contacts (*enchufes*, which literally means a plug) will help you and you will help them – it is the way that things get done. Having the right contacts often means that you can obtain licences quicker than you would otherwise have been able to – or even obtain them where you might otherwise have been refused.

Introductions and contacts mean greater trust between people and is a great way of helping the business in terms of relationships with others, but also introductions to new clients. These contacts are not made by telephone, post or email – they are made personally. Lunch, dinner, the bar, the social club are all good ways of making valuable contacts. You will note that most of these suggestions involve food and/or drink. An informal atmosphere is used to good effect to get to know each other.

Company Hierarchy

The Spanish are very aware of status. When you are trying to develop a new business relationship with another company, you need to make sure that your initial contact is made at the right level. You must deal with the person at the same level as you. If you initially speak to somebody too high up the ladder you will be insulting the person further down the ladder whom you should have spoken to in the first place. Similarly, the same person will be insulted if you initially speak to somebody lower than them. If in doubt, check who your contact should be. At some point it may be necessary to ask whether your superior should speak to their superior to take the matter further and to progress a deal.

Family-owned Businesses

The family is important in Spain – even more so than in the UK. You will often find several generations of a family living together and also working together. If a business is run by the family then the hierarchy of the business will often mimic the family hierarchy, with the youngest gradually working their way up to the top of the ladder.

How to Address Spaniards

The formalities of business etiquette are very important to the Spanish, although this is changing and meetings are gradually becoming less formal. Nevertheless, though Spaniards are aware that other cultures place less importance on dress, they still find overly casual dress to be unbusinesslike. The exchange of business cards is an important part of any meeting. In terms of etiquette, handshakes are a standard part of Spanish business protocol. Women sometimes touch cheeks while lightly kissing the air. While in social situations men and women also do this, business situations demand a handshake. Shake hands when you arrive and also when you leave.

During conversations, Spaniards stand closer, make more physical contact and maintain eye contact longer than you might be used to. Don't be surprised to see them touching each other on the arm, back or shoulder regularly. Once you get to know somebody better you will probably move on to 'manly' pats on the back for men and kisses on the cheeks for women.

First-time introductions with Spaniards should be formal. The 'polite' way to address somebody is by use of their surname. The use of a professional prefix is used in a similar way to the way that we refer to somebody as Dr Smith. If they do not have a profession or you do not know if they belong to a profession, you should refer to them as *señor*, *señora* or *señorita*, as appropriate. Respect is shown by referring to somebody as *Don*. The use of first names and the less formal *'tu'* (instead of surnames and *'Usted'*) should wait until your host suggests moving to this more informal method of address.

Names

A major source of confusion between the Spanish and the British is the Spanish surname. A Spaniard will use the surnames of both their father and mother. Their father's name comes first and their mother's second. Sometimes they will omit their mother's name and use their father's only. When a woman gets married she may substitute her mother's name for her husband's name, but this is unusual.

Meetings

Meetings in Spain can be loud and noisy. They will often start late and go on longer than they should. Generally, it is not considered impolite to interrupt somebody who is speaking, or to take a telephone call during the meeting. Do not expect anybody to write anything down at the meeting or for anybody to take notes. Certainly you should not expect decisions to be agreed in writing. Internal company meetings are usually held simply to communicate any decisions that have already been made by those in authority. Here, too, decisions are made and business discussed only between people at the same level within the firm.

Mañana and *Siestas*

We all know that the Spanish way of life appears to be more relaxed than in the UK and one of the first words most people learn in Spanish is *mañana*. This extends to business and you should not get worked up if a Spaniard is late for a meeting. Being late for a meeting in the UK is frowned upon and is often thought of as being rude to the point of being insulting to the other people involved. It also means that the meeting cannot start on time, so some people are waiting around not being productive. In Spain, being late for anything (apart from bullfighting) is a way of life and is to be expected. It is not meant as an insult. If you cannot get used to this then dealing with Spain and working in Spain may not be for you.

The Spanish tend to prefer to start the day late and work later into the evening. The idea of a working breakfast is almost laughable to many Spaniards. The era of *siestas* in business life have now pretty much disappeared however, particularly when you are working in a more international environment. Despite all the stereotypes, the Spanish are very hard working and have a serious attitude towards business.

Women in Business

Women are paid far more attention in the workplace than they generally receive in the UK. The compliments are normally meant exactly as that – a compliment – and are unlikely to be harassment.

Unfortunately, just as in the UK, few women have made it to the top, although this situation is gradually improving. The most likely place to find a woman in a high position is within a family-owned company.

Things you miss

I set up my own Estate Agency business in 2001 whilst working as a sales person for an agent in Nerja. Clients were coming over to the Costa del Sol with too little money having seen old, repeated, television programmes on the area with out of date prices. I live in the Axarquia area of the Costa del Sol where property is a lot cheaper, so I decided to branch out on my own and offer clients property for prices they could afford. I had no money and didn't intend to borrow any, so I had to set up on a shoestring. A friend of mine had also decided to set up on her own, so although we had our own separate business's we shared a website and a page of advertising each in a local magazine. Axarquia Properties was born! We were sure the Axarquia was about to be "discovered"! And we were right!

I set up with no office, just my mobile phone and my book of properties to show any potential customers. I paid self-employed social security, which is called autonomo and costs 207.20 euros per month regardless of whether you are a single person or a family of 20! My friend and I both became Limited companies, S.L. (Sociedad Limitado) and separated our websites and advertising. I now employ an office manager who is on a contract and two sales girls who work for commission only.

My advice to anyone wanting to set up a business in Spain is go for it. Don't be put off by anyone and don't become a limited company until you've been autonomo for at least a year.

We have a network of English Speaking businesses on the coast that hold monthly lunches and we all get together to help each other and generally network!

Sally Harrison, Owner/agent, Axarquia Properties S.L.

Dress Codes

Spaniards have a great sense of style and pay attention to their appearance. Business dress is generally suits, with darker colours for the winter and lighter colours for the summer, although smart/casual dress is becoming more acceptable – particularly within the less traditional industries. Ties are not worn as frequently as in the past – especially in the south where it gets very hot in the summer. Shoes and watches are status symbols and certain brands will be fashionable at different times – it could be important to keep up!

As elsewhere, labels are important to the Spanish although they should not be too obvious. Good quality brands with small discrete labels will be noticed and appreciated. Your sense of dress will give an indication of your social standing and therefore your success.

Socialising

One of the joys of working in Spain is the potential for socialising – although it can get tiring as the nights tend to be long. If you are going out for dinner do not expect to start before about 9pm and do not expect to get home before the early hours of the morning. Also, do not be surprised if the actual business conversation is started only right at the end of the evening – which can often be difficult to cope with when you are tired, full, and have had one glass of wine too many. The Spanish are very friendly and embrace life with a passion that the British can often only dream of. This is probably one of the many reasons why you are thinking of moving there to work.

If you are honoured enough to be invited to a Spanish home, you know that you are really being accepted and that the relationship is going well. Recognise that this is a big step. Take flowers or chocolate or even a present for the children. Always ask what the dress code is. And don't be afraid to take the initiative yourself – if you want to show that you are eager to make friends, invite them to your house for dinner or a barbecue.

Arguments

The Spanish love to argue. Just go into any bar and you are likely to witness a lively debate taking place. This is part of the culture and can often be misunderstood by people who are new to the country. Just because something looks like the argument to end all arguments doesn't mean that everybody isn't getting on well. Loud voices, waving of arms and pointing of fingers are just part of the rich culture of Spain. Do not take these arguments personally, otherwise you will never get on.

Having said that, it is important to know how to avoid a genuine confrontation. Safe topics of conversation are your home country, travel and sports – especially football. Avoid bullfighting, religion and politics and beware of making personal enquiries, especially during first introductions. Be sensitive to regional differences; making misinformed comments about a Spaniard's region of origin would be offensive (i.e. mistaking a Catalan for a Basque).

If you want to get something done in Spain do not jump up and down and shout – this is likely to mean that you are noticed, but are put to the bottom of the 'to do' list or even thrown off it entirely. You often have to be more subtle than you might be in the UK when complaining. Avoid the 'I have been waiting for a month. If you don't do this I will take you to court' approach and try the 'I want to pay you your money but I can't until you have done that' approach. You will be amazed at the response. If you can explain this over a drink or two at the local bar then you are even more likely to achieve the desired results.

Honour

The Spanish are a very honourable nation and somebody's word and a hand-shake still mean something most of the time. It is very tempting to fall into this trap and not tie up the details of an agreement with paperwork – especially as tying up details in a contract is not the 'Spanish way'. Despite the fact that most Spaniards are honest and a handshake will seal a deal, there is a minority who will not comply with the agreement and documentation will certainly be invaluable should you need to rely on it later. Make sure therefore that you get your paperwork straight.

It is also very easy to fall into the trap of assuming that somebody from your own country is going to be more trustworthy than a foreigner. It is important to remember that almost all fraud in Spain is committed by the British on the British, the Germans on the Germans, and so on – the Spanish are rarely involved.

How to Find a Job

Government Employment Agencies

Every business with a job vacancy is legally obliged to register it with the government employment agency (*Insituto Naciónal de Empleo* – INEM). This is obviously a good starting point as, In theory, all job vacancies are listed there. Check out INEM's website (**www.inem.es**) or they can be contacted at:

Calle Condesa de Venadito

28017 Madrid

t (091) 585 98 88; **f** (091) 377 58 81/377 58 87

Private Employment Agencies

Just as in most countries, there are private employment agencies in Spain that you can approach with your CV to help you find a job. Unlike most countries these private employment agencies are still highly regulated by the govern-ment and are really secondary to the INEM. A list of such agencies can be found at **www. directorio.anuncios-radio.com**.

HR Consultants

HR (Human Resources) consultants in Spain are similar to the employment agen-cies that we are used to in the UK in that they will match up people with jobs. As somebody looking for a job you will register with them, providing a copy of your CV. They will then try to find a job that suits you. HR consultants may even offer a wider range of services, including helping you to modify your CV to make it more suitable.

The *Asociación Española de Dirección y Desarrollo de Personas* (AEDIPE) is a private, non-profit making organisation that works with people in personnel and human resources. They can be contacted at:

Calle Moreto nº 10 Bajo Izd

Madrid

www.aedipe.es

European Employment Service

The European Employment Service (EURES) helps people to find work across Europe. It is a collaboration between the public employment services of the EU countries. In addition to this, certain other associations (such as trade unions and local authorities) are also involved. The EURES network provides various services for workers and employers, including information, advice and placement of jobs. They have a section on their website where you can search for jobs, advertise jobs and also post your CV.

EURES can be contacted through their website (**www.europa.eu.eu.int/jobs**) or by emailing them directly on **empl-eures@cec.eu.int**.

UK Employment Agencies

Some UK employment agencies have lists of vacancies abroad and a number of agencies specialise in providing work for companies abroad – although these are difficult to track down. A list of UK employment agencies can be obtained from the Recruitment and Employment Confederation (**www.rec.uk.com**) although there is a small charge for the list.

Internet

Many people are now connected or have access to the internet, even if it is only through an internet café or a friend's computer. Searching through the internet can provide you with a list of companies with vacancies, although this is likely to take you some time to sort through.

Advertisements

Most people when looking for work will start by looking through the 'situations vacant' advertisements. There is a wide variety of other places where you can look for a job.

National newspapers have the advantage of being widely available no matter where you are based, but the job advertisements are likely to be limited to vacancies in large companies that have the budget to advertise in national papers and who are not targeting people from one particular area. Regional newspapers are going to be more area-specific and are more likely to have jobs in smaller companies. If you are already based in the area, your local newspaper is also a good place to start looking for a job. If you live outside the area you can usually get somebody to send you the local paper.

If your career is specialist and has its own trade newspaper or magazine, it will carry a section advertising industry/profession job vacancies. You will probably know your own UK publication, but may not know whether there is an equivalent trade publication in Spain. The European Directory of Business Associations is a good starting point.

Direct Approaches

Sometimes the best route into work is to take the direct approach. You may know somebody you would like to work for and whom you suspect may be looking for somebody to employ. Providing you have the right skills for that job there is no harm in asking whether they would consider you for the role – although doing so cold can be nerve-racking if you don't know them particularly well. Do not take it badly if they turn you down and don't let that decision affect your friendship with that person – this is business not friendship.

There is also no harm in approaching a business directly. You might be able to solve their recruitment problem without them having to go to the expense of advertising. However, bear in mind that many businesses will be approached by many people each week 'on spec' and you may not always get the warmest of welcomes – particularly if they are busy at the time. Try to choose your timing well and acknowledge that they are busy people and that you do not wish to take up too much of their time.

Networking

Spain is a culture where networking goes a long way. As you get to know more and more people, the chances of their knowing someone who has a vacant situation will increase.

Temporary Work

Unemployment is high in Spain. Nevertheless, there are plenty of temporary positions available, especially during the peak holiday season. Temporary jobs are varied in both the type of work and the duration, from working as a timeshare tout to being a temporary secretary in an office, from gardening to distributing leaflets advertising bars and from being a film extra to office cleaning.

865

There are many illegal immigrants in Spain. Their best chance of making some money is to move from one temporary position to another. Often these illegal workers will compete for the job by offering to work for less than anybody else – often at a rate lower than the minimum wage (see **Setting up a Business in Spain**, 'Employing Staff', p.122). In most cases the employers will pay in cash. Temporary work is generally unskilled, so anybody can do it. Because of these factors there is much competition for each temporary position. It can be difficult to compete for a job – especially if you wish to work legally.

Internships

Another route onto the job ladder in Spain is to work for little or no money. An internship is effectively work experience during an academic career and is treated as a learning experience. The internship is normally, but not necessarily, related to a student's studies. Internships tend to be offered only by the larger organisations and firms. You will need a reasonable understanding of Spanish in order to apply for one – unless the company is very large or run by other British people. If your level of language is not up to scratch then you will need to take a course before you go.

Applications for internships can be made either direct to the company or through an agency. The agencies will charge you for dealing with the application but will have long lists of companies offering such internships. They will also know the relevant person to contact within the organisation. Applying yourself is cheaper, of course, but less likely to produce the results unless you already know somebody within the organisation.

Internships are unpaid in most cases. In some cases the company may contribute to living expenses, but these payments are minimal. Because the internship is meant to be educational you will be supervised at all times. The internship will normally carry a credit towards your studies.

The Leonardo de Vinci programme offers scholarships for people undertaking an internship. In order to apply for such a scholarship, contact the international department of your university or go to **www.europa.eu.int** and follow the links.

The minimum period of internship required in order to receive a scholarship is three months. The scholarship is open to students from the EU on an internship in another EU country and normally consists of a grant of €100-€500 per month and reimbursement of travel costs. If you had to do a language course in preparation for the internship you may be able to get reimbursement for that too.

Voluntary Work

There are many organisations and projects in Spain that rely on voluntary workers. This is seen as good experience for young people who wish to visit Spain and learn more about the country and its people.

Voluntary workers have to be at least 16 years old and some organisations have no upper limit – although others do not take on volunteers aged over 30. Most voluntary work does not require any special qualifications or previous experience – although having some may be an advantage.

In addition to not being paid, you may even be expected to contribute towards the cost of your board and lodgings, even if they are provided for you. If you travel to Spain for the work, you will have to pay your own travel costs and possibly pay to be collected from the airport. Many people benefit from the experience of voluntary work and it may even help when applying for jobs in later life.

A volunteer's working day is around five to eight hours long and you will normally be expected to work five to six days per week. Some projects have work only at certain times of the year, while others are open all the year around.

Basic accommodation (usually shared) is normally provided. Volunteer projects have many different nationalities working for them and the common language is likely to be English or Spanish.

Seasonal Work

In many areas of Spain, tourism is a major part of the economy. Seasonal work is typically for a couple of weeks or even a few months and competition can be fierce. Different parts of Spain have slightly different seasons, but typically the high summer season is between May and September. Seasonal jobs tend to be those not requiring a high level of qualification, although experience in the industry is a major bonus and will help to impress an employer.

Just because a job is temporary and in a country with a warm climate and a relaxed image does not mean that you won't have to work hard – you will. Seasonal jobs tend to be low paid and with long hours. It is a good experience rather than a quick way of making any real money and that is probably the best way to approach it.

The dilemma with seasonal working for most people is that ideally you should not set out without having a job already lined up, but it can be difficult to obtain seasonal work unless you are already on the ground. Most people take the risk and go anyway – assuming that they will either find work or, at worst, spend their time relaxing on the beach. There is a wide variety of possibilities: working in hotels, restaurants, bars and clubs, fruit-picking and packing, holiday reps, sports instructors are just some examples. If you do go to Spain to work for a season, be sure to have an exit plan in case you don't like the job and can't get another one.

Even though you are just working for the season doesn't mean that you don't have to comply with the various different employment laws and regulations. Do not be tempted to work illegally (*see* below).

Illegal Working

Don't do it. Spain has a huge black economy but the government is clamping down on this. They recently announced an amnesty for illegal workers as a precursor to clamping down on this activity even more.

Employers who employ illegal workers and who are caught are fined heavily. These fines run into thousands of euros. Many people do not get caught of course, but it is simply not worth the risk.

If you are an employer, it is tempting to hire illegal workers and to pay them in cash. You don't have to worry about contracts, social security payments, taxes, etc. It seems that you are saving money, time and paperwork. However, it is not as easy as that. It has been known for some employees to sue their employers for wages that they claim they have not received, even though they have! The customers and co-workers see them working. They can easily prove that they have been working for you. You have paid them in cash. You can't prove that you have paid them. They claim they have not been paid and sue you for wages that they have already received and there is little that you can do as you are the person who was employing them illegally.

There are many other problems with working illegally – you are not covered for medical care, you are not entitled to redundancy pay, you have no rights if you are unfairly dismissed, etc. It is simply not worth it.

CVs

Spanish Format

The typical Spanish CV (*currículo*) can be quite different from a UK CV. It is common practice to attach a photograph to the CV and Spaniards generally list all of their qualifications, no matter how irrelevant they may seem.

It is important that you follow the Spanish format when applying for a job with a Spanish company to show that you understand how the system works, but also so that you don't confuse any potential employers. The Spaniards have two surnames – for more information on this, *see* 'Names', p.139. Although this appears strange to us, it is perfectly normal to them and they may initially find it odd that you have only one surname. Further confusion comes when we have middle names, as the Spanish can often misinterpret these as part of your surname. Make sure you stress this point clearly on your CV, otherwise you will end up with your middle name as your first surname and your surname as your second surname – all very confusing for you and for them.

Translations

Your CV will have to be in Spanish if you are applying for a job with a Spanish company. If you are applying for a job with an English-speaking company you may wish to have two versions of your CV – one in Spanish and one in English. If you are not confident about translating your CV yourself then make sure that you get somebody qualified to do this for you. There can be nothing worse than receiving a CV full of spelling and grammatical errors – or even one that simply does not make sense. If you are using an agency to help find a job, then they may assist with translation, but you may need a professional translator if they do not. For a sample CV, *see* **Appendix 1**, p.250.

Employment Prerequisites

Medical

If you are employing somebody or are applying for a job, a medical may be required. Some employers insist on this as a matter of course and in some jobs it is essential. Do not be surprised if you are asked to take a medical test.

Language Tests

Some jobs require your language skills to be of a certain level and some employers may wish to test your ability. This can be done in a couple of different ways. The easiest and most informal way is simply for the employer to speak to you in Spanish. While this can be intimidating, it is a very effective way of finding out how good you are without taking a formal test.

A second way of testing your language skills is for the employer to switch languages at a certain point in the interview and to insist that you do the same so that they can gauge the level of your Spanish. This method is similar to the first method but is a bit more formal in that you know exactly when your language skills are being tested. This can make you feel more pressured and sometimes makes people a bit tongue-tied.

The more formal way of testing your language skills is to make you take a language test. This is likely to consist of both written and oral tests. You may even be sent to be examined at an external institution such as a language school.

If you are going through a recruitment agency then the agency will probably give you some sort of language test as this will help them when they are speaking to prospective employers.

Interview Techniques

In Spain, personal contact is everything. Interviews are usually one-to-one but for high-flying jobs you may have to face a panel and be called back for a second or third 'roasting'. Arrive early, dress formally (suit and tie for men, dress/suit for women) and bring all useful documents such as written references and certificates of qualifications. Above all, be prepared. Make sure you know what the job will require and what questions you may be asked. The first impression is *importantísima*.

During the first interview, shake hands with everyone you are introduced to, looking them in the eye and presenting your business card if appropriate. Use the '*usted*' form, be attentive to everything said to you and reply appropriately, but do not speak out of turn.

Different companies will have different interview procedures. With a smaller business you will probably be interviewed by the owner of the business. You are also likely only to have one interview. If, on the other hand, you are going for an interview with a larger organisation then you may have several interviews.

Many of the same techniques that you would apply to an interview in the UK also apply in Spain, but there is a different emphasis. Avoid monosyllabic answers wherever possible. Show interest in the job and what may be expected of you but be careful not to mention your salary expectations until asked (which you probably will be in the final stage). You should do the same amount of research prior to the interview that you would do back home – what the job is likely to involve, background information regarding the company, information about the industry and so on.

Terms and Conditions of Employment

Written Contracts

If you are successful in an interview and are offered a job, make sure that you have a contract with your new employers. The contract will set out the terms of the employment such as salary, working hours, job description and title, duration of the employment, etc.

An employment contract doesn't have to be in writing, but this is advisable. If there is no written contract there will always be a dispute over what the terms of the contract are. A written contract must be in Spanish. You may wish to have it translated but the legally binding version will be the Spanish one.

Employees should also have a copy of any other company rules and regulations (usually in the office manual) to avoid any confusion over their expected conduct and entitlements.

There are different types of employment contract. These include specific-duration or short-term contracts, which are normally for a specific project, to cover maternity leave, a temporary increase in work, etc.

An employer cannot dismiss a person under a specific-duration contract until the end of that period. There are exceptions to this in the case where both the employer and employee agree to end the contract early, or where the employee has done something that would allow the employer to dismiss him anyway, such as gross misconduct.

Contracts for a specific project will not have a definitive finishing date. The contract will end when the project ends. The most obvious example of a project in Spain is a specific building contract where workers are employed until the construction is finished. With this type of contract it is important to make sure that the project is properly defined and what is meant by it being finished.

Another variation is the work experience contract. These should last at least six months, but no longer than two years. The employee may be paid less than a normal employee as the purpose of the contract is to gain experience and this is seen as a benefit in addition to their pay. The person working under the work experience contract must be paid 60–75 per cent of the amount that they would be paid if they were being employed in a normal capacity. Trainee contracts are similar to the work-experience contract in that the main aim is for the employee to gain experience, but it is not limited to graduates.

If an employee is employed on a permanent basis, or if the employment contract does not specify a specific time period, then they are employed under an indefinite contract. If you employ somebody on these terms they have more rights than an employee on a short-term contract, which is why many employers prefer to employ staff on short-term contracts. This works if the nature of the work lends itself to short-term contracts, but many businesses would suffer if they adopted this approach. They would spend more time interviewing, more time training and they would have less continuity and stability.

The state prefers its population to be employed on a permanent basis rather than on short-term contracts. It therefore encourages employers to recruit on a permanent basis. It does this through a range of incentives, such as reduced social security payments (up to 75 per cent reduction) and reduced redundancy benefits (about 40 per cent) for employing certain types of people such as the disabled, unemployed women and people who have been unemployed for over six months.

Working Hours

As much as employers might like their staff to work around the clock for little pay, there are rules that regulate how many hours a person can work per week and also how much rest they are entitled to. The maximum working week in Spain is 40 hours, with no more than nine hours in any one day – excluding overtime. In addition, the number of hours overtime a worker can work in a week is limited to two hours. The maximum number of days staff can work per week is six. There must be at least 12 hours between the end of a working day and the start of the next working day.

Holidays

Staff must be given a minimum of 14 paid holiday days per year in addition to all the national and regional holidays. The national holidays tend to fall on the same calendar day each year. For a full list of national and local holidays, *see* **References**, p.237.

Training and Education

Employers are expected to provide their staff with adequate training and education during their employment. The government encourages training for employees and will sometimes provide financial assistance, usually in the form of reduced social security payments for the employer.

Dismissal and Redundancy

This is probably the most unpleasant thing that you will have to do as an employer. Unfortunately, no matter how well your recruitment and interview process works there is still the possibility that you may have to dismiss staff at some point for some reason.

The rules in Spain on dismissals are complicated and much stronger than in the UK. You must take care and get advice before dismissing somebody. There is the right to appeal against a dismissal and if the correct procedures have not been followed, or if the reason for dismissal cannot be proved, then the employee will probably win their appeal. There are three different categories of dismissal and within these three categories there are different ways of dismissing staff.

Disciplinary

A worker can be dismissed if he or she does not fulfil their duties to the employer in a serious and intentional way. 'Serious' must mean intolerable behaviour or the inability of the employer to trust the employee. 'Intentional' means that the employee purposely committed the act or acts that breached the employment contract. The employer must give written notice of the dismissal (*carta de despedido*) and the written notice must state that the employee is being dismissed, the grounds for the dismissal and the date of dismissal. The worker may appeal against the decision within 20 days of the dismissal.

There are many types of grounds for dismissal of this category. Some of the most common include:

- **repeated absence from work without justification or prior authority of the employer**
- **disobedience or insubordination**
- **physical or verbal abuse towards the employer or other employees**
- **wilful diminution of job productivity**
- **drug or alcohol abuse that affects job performance**

- **sexual harassment or threats towards the employer or other employees**
- **theft from the employer or other employees**
- **bad behaviour towards clients**
- **unjustified harm to the image or functioning of the company**

Objective causes

Among the types of objective cause for dismissal are ineptitude of the worker (i.e. an inability to actually do the job), the failure by the worker to adapt to the changes in his or her job, intermittent absences from work or the employer's economic, technical, organisational or production reasons. In all cases, the employer must give at least 30 days' written notice. If the employer does not give notice then they must at least pay the salary equivalent of the notice period due. The employee is entitled to 20 days' worth of salary for each year worked up to a maximum of 12 months' worth of salary and may appeal against the decision within 20 days of the dismissal.

Collective lay-off

For an employer to lay off a group of employees he or she must get the approval of the Labour Authorities through an administrative ruling. Employers with up to 300 employees can dismiss up to 10 per cent of staff. If the employer has more than 300 staff then more than 30 employees can be laid off. However, if the business closes entirely then all the employees can be dismissed. Each employee is entitled to 20 days' worth of salary for each year worked up to a maximum of 12 months' worth of salary. A consultation period for the employees or their representatives is obligatory.

In the event that an employee appeals against the dismissal they would go to the Office for Individual Mediation and Conciliation (*see* 'Alternative Dispute Resolution', p.212) and they can also go to the courts. If the employee loses the appeal then the employment is terminated and there is no compensation for the employee. If the employee wins the appeal then they can either choose to have their employment re-instated with the employer (which is unlikely due to the conflictive relationship that will now exist) or they can choose to receive 45 days' worth of compensation per year of service – up to a maximum of 48 months' wages. In addition to this, the employee who wins the appeal would be entitled to back-pay equivalent to the wages they would have received from the date of termination until the date of the appeal ruling.

If a member of staff is being dismissed, the employer must reconsider retraining or relocation. If new staff are employed after redundancies are made there is no requirement to reconsider employing previous staff.

Unemployment benefit (*pago de desempleo*) is paid through the social security contributions for those people working legally.

Benefits

Sickness Benefit

Workers who are ill are entitled to a percentage of their salary in sickness pay (*pago de seguro*). The way that this is calculated will depend on various factors.

Even if you are self-employed you may be entitled to sickness benefit. In order to do this you will need to present a certificate from your doctor saying that you are incapable of carrying out your job. You will then be entitled to 75 per cent of the minimum wage as sickness benefit.

Employees must inform their employers that they are sick as soon as possible on the first day of sickness. If an employee is ill for three days or more then they need to get a doctor's note (*impreso de incapacidad temporal*), which confirms that they are genuinely ill and cannot go to work. If the employee continues to be ill, they have to obtain a doctor's note every seven days until they recover. The doctor's note must be given to the employer.

If an employee is ill for 4–20 days then they are paid 60 per cent of their basic salary. If they are ill for longer than this then they are paid 75 per cent for the period after 20 days.

Maternity Benefit

Should a female employee become pregnant (*emarazada*), she will be entitled to two weeks off work before the birth and up to 14 weeks off after the birth. This period does not vary depending on how long someone has been working for an employer, and Spanish employers tend to be quite flexible over these minimums as the family is very important in the culture. 'Foreign' employers tend to be less accommodating, although they feel under pressure to follow the Spanish custom.

During her maternity leave an employee is entitled to her full salary. If more than one child is born (i.e. twins, triplets) then the period allowed after birth is increased by a further two weeks. In addition to the above, a doctor may decide that the employee needs more time off work and may sign her off for a further period. If this is the case then the employer has to continue paying the employee's salary.

A man is entitled to two days' leave when his child is born. However, there is a curious system by which a man may actually be entitled to more time off – his wife can give him part of her maternity leave. Two weeks of the woman's maternity leave can be transferred to her husband by this means.

If the mother decides to return to work after giving birth, she is entitled to time off work for breast-feeding. This continues until the child is nine months old. The mother is entitled to leave her place of work for an hour each day for breast-feeding. This time can be divided into two separate periods. The father is also entitled to time off to feed the child if both parents work.

Parents can voluntarily take further time off work to look after their child – although without pay. The length of time off will depend on the agreement between the employer and the employee and will often vary according to the seniority of the employee. An employer must keep the job available for the parent to return to for up to a year. However, only one of the parents can keep their job open for this period.

If an employee has a child under six years old, or if they look after a disabled person (providing that the care is not paid), then they must be allowed the opportunity to work fewer hours than they would otherwise. If this is the case then their salary is also reduced – by the same percentage. They are entitled to reduce their hours by between one third and one half of their working day.

Women with children under the age of three years old who are self-employed or employed can claim a personal income tax reduction of €1,200.

Retirement

The Spanish have no compulsory retirement age although the traditional age is 65 years. This applies to both men and women. However, many companies are reducing the staff retirement age and more people are now retiring at the age of 60 or even lower. Employers can effectively force an employee to retire if their age means that they can no longer do their job properly. For pensions, *see* p.192.

Other Benefits

Under certain conditions, employees may be entitled to further time off work. The amount of time off will depend on the situation. An employee can always negotiate with his employer for additional time off or the employee's representative may negotiate this on behalf of the employee.

Unions

Unions (*sindicatos*) in Spain have had an interesting history and were actually abolished during the Franco era. Unions do exist, but few workers are members and only about one in eight workers belongs to one. The two main unions are the *Union General de Trabajadores* (UGT) (general union of Workers), and the *Confederación Sindical de Comisiones Obreras* (CCOO).

Unions are regarded as being unconnected to management and are there to negotiate on behalf of the workers. The unions normally concern themselves with matters such as salary, retirement benefits and working conditions. They don't have any say in the management of the company but are entitled to receive information about a company's performance and also to express the workers' opinion on company strategy.

There is no legal requirement to join a union. Companies with over 50 employees must, however, appoint a representative from its staff to liaise between the staff and the management.

Spain has the European custom of paying staff an additional month or two months' salary (*pagas extraordinarias*) – usually in July and/or December. Unions will negotiate on behalf of its members over rates of salary and also the frequency of *pagas extraodinarias*.

Strikes are not uncommon, and the number of days lost through strike action in Spain has been among the highest in Europe for many years, although this figure is lowering. Spanish workers have the right to go on strike and cannot be dismissed as a result. Certain public-sector professions, for example, the police and army, cannot strike. There are also rules limiting the amount of public transport which can be affected by a strike. The last national general strike was in 2002.

Living in Spain

Learning Spanish 154
Moving 158
Finding Accommodation 162
Communication and the Media 175
Home Utilities 179
Motoring 182
Healthcare 183
Pensions 188
Education 189

07

Learning Spanish

Why is it important to speak the local language?
There are many powerful arguments in favour of learning the language of any country in which you hope to live and work. In Spain there are three co-official languages apart from 'Spanish' (more accurately referred to as Castilian): Catalan, Galician and Basque. In an area where another language is spoken it is advisable to be able to communicate in both Castilian and that one too, since a 'minority' language may actually be the locals' first language (*see* 'Spanish Languages', p.27).

Unless you work in a completely English-speaking environment, you cannot expect to get ahead in the workplace without speaking some Spanish, but equally there are many other aspects of daily life for which speaking in the local language is vitally important – for example getting a drink, ordering a meal, having a medical check-up or a haircut or dealing with repair people. In emergencies it may even be critical. Without some knowledge of the local language, your social life could also be very restricted, unless of course it is limited to socialising exclusively with fellow expats. On the other hand, speaking the language (however clumsily) will earn you the respect of the locals, as it shows common courtesy and a commitment to the community in which you have settled.

Getting Started

You can begin learning the language before setting off or once there, but arriving with a certain level will get you off to a good start. In the UK and Ireland there are many options for studying Castilian, a popular language nowadays, but fewer for Catalan, Basque or Galician. If you look, though, you will find a centre where they are taught. Opportunities for studying these languages are considered below.

Attending Classes

The classic way of learning a language is to attend a course, either at evening classes in a local FE college or at a private institution. Evening classes are generally inexpensive, usually coincide with the academic year and may be aimed at students hoping to take GCSE or A Levels. There may also be less structured, conversation-based classes. These can range from 'survival' level to groups for advanced speakers. It is best to do some structured learning before embarking on a conversation course.

To find out about courses, contact your local education authority or FE college, or look in the Yellow Pages to find a private school. Private courses usually cost more than local authority-run evening classes. Most levels, from beginners through to advanced, are catered for, though demand often determines what is available at any given time. For a price, some schools may tailor courses to your specific needs. Many schools are small, local outfits, which may offer just what you need, but there are also several large language-teaching organisations that offer courses in Castilian Spanish in the UK and Spain:

Berlitz (six UK centres)
Paradise Forum, Birmingham B3 3HJ
t (0121) 233 0974; **f** (0121) 233 1236; **www.berlitz.com/local/uk**

Inlingua
Rodney Lodge, Rodney Road, Cheltenham GL50 1HX
t (01242) 250493; **f** (01242) 250495; **www.inlingua-cheltenham.co.uk**

Check out **www.cactuslanguage.com**, which lets you select courses by place, level and duration – mostly in Brighton and London.

Self- and Online Study

You can also learn through self-study. Self-study methods usually consist of a course book and exercise books and cassettes for listening and pronunciation, and nowadays increasingly incorporate videos and/or CD-ROMs, which offer interactive practice. Much self-study is done via online courses. Look at **www.spanishlanguage.co.uk** for a list of more than 25 such courses. Alternatively, the BBC offers some good courses on its website (**www.bbc.co.uk/languages/spanish**). 'Spanish Steps' is a self-contained introductory course and 'Talk Spanish' is a lively topic-based course also aimed at beginners. 'Sueños', a second course, builds on the language acquired in 'Talk Spanish'. All these courses come with accompanying materials, books, cassettes or CDs.

Private Teachers, Language Exchanges and Language Clubs

You could hire a private teacher, but expect to pay £12–25 per hour, depending on his or her experience and qualifications. Language exchanges with locally based speakers of the language, who wish to learn English or improve their level, provide a cheaper alternative, as well as a good way of making friends. To find a private teacher or someone for an exchange, try advertising in the local press or putting up a notice in a local college or corner shop. Local language clubs can also be informal, friendly and inexpensive, and again are best sought out locally.

Useful Contacts

The Instituto Cervantes (**www.cervantes.es**), a government-backed institution promoting Spanish language and culture abroad, offers a range of courses throughout the year. The Instituto may also provide information on courses elsewhere, and the noticeboards usually have lots of useful ads from private teachers, conversation clubs, or possible exchange contacts.

The Instituto Cervantes has the following centres:

London
102 Eaton Square, London SW1W 9AN
t (020) 7235 0353; **f** (020) 7235 0329

Manchester
26/330 Deansgate, Campfield Avenue Arcade, Manchester M3 4FN
t (0161) 661 4200; **f** (0161) 661 4203

Leeds
169 Woodhouse Lane, Leeds LS2 3AR
t (0113) 246 1741; **f** (0113) 246 1023

Dublin
58 Northumberland Road, Ballsbridge, Dublin 4
t (01) 668 20 24; **f** (01) 668 84 16

Also useful for London-based students is the Hispanic and Luso–Brazilian Council (**www.canninghouse.com**). This organisation runs classes and provides information on where to study Castilian in London, other UK cities and in Spain.

Learning in Spain

Whether or not you begin learning before moving to Spain, there are many options available once there. Information about schools and courses is available both from the Instituto Cervantes and Canning House (*see* above). Otherwise, look in the Yellow Pages under *academias de idiomas*. There are literally dozens in the larger cities and plenty to choose from in areas with a large concentration of expats. English-language publications carry advertisements for language institutions, mainly in Barcelona or Madrid. The Escuela Oficial de Idiomas (EOI), the Official Language School, is cheaper than private schools and has centres throughout Spain. EOIs are now run by the Autonomous Communities but the central school at Calle Jesús Maestro, s/n, 28003 Madrid (**www.eoidiomas.com**), will provide information about all regional schools. The UK-based Open University also offers structured courses in Castilian, either as part of a degree or just for personal satisfaction (OU co-ordinator in Madrid, Calle Serrano 26, 3°, 28001 Madrid, **t** 91 577 7701).

Whether you are studying Castilian, Catalan, Galician or Basque, and whatever method you choose, it is important to be patient and accept that you will make mistakes. Do not aim for perfection from the word go but immerse yourself in the language, surround yourself with it, put yourself into situations where you are exposed to it and have to use it. Watch the TV – news programmes with topics you know about are very useful – read newspapers, listen to the radio, chat to your neighbours. Above all do not be afraid!

Spain's Other Languages

While both Catalan and Galician have much in common with Castilian, they are languages in their own right, not dialects. Basque, unrelated to any other Indo-European language, is another story. No previous language-learning experience will help you here.

Catalan (Català)

Catalan language and literature may be studied at many UK universities, generally in a sub-department of the Spanish or Hispanic Studies departments. Contact the relevant department at your nearest university.

In Catalonia itself many options are available. The Escuela Oficial de Idiomas (*see* above) offers Catalan throughout the whole of Spain and in Catalonia is called (in Catalan, naturally) La Escola Oficial d'Idiomes. The main branch is at Avinguda Drassanes s/n, **t** 93 329 2458. Alternatively, go to the Centres de Normalització Lingüística, central office, Carrer Pau Claris 162, **t** 93 272 3100. It is cheap, covers all levels and offer intensive summer courses. Many private language schools also offer courses.

An excellent series of Catalan-language resources and online courses may be found at **www.languages-on-the-web.com**.

Galician (Galego)

Opportunities for studying Galician outside Galicia are scarce. Some UK universities do have Galician lecturers within the Hispanic Studies departments. Contact the Hispanic Studies Department at the University of Birmingham (**www.bham.ac.uk/GalicianStudies**), which can also facilitate Galician links elsewhere.

Courses are offered at the Escuela Oficial de Idiomas all over Spain and in Galicia. The main branch there is at Calle Pepín Rivero, s/n, 15011 A Coruña, **t** 98 127 9100; **www.arrakis.es~/eoi**. At the Universidade de Santiago de Compostela is the Departamento de Filoloxía Galega, Avenida de Castelao s/n, 15705 Santiago de Compostela; **www.usc.es**.

Basque (Euskera)

Basque is not taught widely outside Euskadi but if you live in Erresuma Batua ('Great Britain' in Basque!), contact the Institute of Basque Studies within the Department of Languages, London Guildhall University (ibs-queries@euskalerria.org). There is also the Basque Association Abroad, the Basque Society (Euskal Elkartea), Oxford House, Derbyshire Street, Bethnal Green Town, London E2 6HD, **t** (020) 7739 7339, **f** (020) 7739 0435; **london@euskaledge.fsnet.co.uk**.

Courses in Basque are offered at Escuelas Oficiales de Idiomas throughout Spain – in Euskadi itself there is one in every province. In the Basque capital the address is Calle Nieves Cano 18, 01006 Vitoria, **t** 94 513 8760. Online Euskera resources can be found at **www.eirelink.com**.

You will know when you have cracked it when you can listen to the news in Spanish on the radio. The news is technical and listening on the radio means that there are no visual clues to help you. The ultimate level comes when you think and dream in Spanish.

Moving

You have made the decision. You are all geared up to move. At some point the big day will come. However, before that happens you need to have done some preparation.

Remember that no matter what people say, things in Spain do not always happen when they should. If you are told that you will sign the title deeds for your new property on one day, do not assume that this will happen. It can therefore be difficult to get the timing of your move right. You may end up with two places to live at the same time, or even worse – none.

If you are employing a removal company to take your belongings to Spain it will normally take a couple of weeks for them to arrive. Again, do not be surprised if they do not turn up when scheduled. To minimise the possibility of delays and problems, make sure that the removal company that you deal with has previous experience of working in Spain.

Talk to several companies before deciding on whom to trust with the removal process. The level of service and the costs can vary. The cost will normally be determined by the space that your belongings take up. There will be extra costs for assistance with packing, and there will also be a charge should you need to keep your belongings in storage for any length of time. The storage of belongings can either be done in the UK or in Spain. Generally, the cost of storage is cheaper in Spain.

Make sure that you have adequate insurance cover for your belongings while they are in transit.

As Spain is a member of the EU, there is (in theory at least) free movement of people and goods between all EU member countries. That doesn't mean that there are no border controls or customs – just that the procedures for EU citizens should be easier. It also doesn't mean that you can take anything with you across borders. There are still restrictions on certain items. It may be illegal to take certain things to Spain – illegal drugs, for example.

Some items that you wish to take to Spain still have some formalities to comply with. These include cars, boats, furniture and pets.

Cars

If you are thinking about taking your UK car with you to Spain, don't.

You will be much better off buying a 'new' car when you arrive. It is much safer to drive a car with the steering wheel on the left-hand side. This is particularly so if you are driving in towns or in country areas without the benefit of a passenger to help you check for oncoming vehicles when overtaking. You will also find that it is easier to get spare parts. Even if you think your present car is sold throughout Europe, you will find that there are many parts that are different on the UK model because its steering wheel is on the right-hand side. It is also widely thought that a local car makes you less visible in the community and thus less likely to be burgled.

Cars in Spain are generally cheaper than in England and so selling your car here and buying another one when you arrive could even prove beneficial.

If you insist on taking your British car you will be able to use it on Spanish roads for a maximum of six months per year without converting it to a Spanish car by having it tested and re-registered in Spain. It can lawfully be used on Spanish roads only when it complies fully with the requirements for use on English roads, which include that the vehicle must be tested and taxed. Insurance will be available only from British insurance companies and you will have to disclose to the company the fact that the vehicle is used primarily abroad.

If you intend to keep the vehicle in Spain for more than six months in any year you must either:

- **Officially import the vehicle into Spain. This can be an expensive bureaucratic nightmare.**

- **Have it 'sealed' by customs each time you leave so that they can confirm it has not been used for more than six months.**

If you are resident in Spain and bought the vehicle and paid tax in another EU country, you should be able to import it free of VAT. If you have owned it for more than six months, you should be able to import it free of municipal registration tax – see below.

If you bought the vehicle tax-free or in another country you will have to pay the VAT immediately upon arrival in Spain. This is normally 16 per cent. You will then need a customs certificate confirming that the vehicle is free of Spanish VAT or that the VAT has been paid. You will also have to pay the municipal registration tax, at around 6–12 per cent. If you import the car from outside the EU there is an additional 10 per cent import tax.

All of these taxes are based on the original price of the car but gradually reduced, so that after it is 10 years old it is calculated on only 20 per cent or the value.

Many people totally ignore all these rules and keep a UK-registered car in Spain for years, though the authorities are taking steps to stop this abuse. If you do decide to ignore the rules, make sure that the insurance is valid.

Boats

You may wish to take a recreational boat with you to Spain. The obvious way to get it there is to sail it, but sometimes (depending on the size) it may be transported by road. Taking any boat other than a recreational craft with you to Spain is an entirely different subject and falls outside the scope of this book.

When you arrive in Spain, the marina or port will inform the authorities that the boat is in their jurisdiction and pass them the owner's details. There may be a charge associated with this.

If you are taking your boat over to Spain for more than six months then you will need to re-register it. This will mean that it will carry the Spanish ensign, which shows that it is registered in Spain and complies with the Spanish regulations.

When you register your boat there will be forms to fill in. The harbourmaster can assist you with what needs doing. There will be a fee to pay and also taxes based on the value of the boat. The current tax is set at 14 per cent of the value of the boat.

If you do need to re-register, it is worth checking your insurance policy to make sure that it is still suitable.

In addition to registering the boat you will also have to qualify for and obtain certification (*patron de yate*). The qualifications for obtaining the *patron de yate* depend on the type of boat and how you intend to use it. You do have to be over 18 and there will be both a theory and a practical test. In addition to presenting your NIE number (*see* 'NIE', p.131) and the boat's documents, you will have to fill in a form to apply for the test (form T130) and pay a fee of around €50.

Remember that your boat will form part of your wealth for tax purposes (*see* 'Business and Personal Taxes', p.109).

Furniture

As a British (or other EU) citizen you will be able to take your possessions with you to Spain. You do not need permission, nor do you need to pay taxes or customs duties if you are becoming a permanent resident.

The most practical way is to use a specialist removal company, who will charge about £2,000 for taking the contents of a medium-sized house from the UK to the south of Spain.

You can of course take the items out yourself. If you do this, you may be asked for an inventory in Spanish and proof of ownership. On the face of it this does not seem to be difficult, but for some items it can be tricky if you no longer have a proof of purchase.

In many cases it is much better to sell your furniture before you move to Spain and to buy new furniture when you get there. Apart from anything else, the furniture that you own in the UK may not be suitable for your new life.

Taking Your Pet

Until recently, taking a dog or cat to Spain involved some soul-searching on the part of the owner. Britain's quarantine laws entailed a level of expense for the owner and distress for the animal which discouraged anyone who thought they might later wish to re-enter the UK.

Thankfully the introduction of the Pets Travel Scheme (PETS), more commonly referred to as the Pet Passport, has made the prospect of moving your animal between Britain and Spain much less stressful – but not necessarily simple. There are definite (non-negotiable) steps which you must go through to get your animal permission to travel.

First your dog or cat must be microchipped and then vaccinated against rabies. A vet must then take a blood sample which will be sent to a government-approved laboratory for testing. Six months must elapse between the date of your animal's blood test and the issuing of a valid PETS certificate. Between 24 and 48 hours before your animal is due to travel, a vet must administer a treatment for ticks and tapeworms and issue a certificate confirming the treatment. Finally, on the day of travel you must sign a declaration of residency (form PETS 3) confirming that your animal has not been in any country *not* covered by the PETS scheme during the previous six months. The PETS certificate is valid for a limited time depending on the date of your animal's rabies vaccination but can be renewed when a booster injection is administered.

It should be stressed that these steps are necessary to enter the UK rather than Spain but it is highly recommended that you get your animal a PETS certificate on leaving the UK even if you have no intention of returning. If unforeseen circumstances mean that you have to bring your dog or cat back into Britain then it is better to have the paperwork already in order.

If you acquire a pet while in Spain – and with so many dogs and cats abandoned it can be sometimes be hard to resist – all the above steps can be performed in the country. However, there is currently only one Spanish laboratory, in Granada, that carries out the requisite blood tests, and results can be very slow in arriving.

If you are in a major city or near one of the main expat communities there will probably be an English-speaking vet or animal organisation which can guide you through the process.

The PETS scheme only applies to dogs and cats and on certain approved routes, either air or sea. Visit the DEFRA website (**www.defra.gov.uk**) for up-to-date details. It should also be remembered that there are regulations inside Spain which govern pet ownership, particularly with regard to dogs. These can vary from region to region but in most cases it is a legal requirement to have your animal micro-chipped and vaccinated against rabies. Consult a local vet for advice. In certain areas regular treatment for particular parasites, such as heart worm, may be advisable or even mandatory.

Finding Accommodation

If you are starting your own business you will be spending a lot of your time at your business premises. It may seem that you spend your whole life at work but you still need somewhere to live. There are basically two options with regard to accommodation – buying and renting.

Buying a House or Flat

The Spanish property market has enjoyed a remarkable boom, particularly in certain areas, with prices rising more than in any other country in the world over the past 20 years. This may seem strange when other statistics, such as high unemployment and low wages, are considered, but it seems that many middle-class Spanish families are willing to spend 30–50 per cent (sometimes more) of their income on housing. Some predict that the bubble will burst and that prices will soon fall. Indeed, a federation of savings banks has predicted that in the near future negative equity could affect property in certain regions, such as Castilla-La Mancha, Extremadura and Galicia. However, it is unlikely that in prosperous regions like Madrid, Catalonia and the Mediterranean coast property values will drop to the levels of five or even two years ago. It is a more likely scenario that prices will level off over the next few years.

Meanwhile, building continues apace. Both in the Mediterranean coastal regions and in the major cities, cranes are as much a part of the skyline as church spires or the shining tower blocks of financial institutions.

Mortgage rates are at an all-time low (below 6 per cent) and are not predicted to go up in the foreseeable future. At the moment, the situation might be described as a buoyant sellers' market. A few years ago it was fairly simple to look around, see a few properties and then ponder which to buy. Today someone doing this could well find that the house they wanted to make an offer on had sold to someone else in the few days after they saw it.

Finding a place to buy is not unlike looking for somewhere to rent in the sense that you can use print media, agents, online resources, word-of-mouth and other channels. The essential difference is that a lease need only be for a limited time: you can start again if you are not happy with the accommodation. Buying property obviously means more by way of commitment.

Buying a property in Spain is as safe as buying a property in England. If you go about the purchase in the right way it is not dangerous and should not be frightening. The same or similar dangers arise when buying a house in England. If you are in any doubt, look briefly at a textbook on English conveyancing and all of the horrible things that have happened to people in England. You do not worry about those dangers because you are familiar with them and, more importantly, because you are shielded against contact with most of them by your solicitor. The same should be true when buying in Spain.

The system of buying and selling property in Spain is, not surprisingly, different from the system of buying property in England or Scotland. On balance, neither better nor worse – just different. It has many superficial similarities, which can lull you into a false sense of familiarity and over-confidence. The most important thing to remember is to take the right professional advice and precautions when doing so. If you do not take such advice there are many expensive traps for the unwary.

One disadvantage of buying a property if you are starting a business is that it ties up some of your money. When you are starting a business you are likely to need all the spare capital that you have. Not only is there the price of buying the property, but also these extra costs in addition to the property price – legal fees, taxes, land registry fees and so on, which add up to something in the region of 10 per cent of the value of the property. Secondly, ownership is less flexible. Too many people buy a property and then once they have been in Spain six months wish they had bought in a slightly different place – particularly if they have bought in a hurry.

Spanish Mortgages

A Spanish mortgage is one taken out over your Spanish property. This will either be from a Spanish bank or from a British bank that is registered and does business in Spain. You cannot take a mortgage on your new Spanish property from your local branch of a UK building society or high street bank. The basic concept of a mortgage to buy property is the same in Spain as it is in Britain. It is a loan secured against the land or buildings. Just as elsewhere, if you don't keep up the payments the bank will repossess your property.

The Main Differences Between an English and a Spanish Mortgage

- Spanish mortgages are almost always created on a repayment basis. That is to say, the loan and the interest on it are both gradually repaid by equal instalments over the period of the mortgage. Endowment, PEP, pension and interest-only mortgages are not known in Spain.

- There are often restrictions or penalties or the ability to impose penalties for early payment of the loan.

- The formalities involved in making the application, signing the contract subject to a mortgage, and completing the transaction are more complex and stricter than in the UK.

- Most Spanish mortgages are granted for 15 years, not 25 as in England, though the period can be anything from 5 to 25 years. Normally the mortgage must have been repaid by your 70th (sometimes 65th) birthday.

- The maximum loan is generally 80 per cent of the value of the property and 75 per cent or 66 per cent is more common. As a guide, you should think of borrowing no more than two-thirds of the price you are paying.

- Fixed-rate loans – with the rate fixed for the whole duration of the loan – are more common than in the UK. They are very competitively priced.

- Calculating the amount the bank will lend you is different from in the UK. As you would expect, there are detailed differences from bank to bank but most banks are limited to how much they can lend you by your net disposable income.

- There will usually be a minimum loan (say £20,000) and some banks will not lend at all on property worth less than a certain value. Some will not lend in rural areas.

- The way of dealing with stage payments on new property and property where money is needed for restoration is different from in England.

- The paperwork on completion of the mortgage is different. There is often no separate mortgage deed. Instead the existence of the mortgage is mentioned in your purchase deed (*escritura de compraventa*). It is prepared by, and signed in front of, a notary public (*notario*).

How Much Can I Borrow?

Different banks have slightly different rules and different ways of interpreting the rules. Generally, they will lend you an amount that will give rise to monthly payments of up to about 30–33 per cent of your net available monthly income. Obviously if your only income is going to come from your business, then this is going to cause a problem in the calculations and therefore the bank is likely to apply different criteria. They will want to see your business plan in order to make their calculations and decision.

The starting point is your net monthly salary after deduction of tax and national insurance but before deduction of voluntary payments such as to savings schemes. If there are two applicants, the two salaries are taken into account. If you have investment income or a pension this will also be taken into account. If you are buying a property with a track record of letting income this *may* be taken into account. If you are buying a leaseback then the leaseback rental income will usually be taken into account. If you are over 65 your earnings will not usually be used in the calculations, but your pension and investment income will be. If your circumstances are at all unusual, seek advice, as approaching a different bank may produce a different result.

e.g.		
	Mr Smith – net salary per month	£3,000
	Mrs Smith – net salary per month	£2,000
	Investment income per month	£1,000
	Total income taken into account	£6,000

The maximum loan repayments permitted will be 30 per cent of this sum, less your existing fixed commitments: i.e. Maximum permitted loan repayment £6,000 x 30% = £1,800 per month

Regular monthly commitments would include mortgage payments on your main and other properties, any rent paid, hire-purchase commitments and maintenance (family financial provision) payments. Repayments on credit cards do not count. If there are two applicants, both of their commitments are taken into account.

e.g.	Mr & Mrs Smith – mortgage on main home	£750
	Mr & Mrs Smith – mortgage on house in Spain	£400
	Mrs Smith – hire purchase on car	£200
	Total pre-existing outgoings	£1,350

Maximum loan repayment permitted = £1,800 – £1,350 = £450 per month. This would, at today's rates, equate to a mortgage of about £60,000 over 15 years.

If you are buying a property for investment (rental) or to invest in the business, then the bank will treat this as commercial lending and apply different criteria and will need to go through more details with you, including your business plan.

Applications for a Spanish Mortgage

Once again the information needed will vary from bank to bank. It will also depend on whether you are employed or self-employed. Applications can receive preliminary approval (subject to survey of the property, confirmation of good title and of the information supplied by you) within a few days.

The Mortgage Offer

Allow four weeks from the date of your application to receiving a written mortgage offer, as getting the information to them can take a while. Once you receive the offer you will generally have 30 days in which to accept it, after which time it will lapse. You cannot accept it for 10 days from the date of receipt so as to give you a 'period of reflection'. This can be very frustrating if the offer has taken ages to arrive and you are in a hurry! Have the mortgage explained to you in detail by your lawyer.

The cost of taking out a mortgage will normally involve charges amounting to about 4 per cent of the sum borrowed. These charges are in addition to the normal expenses incurred when buying a property, which normally amount to about 10–11 per cent of the price of the property. You will probably be required to take out life insurance for the amount of the loan, though you may be allowed to use a suitable existing policy. You may also be required to have a medical. You will be required to insure the property and produce proof of insurance.

The offer may be subject to early payment penalties. Early payment penalties are of particular concern in the case of a fixed-rate mortgage.

The Exchange Rate Risk

If you are running a business in Spain, you will probably be paid in euros. You will want to be paid in euros as that is the currency that you will be spending when you are in Spain. However, you may receive income in some other currency, if for example you are running some sort of e-commerce business, as your customers may feel more reassured paying in their own local currency.

If the funds to repay the mortgage and support the business are coming to you in a currency other than euros, then the amount you will receive will be affected by fluctuations in exchange rates between the currency that you receive and the euro. Do not underestimate these variations. Over the last 15 years – a typical period for a mortgage – the Spanish peseta has been as high as 162 pesetas = £1 and as low as 285 pesetas = £1. This means that sometimes the sterling you would have had to send to Spain to pay the mortgage would have been almost double the amount at other times. This is less of a worry if your income is in euros – for example, from renting the property.

It is possible to mortgage your home in Spain but to borrow not in euros but in sterling – or US dollars or Swiss francs or Japanese yen.

There may be some attractions to borrowing in sterling if you are repaying out of sterling income. The rates of interest will be sterling rates, not euro rates. This will currently mean paying more. Usually the rates are not as competitive as you could obtain if you were re-mortgaging your property in the UK, as the market is less cut-throat. You will have all the same administrative and legal costs as you would if you borrowed in euros – i.e. about 4 per cent of the amount borrowed. This option is mainly of interest to people who either do not have sufficient equity in their UK home or who, for whatever reason, do not wish to mortgage the property where they live.

A Spanish mortgage will usually be paid directly from your Spanish bank account. Unless you have lots of rental or other euro income going into that account you will need to send money from Britain in order to meet the payments.

Every time you send a payment to or from Spain you will face two costs. The first is the price of the euros. This, of course, depends on the exchange rate used to convert your sterling. The second cost is the charges that will be made by your UK and Spanish banks to transfer the funds – which can be substantial.

There are steps that you can take to control both of these charges. As far as the exchange rate is concerned you should be receiving the so-called 'commercial rate', not the tourist rate published in the newspapers. The good news is that it is a much better rate. The bad news is that rates vary from second to second and so it is difficult to get alternative quotes. By the time you phone the second company, the first has changed! In any case, you will probably want to set up a standing order for payment and not shop around every month.

There are various organisations that can convert your sterling into euros. Your bank is unlikely to give you the best exchange rate. Specialist currency dealers will normally better the bank's rate, perhaps significantly. If you decide to go to a currency dealer you must find one that is reputable. They will be handling your money and, if they go bust with it in their possession, you could lose it. Ask you lawyer for a recommendation.

Another way of saving money involves 'forward-buying' the currency that you are going to need in the future. You could agree with your currency dealer that you will buy all of your euros for the next 12 months at a price that is, essentially, today's price. You normally pay 10 per cent down and the balance on delivery. If the euro rises in value you will gain, perhaps substantially. If the euro falls in value – *la vida es dura*! The main attraction of forward-buying is the certainty that the deal gives you. Only enter into these agreements with a reputable and, if possible, bonded broker.

Bearing in mind the cost of conversion and transmission of currency it is better to make fewer rather than more payments. You will have to work out whether, taking into account loss of interest on the funds transferred but bank charges saved, you are best sending money monthly, quarterly or every six months.

Mortgaging your Spanish Property: Summary

Generally speaking, Spanish euro mortgages will suit people who are running a business in Spain. The main advantages are:

- **You will pay Spanish interest rates which, at the time of writing, are lower than UK rates.**

- **The loan repayments will usually be in euros.**

- **If the funds to repay the mortgage are coming from income paid to you in euros then you have no exchange rate changes or fluctuations.**

Some of the main disadvantages of taking out a Spanish euro mortage for your property in Spain are:

- **The loan will probably be expensive to set up (arrangement fees, inspection fees, notary's fees and land registry fees will come to about 4 per cent of the amount borrowed).**

- **The loan repayments will usually be in euros. If the funds to repay the mortgage are coming in a form of currency other than euros, then the amount you have to pay will be affected by fluctuations in exchange rates.**

- **You will be unfamiliar with dealing with Spanish mortgages and all correspondence and documentation will usually be in Spanish.**

- **Normally only repayment mortgages are available – i.e. mortgages where you pay off both capital and interest over the period of the mortgage.**

- **You will probably need extra life-insurance cover. This can considerably to the cost of the mortgage, especially if you are getting older.**

Finding a Property to Buy

There is a variety of ways to find out about properties available for private sale. First of all, wherever you go in Spain – in the entrance halls of city apartment blocks or at the end of farm tracks – you will see a wide assortment of DIY for-sale signs (with the words *se vende* or *en venta*), nearly always with a contact phone number. To take advantage of property offered in this way you obviously have to be in the area, and will probably need to speak at least some Spanish. Even if you can't carry on much of a conversation in Spanish, though, it's still worth a trial phone call; if the person who answers does not speak English there may be a local English-speaker – perhaps in your hotel – who can make contact on your behalf. With rural properties you can often just walk up and knock on the door but, if a phone number is given, it's best to call first, and the chances of finding any English-speakers are wholly unpredictable. As a last resort you can phone your lawyer, who should be able to find out the necessary details for you and, if you wish, make arrangements to view. He will charge for this but the saving on estate agents' fees will still work out to your advantage.

Local newspapers (which in Madrid and Barcelona include the local editions of national papers like *El País*) also carry lots of property ads in their classified sections, especially, in most cities, on Sundays. Most will have been placed by agencies, but there will be plenty from private sellers too. Another very good place to find private sales ads placed by Spanish owners is the free advertising magazine *Segundamano*, which has editions in many parts of the country. Again, you will have to phone to make contact. Local English-language papers also carry plenty of property ads, but beware of anyone advertising in this way who suggests a friendly Brit-to-Brit sale cutting out some of the Spanish formalities – there have been reports of property sharks working a variety of scams on other foreigners by this means, especially on the Costa del Sol. It is surprisingly common for people in the big expat clusters to think that they can agree property sales 'between themselves', ignoring most or all of the Spanish legal obligations, failing to register proper title and so on, and storing up big problems for themselves in the future. Even leaving aside the types who make a living out of exploiting this sort of naïve chumminess, this is absolutely to be avoided. Get a lawyer and do things by the book.

Buying at Auctions

Property in Spain can be bought at auction, just as in the UK. Some auctions are voluntary, while others are run by court order following compulsory repossession. Low prices can make them very attractive – a few years ago, during Spain's last major recession, it was possible to find incredible bargains at auctions, with prices equivalent to only 30 per cent of normal market value. Today auctions no longer offer such spectacular discounts, but the prospect of getting large properties at prices well below the local norm still draws many buyers. Prices are so low primarily because, in judicial auctions in particular, the process is intended first and foremost to recover debts of various kinds, and once these and the costs have been covered there is little reason for auctioneers to press for a higher price.

Buying property at auction is not simple for non-locals, and if you are interested in trying it out it is vitally important that you have taken all the normal preparatory steps – including seeing a lawyer – before you embark on the process. Auctions are usually advertised six to eight weeks in advance: auctions ordered by the court will be officially announced in local papers and notices posted in the area, while non-judicial auctions will just be advertised in the press. Brief details of properties to be sold are published, but these are often very uninformative. To make any preliminary decisions you will need to inspect the property and decide whether it is of interest, a time-consuming and potentially costly process. An alternative to looking yourself is to get someone to do it for you: this is not as satisfactory, but a local estate agent will, for a fee, go to look at the property and give you a description of it, and can perhaps post or email you some photographs. Buying blind at auctions, on the other hand, is really for confirmed gamblers.

Another important preliminary, before the date of the auction, is to check out the legal situation of the property and, since many properties sold at auction are not in the best condition, to get estimates of the likely cost of repairs or improvements, to make sure that the price you are going to bid plus these costs is not so high as to make the whole project non-viable. Finally, you should appoint a lawyer to act for you at the auction itself – only very brave or foolish foreigners take on these events without a lawyer to represent them or at least help them on the day. Your lawyer will explain precisely what needs to be done at each stage, while you will have to tell him the maximum price you want to offer and give him the bidding deposit – a refundable deposit levied by the auctioneer to allow you to enter a bid. You will also have to give the auctioneer various personal details, and a deposit amounting (usually) to 10 per cent of the price you are offering, less the bidding deposit. This deposit must be paid over at the time your bid is accepted. You do not need to attend the auction in person, as your lawyer can do so for you, for which he will require power of attorney and the required funds.

Although auction prices are low you should be aware that you will face additional costs over and above those you would have to pay in a normal house purchase, including the extra fees you will owe to your lawyer for dealing with the auction. These costs are likely to raise the overall transaction costs of the sale from the 10–11 per cent of the purchase price normal in Spain to around 13–15 per cent.

Estate Agents (*Agencias Inmobiliarias*)

Whether you buy through an estate agent or by private agreement with the seller, estate agents serve as a shop window for the housing market. Properties are displayed, complete with photo, description and price – so you can easily get an idea of what is available and for how much.

If you choose an estate agent, there are a few things you should know about them before committing yourself to using their services. Estate agents may be small, locally run outfits or large multinational companies with central offices in Zurich, London or Paris. Between these extremes are franchise establishments which, though bearing the same logo and colour scheme, operate independently from each other. Some common names you see are Tecnocasa, Frimm, Don Piso and Remax. Others may be 'cowboy' outfits, though happily these are the minority these days.

Searching on the Internet

The internet is the perfect place to see what properties are for sale. Opposite is a list of some of the many internet sites dedicated to purchasing property in Spain. The list is by no means exhaustive and is principally aimed at those looking to buy before setting up in business in Spain.

Renting

There could be many reasons why you would wish to rent a property in Spain rather than buy one. For one thing, renting a property is more flexible than buying. If you decide that you don't like the area, if you need a bigger or a smaller house, or even if you just fancy a change, it is much easier to do this if you rent. Secondly, you can use your capital for other uses. If you are running a business then you will be able to think of a million and one uses for extra capital. It also costs much less to organise. When you buy a property you will probably pay in the region of 10 per cent of the value of the purchase price in miscellaneous fees and taxes. When you start renting, you will have to pay a security deposit of normally a month's rent. If you are renting a furnished property then it is normal to pay a deposit equivalent to two months' rent. If the property includes a telephone, you will probably be asked for a deposit for that too. Finally, you will be making sure that the area you have chosen is the right one for you and your business before you buy. No matter how often you go to Spain, and an area in particular, you won't know it as well as the UK.

On the down side, property prices have risen in many areas. If you are renting and property prices continue to rise, it will be more difficult for you to get onto the property ladder as the years go by.

Property Websites

www.4seasonsestates.com	Apart from property searches, this site also has information on legal questions and more.
www.andalucia.com	Property information and much more, focused, as the name suggests, on Andalucía.
www.apartmentspain.co.uk	This site caters more for the cheaper end of the market.
www.buyaspanishhome.com	Run in association with Fincas Corral, Spanish estate agents, so has access to lots of local agents.
www.countrylife.co.uk	An offshoot of the well-known magazine which focuses on the upper end of the market.
www.findahomeinspain.com	Based on the Costa del Sol but with an office in Dublin, this site offers search facilities and lots of useful information about living in southern Spain.
www.idealspain.com	Legal and financial advice plus lots of links to property companies.
www.marbella-lawyers.com	A very useful site covering all aspects of law affecting the foreign resident in Spain, from conveyancing to drinking and driving.
www.propertyfile.net	Information about renting and buying in the Canary Islands, the Costa del Sol the Costa Blanca and many links to other sites.
www.propertyfinance4less.com/spain	Info on mortgages for those intending to buy in Spain, Portugal, France and Italy.
www.property-in-spain.com	The website of Harringtons International, property consultants specialising in all the costas.
www.spain-info.com	General tourist information and property links for most of Spain.
www.spanish-living.com	Property and much, much more.
www.spanishpropertyco.com	Lots of useful information about many aspects of living in Spain.
www.vivendum.com	A joint site of thousands of local estate agents in Spanish.

Housing Jargon

Frequently employed abbreviations, as often seen in classified ads, are in brackets after the full word.

a estrenar	brand new
aire acondicionado (a/a)	air-conditioning
alquilar/se alquila	to rent/for rent
(el) alquiler	(the) rent (i.e. what you pay)
amueblado	furnished
armario empotrado	built-in wardrobes
ascensor	lift/elevator
aseo	small bathroom usually with just a toilet and washbasin
ático	roof or attic apartment/flat
aval or *aval bancario*	bank guarantee equivalent to a letter of credit
bajo	ground floor apartment
balcón	balcony
baño completo	full bathroom
bien comunicado	well located for public transport
buhardilla	loft or attic apartment, usually with sloping ceilings
calefacción central (c/c)	central heating
calle (c/)	street
chimenea	fireplace
cocina americana	integrated kitchen (generally in an open-plan kitchen-diner-cum-living room)
cocina amueblada	kitchen complete with pots, pans, utensils, etc.
cocina independiente	separate kitchen (from the living room)
(gastos de) comunidad	community expenses such as rubbish collection or cleaning of common areas (stairwells, lobby, etc.) that may or may not be included in the monthly rent
dormitorio	bedroom
dúplex	maisonette (duplex apartment in US English)
electrodomésticos	kitchen appliances, e.g. fridge, microwave, food mixer
entresuelo	mezzanine
estudio	studio apartment

exterior (ext)	exterior (i.e. looking on to the street)
fianza	deposit paid to landlord (usually one or two months' rent)
garantías	guarantees (financial)
gas ciudad/natura	piped gas (many apartments do not have this, using bottled butane – *butano* – gas instead)
habitación (hab)	room (can also mean bedroom)
hall	hallway
hipoteca	mortgage
interior (int)	looking on to an interior patio
luminoso	bright, with lots of sunlight
luz	electricity (literally 'light')
moqueta	wall-to-wall/fitted carpet
nómina	salary/wage slip (often required by landlords as proof of steady income)
office	utility room (usually attached to kitchen)
parabólica	connected to satellite dish for TV
parqué/parquet	parquet flooring
piso	apartment or flat
planta	floor
plaza de garaje	garage parking spot
portero/a/conserje (físico)	concierge or caretaker, man or woman who takes care of the building
portero automático	automatic door
puerta blindada	reinforced/security door
razón portería/portero	contact the concierge/caretaker
reformado	renovated/'done up'
salón	living room
salón-comedor	living room–diner
semi amueblado	partially furnished
sin muebles	unfurnished
soleado	sunny, with lots of sunlight
sótano	basement apartment
suelo	floor
terraza (acristalada)	terrace (glazed/glassed over)
trastero	storage room
vacío	empty/unfurnished
vender/se vende	to sell/for sale
vistas	views

Rental Contracts

It is important to get a rental contract. Although most rental contracts are taken from standard forms, make sure that you get a lawyer to check it for you. Long-term rentals (*arriendo de viviendas*) are defined as being for more than a year. If you are in a long-term rental contract (*contrato de arrendamiento*) then the laws are much more favourable to the person renting than they are in the UK. The law on rental is called the *ley de arrendamientos urbanos*. The law basically means that a long-term rental contract has a minimum period of five years and the contract is automatically extended after that period unless the landlord gives notice.

Most properties in Spain are rented unfurnished but it is possible to rent furnished (*amueblado*) properties. If you are renting an unfurnished property it is important to establish what, if anything, is included in the property. If you are renting a furnished property then you must make sure that you have got an inventory. Check the contents carefully before you sign the inventory and make sure that you sign the inventory after you have moved in to ensure that items do not go missing between the signing of the inventory and your moving in.

When you rent a property, you will be responsible for the payment of the utilities, rates (IBI), water rates and community fees (*comunidad*) if appropriate.

Finding Rental Property

Finding rental accommodation in Spain is not much different from looking elsewhere, though there are some things to bear in mind. Spain has the smallest rental market in Europe; only about 13 per cent of all housing stock is rented compared with an average of 40 per cent across the continent.

The most common search method is through the print media, or their online versions. It helps to be *au fait* with the language of adverts (*see* 'Housing Jargon', p.176). *Segundamano* is a classifieds magazine published three times weekly (similar to *Exchange and Mart*). Although published in Madrid and sold only in central Spain, *Segundamano* does have property ads for the whole country, organised by Autonomous Communities, and price bands. The online version for rentals all over Spain is **www.segundamano.es**. The same publishing group also distributes two freesheets in Catalonia, *Claxon* and *Revenda* (**www.claxon. segundamano.es** and **www.revenda.segundamano.es**). The major dailies also have classified property ads.

Agencies (*agencias inmobiliarias*) are to be found on practically every major street. They charge a fee, usually a month's rent on whatever acceptable property they find you. (This is in addition to any deposit payable to the landlord.) Most agencies specialise in buying and selling property. Rentals may represent only a small percentage of their work and not all provide as good a service as they claim, so talk to people who have used their services. Above all, do not let yourself be bullied into accepting anything below the standard you require.

Those with time to spare may prefer to search independently, pounding the streets looking for '*se alquila piso/apartamento*' signs. This can produce results, especially since many landlords who advertise this way include *razón portería* (contact the caretaker) in the advertising poster, which means you can view the flat without making an appointment. If you choose this method, go armed with patience, pre-prepared questions if your language skills are not too good, and a comfortable pair of shoes!

When viewing flats, have your 'spiel' ready if you are not yet confident in the language. If your level is really basic, take someone along to do the talking. You may have to be more convincing than locals if you are a foreigner, as some landlords are wary of renting to *extranjeros*. Remember to dress well and appear trustworthy. It also helps to have some cash ready to put down as a partial deposit (*seña*) if the property is just what you are looking for. This is common practice and avoids the landlord renting to the next person who comes along. It need not be a full month's rent and will be deducted from the actual full deposit paid on signing the lease. Do not be rushed into renting the first thing you see; rather have a clear idea of what you are looking for and when you see it, grab it!

Communication and the Media

Telephones

Business relationships in Spain are made face to face, often over a coffee or a beer. However, you cannot run a business without a telephone. Telephones have had a chequered past in Spain. It stretches from a time not so long ago when the installation of a telephone was a cause for celebration, and in some instances led to an opening ceremony and a long party, to a time when everybody seems to have mobile phones.

Telefónica is the Spanish equivalent of British Telecom. For many years Telefónica enjoyed a monopoly on telephones, but recently the industry has been opened up and other companies have been able to provide call services. The second largest telecoms group in Spain is Auna.

Statistically, the cost of calls in Spain is among the lowest in the EU and promises to get even cheaper. Telefónica announced at the beginning of 2005 that it has implemented a new billing platform, which should see it saving 60 per cent on maintenance costs over the year. The savings that this new system will make should reduce prices and bring in special offers on calls and the introduction of new broadband services.

For comparisons of the different rates from call providers, check out **www.teltarifas.com**. For a list of the telephone codes for various different cities and towns, *see* 'Spanish Area Telephone Codes', p.227.

Mobiles

Spain has increased its mobile phone use faster than any other EU country. This increase has been caused by the drop in price of both the phones and the calls. There are three main Spanish mobile phone companies: Amena, Vodafone, and of course Telefónica. All three offer both contract and pre-paid services. Coverage for mobile phone reception in Spain is good on all three networks, unless you are in an area with low population.

Post

The Spanish postal system remains in state ownership and for the most part is as efficient as any modern European country. Standard letter post to the UK, or anywhere else in Europe, costs €0.51, and parcels sent to the UK should arrive within a week. Of course letters and packages do occasionally get lost and if you are sending anything particularly important or are sending items as part of your business then it pays to use recorded delivery (*certificado*), which is available at a small supplement. There are various tariffs available for parcel post that offer a range of insurance or urgency. The Postal Express courier service is every bit as good as any private company. If you are sending small items through the post, you can also send goods *contra reembolso*, which means the recipient must pay a given price for the package on arrival and you receive the cash one or two days later.

Faxes

Most businesses will require a fax machine. Telefónica offer deals on a second line, either business or domestic, and you should expect to pay an additional standing charge of around €30. In theory a UK fax machine will work on the Spanish telephone system. The phone-jack socket is different, however, which, together with the need for a different mains plug, will be sufficient to invalidate any guarantee and means that it is probably not worth the effort of bringing a fax machine from home. Fax machines have in any case dropped massively in price in recent years owing to the growth in email use, so you can pick up a decent model cheaply. If you have only occasional need to send or receive a fax, some photocopy shops, stationers and *estancos* may offer fax services.

Internet

As with mobile phones, the lowering of internet charges has led to the Spanish taking to the internet in a big way. Just a few years ago, connection to the internet was difficult. Now broadband use in Spain is among the highest in the world, although it is still not available in all areas. If you are going to rely on broadband use for your business then it is important to make sure that broadband connection is available where you are going to base the company. Add this to your list of things to check.

Just like in the UK there is much competition in the internet service market. There are many providers and it pays to shop around to make sure that you get the best deal. Some internet providers include: **www.terra.es**, **www.ya.com**, **www.jazztel.com**, **www.tiscali.es** and **www.telefonica.es**.

Television and Radio

If you are going to be running your own business you are not going to be able to have much time to watch television! In any case, most Spanish television is pretty awful – after all '3-2-1', with the walking dustbin 'Dusty Bin', was a Spanish invention (although it was originally called '1-2-3').

In most parts of Spain viewers can choose from five or six open-access channels, the main ones of which are: TVE1, state-owned, middle-of-the-range programming; TVE2, the 'quality' state channel with films, arts programmes, documentaries, etc.; *Antena 3*, a private commercial channel (though often criticised for being a mouthpiece of the government) offering safe, middle-of-the-road programming; *Tele 5*, another private channel with game shows presented by scantily clad females, etc. but offering fairly independent news coverage. There are also various regional channels.

The Spanish radio scene consists of an extraordinary number of stations, some of them just serving one town, although the bigger ones tend to be part of four groups, the state-owned RNE and the private SER, COPE and the more youth-orientated Onda Cero. Within all this apparent diversity, programming tends to divide into just two kinds, continuous chat (phone-ins, rambling discussion-interviews) and continuous music, with few surprises in between. When you do find an interesting station, it is another way of improving your Spanish.

To get the BBC World Service in Spain you need a short-wave radio. The best frequency to use can change slightly through the day; the World Service website (**www.bbc.co.uk/worldservice**) has a worldwide frequency guide, and an excellent information service to help listeners get the best signal. If you have satellite radio you can get BBC Radios 1, 2, 3, 4 and 5 and some other UK stations. There are also several local stations that broadcast in English for all or at least part of the day, such as Central FM (98.6 and 103.8), Coastline Radio (97.7), Spectrum (105.5) and Radio Gibraltar (91.3) on the Costa del Sol, or Waves FM (96.8) in the Canaries. Frequencies and even stations can change frequently, so check the current ones in the local English language press.

It is possible to install satellite TV that can pick up the same channels that you would in the UK. You need never miss another re-run of 'Only Fools and Horses' again. However, it is important to remember that the signal that is transmitted in Spain is different from that in the UK. This means that if you bring your UK equipment to Spain it may not work correctly, unless your equipment has the capacity to run on both systems. It is possible to convert most equipment to run on the Spanish system, although you may decide that this is the opportunity you have been looking for to get that newer model in Spain – especially as the prices are often cheaper.

Newpapers

Nationally, the most important and widely read newspaper is *El País*, founded in 1976 and seen as synonymous with the country's transition to democracy. A serious paper, *El País* has a liberal, centre-left editorial line but gives space to writers and intellectuals from across the political spectrum. Printed in both Madrid and Barcelona, throughout the week it comes with various supplements covering new technologies, education, arts and music, a quality literary supplement plus a well-regarded pink-paper financial section and a glossy magazine on Sundays. A selected digest of the paper's main stories is available in English, in a pull-out section distributed with the *International Herald Tribune*.

Second in circulation is *El Mundo*, also distributed nationally, which is printed in Madrid, Barcelona and the Balearics with supplements catering for other regions. It also has an array of supplements and an online edition, **www.elmundo.es**, with free content.

Spain's third most popular newspaper is the conservative, monarchist, tabloid *ABC*, published in Madrid, Seville and Córdoba. The weekly arts supplement *ABC Cultural* is more open-minded than the main paper, with excellent book reviews, art criticism and special features.

Most regions also have their main dailies, some available nationally, such as Catalonia's *La Vanguardia* or locally such as *Diario de Mallorca* or *Diari de Balears* (in Castilian and Catalan respectively) in the Balearics or *Sur*, in the Costa del Sol. Those interested in finance and economics can choose from *Cinco Días*, *Expansión* and *Diario de los Negocios*, all with company reports and daily market news.

Those only interested in English-language newspapers have few problems nowadays as most major British, North American and Irish papers are available at news kiosks in major cities and expat areas, arriving around midday, or earlier where there is an airport nearby. There is also a fair smattering of locally published, often free, English-language newspapers and magazines. Quality varies, and news coverage is at times superficial, but they do carry features of interest to expats. They can also be useful for finding accommodation. Look out for: *The Broadsheet*, published in Madrid but distributed in Barcelona; *Metropolitan*, Barcelona's monthly magazine in English; *Sur in English*, a weekly English edition of the Spanish-language newspaper, and *Costa del Sol News* and *Costa Blanca News*.

Home Utilities

Electricity (*Luz*)

New properties must be connected to the electricity supply. If the property is rented, then the landlord should take care of this. If it is your property, contact the distributor and stipulate how much electricity you want. If you are not sure, consult an electrician or the company, stating the number of appliances you might want to use and how much wattage would cover the demand at peak usage times. Be careful not to underestimate the amount of power needed, especially during winter. If you contract too little, your supply will cut out at times of highest demand.

If you rent or buy a used property, you simply take over the existing supply and have the account transferred to your name. The process is straightforward and involves a small fee. If you think the existing supply will not be sufficient, ask for it to be upgraded, again for a small fee.

To contract supply, you will need to produce the usual documents (passport, NIE, bank details – if you wish to pay by direct debit). Being a resident is not, *un requisito*, a requisite for getting supplied. Before moving in, ask the company to make a special meter reading to avoid paying the previous occupant's bill. If your house is in a remote rural area and is not already connected to the electricity supply, get a quotation for connection before committing yourself to the purchase. It may prove expensive.

If you are renting, there will usually be an existing electricity supply. It may be in the landlord's name, so he will either charge you or include it in the rent. Some landlords may insist that you have the contract put in your name, depending always on the terms of the lease. Others may insist that you contract electricity from the outset, in which case you will have to contact the company yourself. Make sure to terminate the contract with the company on leaving the flat!

There are several different tariffs available from the electricity company. Check them carefully. If you are thinking of renting the property it is better to go for the standard tariff because otherwise inconsiderate tenants can run up enormous electricity bills by connecting to the supply at costly times.

Normally, you will be billed every two months with the standing charge payable in advance and the consumption in arrears. Electricity bills can most conveniently be paid by direct debit from your Spanish bank account. The electricity company is quite quick to cut off non-payers – though they must send you a warning first. As the warning will be sent to the house (probably empty) this does not solve the problem. As the inconvenience of arriving at your house late at night to find you have been disconnected is considerable, make sure that there are sufficient funds in your bank account to cover the likely charges.

Wiring

Electrical wiring in Spain is done differently from in England. Do not be tempted to have a friendly English electrician re-wire your property in Spain. If the authorities find that this has been done and that the wiring does not comply with their standards, they can condemn it and disconnect the electricity supply. In any case, mixed or incompatible wiring is dangerous both to you and to any workmen working in the premises.

You have probably already noticed that electrical sockets in Spain are not installed as liberally as they are in the UK, and that the use of extension cables and adapters is frequent. You will also notice that the electrical sockets are often installed in strange places or at funny angles. There is certainly a market for Spanish-qualified electricians to install extra sockets or to relocate sockets to more logical and useable points.

Voltage

Electricity in Spain is normally supplied at 220v, although it is still possible to find some places that supply 110v – sometimes even in the same building! The lesson to be learnt here is check the electrical supply. Any property still connected at 110v can be converted – at a cost

Interruptions of Supply

These are surprisingly common, especially outside main cities and major tourist areas. Things are getting better. Much of the problem stems from the Spanish not being prepared for rain. They tend to build sub-stations and junction boxes in stream beds. As soon as it rains they flood and short. Cuts can vary from a split second to many hours. Get a UPS (uninterruptible power supply) to protect computers and other vital equipment. Get a surge protector to guard sensitive devices. Both are cheap.

However, the power cuts are often the fault of the owner of the property. The electricity contract you have with the company is based on the maximum power you can be using at any one time and if you exceed this, there will be a failure in the power supply.

Solar Power

Spain is a fantastic place for solar panels as, once these are installed, they are a very cheap way of getting electricity to your property. Spain is one of the largest manufacturers of solar panels.

The new government is keen on encouraging the use of solar power as a way of reducing fuel costs and helping the environment – so much so that they recently passed a law that all new and renovated buildings from 2005 have to have solar panels on them. The government wants to increase the use of solar panels by 10 per cent by the year 2010.

Air-conditioning

Air-conditioning is not an unnecessary luxury in southern Spain; consider installing at least a minimal system. If the 2am temperature is 30°C (86°F) you will not regret the outlay. Portable air-conditioning units can be bought in hypermarkets and electrical stores, and installers of larger, built-in systems advertise frequently in the local expat press, or can be found in the *Yellow Pages* under *aire acondicionado*. Anyone with a record of asthma or any other respiratory problems should be doubly careful when buying any air-con system, and get independent advice on its health effects.

Gas

Mains Gas

Mains gas is widely available only in larger cities, although the network is slowly extending to other areas. Until January 2003, mains gas supply was the monopoly of Gas Natural, and you must still contract supply via them. However, you can now choose to be billed by a competitor. The other three big energy suppliers are now beginning to compete by offering '*gas + luz*' deals.

Getting connected involves contacting the company – providing the necessary identification and your NIE, plus bank details if you plan to pay by direct debit. You will almost certainly be asked for a safety certificate from an authorized gas fitter (*fontanero de gas*) before supply can commence. Bills are issued bi-monthly. Payment is best done by direct debit, though if you wish you can pay directly into one of the specified banks. As with electricity, you pay standing charges in advance and consumption in arrears.

Bottled Gas (*Butano*)

Many Spanish homes still use bottled butane gas. This form of energy is cheap: the standard 12.5kg bottle (*bombona*) costs around €9.50 when delivered, usually paid in cash to the man who brings it. It is slightly cheaper if you fetch bottles yourself.

Repsol Butano (**www.repsolypf.com**) has a near monopoly on butane supply and you have to sign up with them to be supplied. Check in the telephone book for their local number. They usually order a safety check first, and older properties often need modifications (such as air vents) to meet safety standards. Some form of ID will be necessary, otherwise contracting is straightforward. If you are taking over a flat or house from a previous occupant it is simple to have the contact changed to your name.

On signing the contract, a deposit of around €17 per bottle is payable. Keep a spare to avoid running out. Ask a neighbour to show you how to change gas bottles. The snap-on regulator valve, known as an *alcachofa* (artichoke), requires a certain knack to fit and, if incorrectly fitted, can be extremely dangerous. Repsol also insist on five-yearly inspections and may send an authorised technician to carry them out, usually with advance warning. Be wary of 'cowboy' operators with a fake Repsol logo on their overalls who arrive unannounced, change tubing and *alcachofas* unnecessarily, charge the earth (on the spot) and then disappear without trace. The orange gas tubes that connect to your appliances have the date printed on them, are sold in hardware stores and can be changed easily without the help of a technician.

Water

Water is scarce in many parts of Spain and is a precious resource. Average rainfall provides sufficient water overall but 'green Spain' gets too much, the rest not enough. To offset this problem, various expensive engineering projects have been set up, including the government's controversial national hydrological plan – still far from completion – to canalise water from north to south. Water may therefore be expensive, depending on where you live.

Water supplies are generally metered in Spain and you pay for the amount consumed. Contracting is much the same as for other utilities. Most companies bill quarterly and the best way to pay is by direct debit.

Motoring

Spain has the dubious honour of having some of the most dangerous roads in the EU. In particular, the coastal road N340 in the Costa del Sol is one of the most dangerous roads in Europe. If you run your own business, you will probably need a vehicle to collect stock, make deliveries, go to meetings, get to work and so on. You may even decide that a vehicle could turn into a mobile advertising hoarding. If you buy a Spanish car from a dealer they will usually register it for you. If you buy it privately you will need to apply for registration within 10 days of buying it. You will need:

- **completed application form**
- **registration document (*permiso de circulación*)**
- **vehicle tax receipt**
- **test certificate if it is over four years old**
- **transfer tax receipt**
- **residence papers, or a copy of your *escritura* or rental agreement if you are not a resident**
- **receipt for registration fee**
- **stamped self-addressed envelope**

Most people will have a *gestor* do this for them. His fee will be about £50. For more information about the *gestor, see* 'Using a *Gestor*', p.132.

Driving Licence

Whether you buy a car in Spain or import your own car you will have to decide what to do about your driving licence. Until recently it was a legal requirement that if you were going to stay in Spain you had to convert your foreign driving licence into a Spanish one. There was a certain amount of paperwork connected to this exercise but it did not involve taking a Spanish driving test. Following the latest EU directive on the mutual recognition of driving licences this is no longer required for EU nationals but it can still be a good idea to get a Spanish licence. It can reduce problems on roadside checks and, in any event, you will be forced to do so in the likely event that at some stage you pick up a penalty point under the Spanish traffic system.

As you will be resident in Spain, if you do not obtain a fresh driving licence you must produce your UK licence for the traffic department (*jefatura provincial de trafico*) so that they can enter details into their IT system.

Healthcare

National Health Service

Many people get worried about doctors and hospitals abroad, in a mistaken belief that they are not as good as the ones back in their home country. Some Spaniards reckon that the health system in Spain is better than in the UK, but the British maintain that the health system in the UK is superior. The reality is that in every country you get some good experiences and some bad experiences when dealing with doctors and hospitals. As in the UK, Spain has public and also private healthcare. Generally you will find that the Spanish are quite a healthy lot – a trend that is followed all along the Mediterranean. The hospitals in Spain are generally modern with good equipment.

Who Qualifies?

If you are over retirement age or you are working legally in Spain, then you will be entitled to free state healthcare just as if you were a normal Spanish national. Because you are working legally you will be paying social security payments (about 6 per cent of gross income).

In order to use the Spanish healthcare system you must present a *cartilla*, a card which shows that you are entitled to use the service. In order for a non-Spanish national to obtain this card they have to fill in a form for the Spanish Social Service. It is therefore important that before you move to Spain you contact the Overseas Branch of the Department of Health in Newcastle and inform them that you will be moving to live in Spain. They will send you the relevant forms to fill in so you can apply for your *cartilla*. When you present the *cartilla* you will be entitled to free healthcare and it will also entitle you to 90 per cent off prescription charges. Some people get worried about going down this route as they think that they will no longer be eligible for UK medical care. This is not true, as the *cartilla* will allow you to have full health benefits when you visit the UK as a tourist, or indeed any other EU country.

Some people are tempted not to register as a resident or to work illegally in Spain. While it may appear that they are being clever by not paying the proper taxes and seem to be successfully cheating the system (assuming that they do not get caught) one major problem of going down this route is that if you become ill or need some form of medical assistance then you may not be able to afford it.

If you are an employer then it is your responsibility to register your employees for social security (*see* 'Benefits', p.153), which will mean that they are covered for healthcare. It is illegal not to do this.

Under international treaties for reciprocal healthcare, healthcare in Spain is also covered for up to three months' stay. Many people believe that this applies whether you are visiting for three months or for the first three months of a more permanent stay. Do not fall into this trap. This three-month cover is only available to those who are not permanently resident in Spain and covers only accidents and emergencies.

Doctors

Finding a doctor (*doctor* in Spanish) in Spain is not a problem apart from in the most rural areas. However, finding a good English-speaking doctor can sometimes be difficult. Depending on your level of Spanish, it may be important for you to find a doctor who speaks your own language. There can't be anything more frustrating than being in pain and not being able to communicate with the person who is supposed to be able to make that pain go away. Obviously in the areas that are popular among holidaymakers, you are much more likely to find doctors who speak English.

Before moving to Spain, it makes sense to get hold of a copy of your medical records from your existing UK doctor, get them translated into Spanish, and give them to your new doctor when you register with him.

Your local embassy or consulate will often have a list of English-speaking doctors in your area. In addition, in the areas that are popular with foreigners you will often find English-speaking doctors advertising in the local expat press. However, a recommendation by somebody that you know in the area will probably be worth following up.

Opening hours will depend on whether the doctor is private or public. Public doctors tend to be open for longer – often from 8am until 6pm. Private doctors will typically work between 9am and 2pm and then from 5pm until 7pm Monday to Friday.

Hospitals and Clinics

Spanish hospitals (*hospital*) tend to be modern and well equipped in the major cities and towns. The staff are well trained and generally you will get a good level of service and treatment. In smaller towns the hospitals may not be so up to date. In the major towns and those areas that are popular among holidaymakers you will probably be able to talk to the doctors and nurses in English. In the more rural areas you are more likely to have difficulty talking to the hospital staff unless you speak some Spanish. If in doubt, take somebody along with you who can speak both.

Public hospitals can be used by anybody who is contributing to the social security system. You are normally referred to a hospital through your doctor unless it is an emergency. You will have to present your social security card, evidence of insurance cover or the ability to pay, before treatment will start. However, if it is an emergency, such details will be sorted out afterwards.

Private hospitals are often advertised in the local press in the area that they are located, or in the yellow pages (**www.paginasamarillas.es**). The majority of private hospitals tend to specialise in one particular field. It is rare for them to cover general practice. In certain areas of Spain there has been a definite increase in the number of private hospitals and clinics that specialise in cosmetic surgery. Not surprisingly, the Costa del Sol has no shortage of hospitals dedicated to making people 'more beautiful'.

Hospital Terminology

Departamento de emergencies	Emergency department
Consultas externas or departamento de enfermo externo del hospital	Outpatients department
Ambulancia	Ambulance
Hospital general	General hospital
Hospital distrito	District hospital
Hospital de la seguridad social	Public hospital
Hospital privado	Private hospital
Hospital comarcal	Regional hospital
Hospital provincial	Provincial hospital
Hospital comarcal o local	Local hospital
Hospital militar	Military hospital
Clinica de reposo	Nursing home
Clinica de emergencia	Emergency clinic
Clinica privada	Private clinic
Centro medico	Medical centre
Ambulatorio or casa de socorro	24-hour public health clinic
Centro de salud	Medical centre

Dentists

Dentists (*dentistas* or *dentistas odontógos*) are generally very good in Spain. Only limited work by dentists (usually following an accident) is covered by the public health system and therefore you will either have to pay for dental treatment or have some form of insurance to cover any work that may need doing. Prices are not hugely expensive compared to the UK and there are normally payment plans available for the more expensive treatments.

Your local embassy or consulate should have a list of English-speaking dentists in your area. In addition, in the areas that are popular with foreigners you will often find English-speaking dentists advertising in the local expat press. However, a recommendation by somebody you know in the area will probably be worth following up.

Typical opening hours are 9.30am–2pm and then 5–8pm Monday to Friday. Some may open on a Saturday morning for a couple of hours – typically between 9am and noon.

Opticians

Opticians (*optica* or *medicos oftalmólogos*) work in a similar way to opticians in the UK – you don't have to register and you simply make an appointment with an optician of your choice. Opticians can be found in the local press and the yellow pages (**www.paginas.amarillos.es**) – although recommendations from friends and family are better.

Many opticians provide free eye tests. Public health eye tests and prescriptions are available, but these have to be at public hospitals after referral by a doctor.

Just as in the UK, it is important to get quotes before having an eye test, buying lenses and so on. The cost of opticians' services are not regulated and therefore the prices can vary quite a bit.

'Alternative' Medicines

The use of 'alternative and complementary' medicines (*medicinas alternativas* or *medicinas complimentarias*) throughout the western world is generally on the increase and Spain is no exception to this (although they are probably still not as popular as they are in the UK). Spain has a long history of alternative medicines, with the first homeopathic hospital (Fundación Instituto Homeopatico y Hospital de San Jose in Madrid) founded in 1878, and quickly followed by the Homeopathic Academy in Barcelona (Academia Medico Homeopatica de Barcelona) in 1890. Until 1987, alternative or complementary medicine other than homeopathy played only a small role in Spain.

Alternative medicine, however, is still not fully integrated into the Spanish health system. Treatment cannot be covered for free under the INSALUD, for example, and the majority of insurance companies refuse to provide cover for this sort of treatment. It is illegal to practise medicine – including alternative and complementary medicine – without the relevant medical certificates.

It has recently (January 2005) been announced that four hospitals and 60 pharmacies in Catalonia are to distribute cannabis to patients suffering from AIDs, cancer, multiple sclerosis and chronic pain of nervous origin. The use of cannabis is otherwise illegal. The Catalonian regional government reached an agreement with the Spanish health ministry to try this experiment for a year. The cannabis will be distributed in the form of capsules containing powder made from cannabis rather than any other form.

As alternative and complementary medicines increase in popularity there is more opportunity for you to start practising in this field – assuming that you have the relevant qualifications of course. Even if you are not qualified to give this type of treatment, this does not necessarily mean that you cannot set up a business offering alternative medicine. You can always employ somebody who does have the relevant skills and certification. In some areas – particularly the south of Spain – there are resorts with clinics specialising in the provision of alternative and complementary medicines. One example of this is the Gefion Clinic in Mijas that not only provides alternative practices but also offers courses and support on starting new clinics or centres; see **www.gefionclinic.com**.

Private Health Insurance

Many Spaniards have private health insurance. You can use any doctor anywhere at any time – you don't have to register. The use of specialists is normally upon the recommendation of your doctor – and insurance companies prefer this, but you have free choice. However, it is important to read the small print – as in the UK, you may find that the terms of the policy stipulate that you can use only specific doctors approved by the insurance company.

The cost of private medical cover will obviously depend on a number of factors – your age, your medical history, the level of cover and so on. The cost of such policies can vary considerably so it is worth shopping around to make sure that you get the best deal. When comparing costs, make sure that you are comparing like with like, as often the policies will cover different things. Because of this it can be difficult to compare policies.

It is also important to make sure that you understand how the policy will work. For example, some treatments may not be available until after six months from the date of starting the policy.

Policies aimed specifically at foreigners living in Spain are likely to be more expensive but may be worth looking into. They will probably be more suitable for your circumstances as, for example, they may cover repatriation costs and also treatment in countries other than Spain.

Pensions

State – UK

Your state pension will be paid in the way described in **Working in Spain**; *see* 'Benefits', p.153.

If you have a government pension (army, civil service, police, etc.) your pension will still be taxed in the UK. Otherwise, the pension should be paid gross (i.e. tax-free) and it will be taxed in Spain; *see* 'Business and Personal Taxes', p.109.

State – Spain

Just as in the UK, if you pay into the social security system you will be entitled to a state pension upon retirement, provided that you have been paying into the system for 15 years. The age for claiming the state pension in Spain is 65 for both men and women.

If you have already paid social security payments in another EU country then it is possible to 'transfer' the credit for pensions that you have built up in your previous country to Spain so that the years of paying into the system are counted towards your 15 years in Spain. However, depending on your circumstances you may wish to continue paying into the system in the UK. It is important that you take individual advice on this point.

Just like normal workers, pensioners will receive more payments than there is months – they will receive 14 payments over the year.

We tend to complain that the UK state pension will soon be worth nothing and are all encouraged to make our own pension arrangements. The position in Spain is similar where the state pension is a burden on the economy and the government is looking at ways of reducing its commitments.

Private/Company

If you have a company pension it will be paid wherever the pension scheme rules dictate. Some permit the administrators to pay the money into any bank anywhere and others, ostensibly for security reasons, insist on the money being paid into a UK bank account.

If your pension has to be paid into a UK bank account, you can, of course, simply ask the bank to send it on to you in Spain. Bank transfer costs mean that it is probably best to do this only three or four times a year. You can also make an annual arrangement with some currency dealers whereby they will send the money at a fixed exchange rate that will apply for the whole year. This provides certainty of income. Whether you will do better or worse than you would have done by waiting, is in the lap of the gods.

Tax Treatment of Pensions

We often think that a pension is a pension and that is it. Unfortunately, this is not the case and there are many different types of pensions and different ways of structuring your pension. How you structure your pension will affect how you are taxed.

As a tax-resident in Spain you will pay worldwide income tax on your worldwide income; *see* further 'Business and Personal Taxes', p.109. This includes pensions – although not, interestingly, government-service pensions, which remain taxable in the UK (and therefore not in Spain).

Depending on the structure of your pension you can make considerable savings on its tax liability. These savings can be between 55 and 80 per cent. It is therefore of vital importance that you take professional advice on this. You should take this advice before you move to Spain as once you are over there some of the opportunities may be lost.

Education

Starting a business in Spain usually means taking your family with you. This can necessitate some difficult decisions – particularly for your children. English-speaking parents face some tough decisions when it comes to educating their children in Spain. It really comes down to two or three choices which depend on your income level and/or expectations. First there is the state, or public, system, which is basically free apart from school books, lunches, possibly uniforms and extra-curricular activities. In the state system, your child will be taught in Castilian and/or in one of the other co-official languages in areas where these are spoken. Then there are private schools, generally quite expensive, whose principal language of instruction is English. There are also many other private schools where the education is in Castilian. In between there are the *concertados*, which are basically private but which receive some state funding. These are roughly equivalent to grant-assisted schools in the UK. Alternatively, you could send your children abroad to a boarding school.

There are plenty of English-speaking schools in Spain, and schools that teach the English curriculum. These have several advantages – particularly if your children are a bit older.

English-language teaching is going to be privately funded and therefore, if you are going to send your children to such a school, you will need to budget for this – at a time when you are setting up a new business and need all your spare cash to make the business work.

English-based teaching will sometimes teach a UK-based curriculum. This certainly makes it easier for young people to integrate back into the UK education system at a later stage should the need arise.

The State School System

Infant Education (3–6 Years)

Pre-school (*pre-escolar* or *educación infantile*) is universally available. Pre-school education aims to encourage the child's physical and personal development, promote independence and personal hygiene and create awareness of self and others.

Primary Education (6–12 Years)

Educación primaria is compulsory. Over three two-year cycles, it aims to further the child's socialisation and independence. The broad subject areas are: the natural, social and cultural environment; art and music; PE; Castilian (or the co-official language where appropriate); mathematics and, from age eight, a foreign language, usually English (Castilian in Catalonia!). Evaluation is continuous and under-achievers sometimes repeat a year. Classes have a maximum of 25 pupils. The school year runs from mid-September to late June, with two weeks' holiday at Christmas, just over a week at Easter, several public holidays throughout the year and some local holidays.

Secondary Education (12–16 Years)

Compulsory secondary education (*educación secundaria obligatoria* ESO), comprises two two-year cycles and prepares students either for baccalaureate (*bachillerato*) or vocational training (*formación profesional*). Students cover a comprehensive range of subjects from the humanities, the natural and social sciences and the arts and can choose from several optional subjects according to their talents and interests. Evaluation is similar to that in primary education and insufficient progress can again mean repeating a year. The school year is basically the same as that in primary education but the day is shorter, usually from 8 or 8.30am until 2.15 or 2.30pm.

After Secondary Education (17–18 Years)

Those who do not pass ESO can either leave school or proceed to *formación profesional*. Those who pass receive their Secondary School Graduation Certificate (*Graduado en Educación Secundaria*) and may go on to either specific vocational training or the more academic *bachillerato* programme. This two-year course prepares them for university entrance exams (*selectividad*), although they can enter specific vocational training at this point. The university entrance exam may be abolished in the future.

Enrolment in Spanish State Schools

Enrolment in a Spanish school may require an interview and possibly an examination, although this is rare for foreign children. Schools have annual quotas and places are allocated on a first-come, first-served basis. Enrolment is usually during the spring term prior to the year the child is to enter school but may vary from one region to another. Check exact dates with any school in your area.

For children who are of an age to enter the ESO third grade, at about 14 or 15, you need to produce your child's birth certificate, school record book and/or examination results. Contact the Ministerio de Educación, Cultura y Deportes, Calle Alcalá, 36, 28014 Madrid, **t** 902 218 500; **www.mec.es/educacion**. Alternatively, contact the ministry's representation at 20 Peel Street, London W8 7PD, **t** (020) 7727 2462. All necessary forms may be obtained and presented there. Try to complete the process before arrival in Spain. Theoretically a child will not be admitted until the official papers have been received and stamped by the Department of Education. Allow three to six months for this process.

Private Schools

The state education system (*see* above) has improved greatly, but as everywhere else has its drawbacks. For instance, you may not want to throw your child directly in at the 'deep end', since this could prove traumatic. Having to learn another language and use it for school work is only one aspect of the problem; there is also the impact of a totally different culture – something frequently underestimated by parents.

Integration is generally easier with younger children. Adolescents may find it more difficult. Children *are* adaptable, but do not expect too much of them too quickly. If you choose to put your child into the state system, then you are well advised to find them a private language tutor to get them to a reasonable level before they start school. You should also learn the language yourself, as quickly as possible, to allow communication with teachers (vital) and enable you to help your children with homework.

You may decide on a year's private English-speaking or bilingual school to get around these problems before going into the Spanish state system. Much depends on your income, since private schooling does not come cheaply. Some 40 schools are listed on the website of the National Association of British Schools in Spain (**www.nabss.org**). They are found mainly in the major cities, the Mediterranean coastal areas and in the islands, both the Balearics and the Canaries. Annual fees vary but you should expect to pay about €4,000 per child for primary schools and €5,000–6,000 for secondary level. On top of this you may have to pay for uniforms, transport, school lunches, extra-curricular activities and a variety of school trips (often somewhere more expensive than the local museum).

Most of these schools take children aged from three to 18 and follow the national curriculum leading to GCSE and A-Levels, their American equivalents or the International Baccalaureate. They may prepare students for Spanish ESO and *bachillerato* exams too. They provide a good, across-the-board education both academic and extra-curricular. Facilities vary but often include sports halls, playing fields, swimming pools, music rooms, auditoria and even stables. Membership of clubs and societies and the pursuit of hobbies are often important features in these schools, as are trips to skiing resorts and even abroad.

Staff tend to be from Britain and other Anglophone countries along with some Spanish teachers. Students may be a mixture of Spanish with a sprinkling of other nationalities, but foreigners are sometimes the majority. Students usually leave completely fluent in English and Castilian Spanish and perhaps another language or two. Academic results can be excellent – a very high percentage go on to university after leaving.

Sending your child to such a school may, however, isolate them from the local culture and reduce their chances of making friends locally, which could mean a social life dependent on children of other expats. You could easily find yourself driving miles to birthday parties and other social gatherings, which could just as well have been held in your own neighbourhood.

Legal Matters

Business Law 194
Insurance 199
Disputes and Debt Collection 204
Bankcruptcy 210

08

The following pages aim to provide a basic background in Spanish law as it relates to some key areas including contract law, insurance and debt collection. However, there is no substitute for seeing a lawyer face to face. If you have not yet started your business then you may choose to go to a UK lawyer who specialises in Spanish law. Alternativley, you might use a Spanish lawyer who also knows about the legal system in the UK. Either way, getting sound legal advice can pay dividends in the long run. British, American and Irish consulates can supply a list of English-speaking lawyers in your area. However, inclusion on the list does not constitute endorsement of the lawyers in question. A physical meeting is still the best way to start an important relationship as it is usually easier to make certain that you understand each other in a face-to-face meeting than it is by letter.

Business Law

Each country has its own laws. Laws can be on a local (regional) basis or on a national level. Over and above national laws there are international laws, treaties, etc. Within Europe there are European laws and directives. All these laws have effect and are often drafted in different languages. Unsurprisingly, different laws can sometimes conflict. When two or more laws come together but don't work well together it is called conflict of laws. Spanish law, like all law, is complicated and there are many ways in which two or more sets of laws can conflict.

What has this to do with your business? In an increasingly international world you are more likely to be affected by a clash between laws. For example, when you bring goods into or out of Spain, or sell goods over the internet, or enter into agreements with companies and bodies in other countries there is a potential for conflicts between laws to arise.

Do take advice on this point. Your legal adviser should understand both the UK law and the Spanish law so that they can be sure that what you are trying to achieve in one country does not impact on the other country. If you are dealing with countries other than Spain and the UK, then your legal and tax advisers must also understand the respective legal and tax systems.

Contract Law

This is another huge subject on which entire books have been written. It is very important if you are starting a business or working for somebody else. Undoubtedly you will come into contact with contracts. Each time you buy something, sell something, employ somebody or enter into an agreement with somebody you are entering into a contract of some sort.

The Spanish law of contract is set out in the civil code. A contract (*contrato*) can be made between two or more people or companies. In order for the contract to be valid it must have three elements:

1. Agreement. Basically adults who are not mentally incapable can enter into a contract. There must be an offer by one party and an acceptance of that offer by the other party.
2. An object. This basically means that there must be certainty about what the contract is about. The object of the contract must be both legal and moral – meaning that if you wished to sell something that is not yours to sell then the contract does not have any validity. You are however allowed to enter into a contract to sell something that will be yours and that you will be able to sell when it becomes yours.
3. Legal basis. There must be some legal basis as to why you are entering into the contract and why you are complying with this.

There are different types of contract in Spain. Each of these works in a slightly different way.

Agreed Contracts, Formal Contracts and Contracts Relating to Property

These contracts are some of the most common and have as their purpose the delivery of something – such as a property – which requires a deed to effect the transfer.

Bilateral and Unilateral Contracts

Bilateral contracts have legal obligations on both parties. For example, you do something and in return I do something else.

A unilateral contract, on the other hand, is one where only one of the parties has to do something. An example of this is a loan, where one party's obligation is to return the money borrowed.

There are many other different types of contracts and your lawyer will explain the differences between them.

If you breach a contract then the other party will be entitled to compensation. Sometimes the parties try to limit the level of compensation through the wording in the contract. Sometimes this protection is legal and sometimes the parties will try to remove rights that are there by law.

If you enter into a contract with somebody it is important to make sure that there are penalty clauses, so that if they do not comply with the contract, you are compensated in some way. For example, if you are paying a deposit for something (say a house) and the seller later refuses to sell to you, you can draft the contract in such a way that the seller has to return double your deposit to you. This can be a very effective way of stopping the other party selling to somebody else.

If a contract involves some transfer of money then it is important that the price is clearly defined in the contract. You do not want an argument later about how much was supposed to be paid!

Rental Contracts

If you are renting a property in Spain, there should be a rental agreement. The duration of the rental contract is freely set by the parties. However, if the contract is for less than five years then the person renting has an automatic right to extend the rental for a further year at the end.

The owner of the property can stop the rental contract by giving 30 days' notice to the person renting.

Deposits are normally a month's rent. A tenant will need written permission from the owner before they can make alterations to the property.

Contract for the Rental of a Business

The deposit for this type of contract is usually two months' rent.

A tenant will be allowed to sub-let the property to another person without needing permission from the owner.

Exchange Contracts (*Permuta*)

An exchange is similar to the old bartering system. I own something that you want; you own something that I want. We swap what we have and we are both happy. No money changes hands – we simply exchange what we own. Although uncommon in business this does still happen. For example, you may own a plot of land and a friend of yours may own another piece of land. You each think that the other plot of land is more suitable for your needs. You swap.

Commercial Leasing Contracts

This is normally used for industrial equipment. You may, for example, enter into a lease for machinery, vehicles or buildings. These contracts are normally drafted by the entity leasing the object and are rarely negotiable.

Contractual and Performance Guarantees

If you are entering into a contract, make sure there are guarantees in place. For example, you may wish a builder to construct a shop for you. You are relying on him to have the shop ready by a certain date. If the shop is not finished by that date, this is going to have a knock-on effect on when you can start installing all the shop fittings, bringing in stock, advertising the business, bringing in customers and ultimately starting to make money. One way to avoid this situation is to have specific clauses in the contract relating to the performance. You would set out the standard that the shop is going to be finished to and when it is to be finished by. If the shop is not finished by that date then the contract should provide you with compensation for late completion. This normally focuses the mind of the other party.

Breach of Contract – Your Legal Remedies

Unfortunately, no matter how well a contract is drafted and how good the intentions of the parties entering into the contract, there are always times when there is a breach of contract.

The first reaction of many Spanish legal advisers is to jump into court and sue the other party. While this is one option it can often be an expensive and time-consuming exercise. If there is a breach of contract it is a good idea to think about your options carefully.

First, speak to the other party. Why have the contractual obligations not been fulfilled? There may be a perfectly reasonable explanation. You may be able to resolve the problem. Trying to settle the matter in an amicable way is often the best way to proceed. It is cheaper and less time-consuming than going to court. It also usually ensures that the parties can continue to work together in the future rather than the whole relationship breaking down.

If this does not work then you may have to revisit the idea of some sort of litigation – or at least the threat of litigation. A well-worded letter from your lawyer will often solve the problem.

Limitation to Your Legal Rights

If there is a breach of contract or some other circumstances in which you can claim from somebody else, make sure that you claim in time. In Spain, just as in many countries, there are limitation periods. This means that unless you claim within a certain period you lose the right to bring the claim. This can work to your advantage. The tax office, for example, sometimes loses the right to recover the tax due unless you have paid within a certain period. The planning authorities may lose the right to pull down an illegally built house unless they do so within a certain period.

Different claims have different limitation periods. This limitation may be for a certain period agreed in the contract or it may be for a period set out by law. For example, a claim for a personal injury generally has a limitation period of one year (although there can be circumstances where this can be different). In the case of a contractual claim the limitation period is 15 years, although in employment cases this can be one year.

One of the important points about limitation periods is exactly when the limitation period starts to run. This is not always obvious.

Industrial and Intellectual Property

This means the legal rights that you receive from creating something – whether it is an object or an idea – for example, literary works, musical compositions, works of art, maps, drawings, photographs, computer programs, etc. In Spain, as elsewhere, there are two different types – 'industrial property' and 'copyright'. Basically, the person who creates the 'thing' has the rights. If two or more people were responsible, then the intellectual property rights belong to both or all of them.

Rights

The person who holds intellectual property rights has certain rights arising:

- **to claim acknowledgement as the author of the work**
- **to modify the work**
- **to decide how the work is to be made available to the public**
- **to decide how and when the work will be used and exploited**
- **to exploit the item for their lifetime plus a further 70 years after their death**

In the case of an employee, it is the employer who has the benefit of the intellectual property, providing that the work was carried out during the course of their employment.

If you are producing something, be very clear about the ownership of any intellectual property rights. You do not wish to have a situation later on where you are having to pay compensation to somebody else.

The intellectual property registry in Spain (*Registro de la Propiedad Intelectual*) protects the rights of the owner of the intellectual property rights.

There is no requirement to register intellectual property rights, but this will obviously help, should a dispute arise in the future. Registration is carried out at the provincial office of the general registry of intellectual property (*Oficina Provincial del Registro General de la Propiedad Intelectual*) or at Spanish consular offices (*oficinas consulares de España*) abroad. Registration requires some forms to be filled in and a fee to be paid.

There is no need to register documents to which you wish to add the © sign. If you are the author of the work then you are entitled to claim copyright by adding the © symbol. This will notify anybody reading the work that you own its intellectual property.

Product Liability

Product liability is the responsibility that is imposed upon a manufacturer or a distributor of a product for any injury or damage that results from their product. As the owner of a business in Spain you are required to make sure that the products you supply are safe to the public. If you simply supply the products and buy them from the supplier, then you still are obliged to make sure that you are supplying safe products. If you are in any doubt, don't sell the products – this could be used against you in the event of a claim. Your failure to withdraw a product from sale that you know is unsafe is enough to make you responsible for the injuries that result.

The first thing that you need is a complaints book (*hoja de reclamación*). All Spanish businesses are obliged to keep a complaints book. Should a customer have cause to complain they will fill in a report. There are three copies of the complaints book – one is kept by the owner of the business, one is kept by the person complaining and one is sent to the municipal office for information to the consumer (*Oficina Municipal de Información al Consumidor* – OMIC). The OMIC is located in the town hall or in the municipal market and is the local representation of the ministry of health and consumer affairs (*Ministerio de Sanidad y Consumo*).

The OMIC does not have legal power to force companies to do things, but it will make sure that the relevant authorities are informed of any wrong-doings.

If a customer makes a complaint against you, you have 10 days to deal with it or else the OMIC will get involved. If a customer complains and does not get satisfaction through the OMIC then the person complaining can go to the defender of the public (*Defensor del Pueblo*), an ombudsman on a regional and national level. Another consumer organisation is the *Organización de Consumidores y Usuarios* (Organisation of Consumers and Users). The other option available is to proceed through a lawyer, or even the courts.

Insurance

Any business should make sure that it has adequate insurance. Nobody likes to pay for insurance (*seguro*), of course, especially when you pay for a whole year and don't make a claim. But insurance can protect you in any number of ways. For one thing, it is worth making sure that you get an insurance policy that covers you for product liability claims (*see* p.205) or at least legal expenses.

Brokers

An insurance broker in Spain is a *corridor de seguros*. Just as in the UK some insurance brokers are better than others, so try to get some personal recommendations of brokers who have provided good service in the past. Remember that the cheapest policy is not always the best and that good advice when taking out the policy, and a good record of assisting clients when claims have to be made, are also important.

Spanish-based Brokers

There are obviously plenty of Spanish insurance companies that provide insurance. These companies, while they may have English-speaking staff, will provide all the documentation in Spanish. Should you need to make a claim, the claim form will be in Spanish and you will have to deal with Spanish staff in making your claim. Some Spanish-based brokers may provide some documentation in English.

English-based Brokers

There are a number of insurance companies in Spain that cater specifically for the British community. Their staff can speak English and as much documentation as possible will be in English. The insurance policy is likely to be in Spanish, but the broker may provide an English translation. To start with, many people will use an English-based broker because it is more convenient – after all, making a claim is stressful enough without having to do it in a foreign language. However, this convenience usually comes at a price and the policies are likely to be more expensive than if you went to a Spanish-based broker.

Brokers within the EU

You are free to take out insurance for cover in Spain with any insurance company within the EU, even if the insurer is not registered in Spain. For some people this may seem convenient as they can deal with an insurance company that they have used in their home country. However, this is probably not worth considering as the insurance company will not understand how things work in Spain and this can cause problems should you have to make a claim.

Duration and Policies

Insurance policies usually run for a year. These days many insurance policies are automatically renewed at the end of the policy and it is your obligation to cancel if you do not wish to extend the policy for a further year. Check the terms of the policy to see how much notice you have to give. Notice periods will change from policy to policy but are typically a couple of months from the end of the policy. To terminate a policy you have to write to the insurance company and inform them of this. It is sensible to send the letter by recorded delivery.

In return for the policy you will have to pay the premium (*premios* or *primas*). The premium is paid for the duration of the policy and may be paid for the whole year at the start of the policy or over the duration of the policy.

It is essential that you go through the policy carefully to make sure that it covers everything you wish to have cover for.

Claims

Should you have to make a claim, do it as soon as possible. The notification period will depend on the type of policy and the nature of your claim. Again it is worth reading through your policy to make sure that you understand what the time limit is for making a claim. If you try to claim outside the time period, the insurance company may well refuse to pay out.

Insurance companies can refuse to pay out on a policy for various reasons. For example, they can refuse to pay out if you have lied to them on the application form, if the value of the item insured has increased without their being notified, or if you do not keep up the premiums on the policy. It is important to be absolutely straight with the broker and the insurance company to make sure that there are no excuses not to pay out in the event of a claim.

In addition to making the claim within the specified time you will have to provide whatever documentary proof is possible to support your claim. This could be a police report in the event of theft, photographic evidence of the damage, copy receipts for goods damaged, etc.

Disputes with Insurance Companies

Disputes with insurance companies over some aspect of their service, the policy or a claim are not unusual. If such a situation arises, the insurance company will have a complaints department. If you do not get satisfaction through the internal complaints procedure and you still feel that you have a valid reason to complain then you can make a complaint to the equivalent of the insurance ombudsman in Spain – the *Servicio de Reclamaciónes* at the *Dirección General de Seguros y Fondos de Pensiones* (DGSPF). For contact details of the DGSPF, *see* 'Contacts', p.220. If you do not feel that you have obtained satisfaction through the DGSPF, you may be able to claim against the insurance company through the courts, but bear in mind that they have much more money and time than you and that claims against insurance companies are never easy. They can afford to drag the case out until you run out of money.

Third Party Liability and Public Liability Insurance

Do investigate taking out insurance when you open a new business. Obviously, the type of business will dictate the type of insurance. If you are running a business that has members of the public coming to your business premises, you should consider taking out public liability insurance or third-party liability insurance (*seguro de terceros* or *riesgo a terceros*). This insurance will mean that if somebody injures themselves on your premises you will be covered for any damages that they might claim. This type of insurance can often be included in your buildings insurance but it is worth looking at the terms of the policy to make sure that you are sufficiently covered and that the terms of the insurance are suitable for your needs, as running a business is different from just owning a property.

Buildings Insurance (*Continente*)

The building itself is likely to have insurance of some type, but it is important to double-check this, as it is not compulsory. If you own the property then it will be your responsibility to take out this insurance. If you rent or lease the property then it is equally important to establish who is responsible for arranging the insurance. If it is the property owner's responsibility then it is prudent for you to check that he has done this and if possible get a copy of the policy to make sure that it covers your needs. This insurance will cover damage to the building from a variety of incidents such as fire, flood, vandalism, etc.

Contents Insurance (*Contenido*)

You are building up a business, everything is going well, your shop is full of stock, you have just had a new delivery and you are feeling good about the future. Unfortunately, that night a fire breaks out in the building next to yours, which in turn spreads to your business. The stock is ruined. If this happens your business would be over, unless you have either sufficient funds to replace all your stock as well as refurbish the business premises, or you have insurance that will pay for this for you. Typical contents insurance refers to the contents of your home, but commercial contents insurance also covers the contents of your business – particularly stock.

Farm Insurance (*Seguros Agrario*)

You have been working for years to get your vineyard working. It has taken years for the vines to produce their first grapes and a further year for the grapes to be useful. You have been living on your savings for several years, money has been tight and you can finally see the light at the end of the tunnel and the possibility of some income coming in. Then there is a fire that destroys your whole crop. Faced with a further four years of not receiving any income your business disappears in a matter of hours. All sorts of things can happen that can destroy crops – you only have to look at the locust swarm in Lanzarote and Fuerteventura at the end of 2004 to realise this.

To safeguard against such eventualities it is sensible to take out insurance. There is a special insurance scheme for farmers, which is run as a joint venture between the insurance companies and the government, who subsidise the scheme. Further details of the insurance scheme can be found at the *Entidad*

Estatal de Seguros Agrarios (ENESA), which is the state entity for agricultural insurance. Details of ENESA can be found at **www.enesa.mapa.es**.

You can still arrange your own insurance outside the special agricultural insurance scheme, but few people do this as the scheme is particularly geared for the agricultural sector.

Employer's Liability

If you employ staff you should take out employer's liability insurance to cover any injuries or losses that your employees may suffer while at work and on your premises. Employer's liability insurance will protect you against claims made by employees who are injured or who are ill because of their work. If there is an accident at work, the employee will have a general limitation period of a year in which to make a claim.

Professional Negligence

Insurance of professionals is normally done through the regulatory body for that profession (*colegio*). Professional negligence insurance is a type of policy that covers the work or advice that you do for a client. For example, you are a surveyor and advise a client that there is nothing wrong with a property. The client then goes to buy the property and, after a week, finds that there is a major problem with the foundations that you had not spotted. Your professional negligence policy will compensate the client for their loss.

Surprisingly, many professions are not required to carry professional negligence insurance. For example, in the UK it is compulsory for lawyers to have professional indemnity insurance cover of at least £1 million. In Spain many local law societies do not require professional negligence insurance and where they do the level of cover that they insist on is far less than in the UK.

Health Insurance

For details on this topic, *see* 'Healthcare', p.187.

Life Insurance (*Seguro de Vida*)

Life insurance that will pay out an agreed sum in the event of your death can provide peace of mind. The person specified under the terms of the policy who will receive the lump sum can be anybody you wish, but it is normally your spouse, partner or children. The death of a partner who you are working with can have devastating effects on a business so it is especially important to take out adequate life cover if you are starting a business.

Salary Insurance (*Pago de Seguro*)

In the event that you have an accident and are unable to work, salary insurance will continue to pay your salary even though you are not working. This insurance is provided by the Spanish social security system. If you are a legal employee and are paying into the social security scheme then you will be entitled to this once you have been off work for a certain number of days. There is no set number of days that you have to be off work to be able to claim salary insurance as this will depend on the employer and also sometimes how long you have been working for the employer.

If you are self-employed then it is possible (but often difficult) to take out a private insurance policy to cover loss of earnings.

Unemployment Insurance (*Pago de Desempleo*)

Again this is compulsory if you are an employee and is provided by the social security system. If you are self-employed you would have to take out private insurance, which is difficult to find.

Vehicle Insurance

Depending on the type of business you run, you may well need a vehicle of some sort. This may be a car to get you to and from clients, or a van to transport your stock or make deliveries. It is compulsory to take out insurance for vehicles in Spain. There are basically two different levels of vehicle insurance:

- **Third-party liability insurance (*seguro de terceros* or *seguro de responsabilidad civil obligatoria*). This is obligatory and is the lowest level of insurance that you can legally have for your vehicle. This covers the situation where you cause damage to a third party or their property.**

- **Fully comprehensive (*seguro a todo riesgo*). This covers a variety of other insurable situations, such as fire, theft, damage to your own vehicle, personal injury to yourself and the occupants of your own vehicle, damage to the contents of the car, etc. It is important to specify what you wish to be covered under fully comprehensive insurance.**

Disputes and Debt Collection

For any business, unpaid bills cause a major problem. Most businesses that fail do so not because the business itself is flawed, but through cash-flow problems. Such problems are often caused by the failure of clients and customers to pay their bills on time, or in some cases at all.

In some cases there can be disputes with people that you come into contact with in a business environment, which are not directly related to monetary issues – although the failure to pay an invoice may be attributed to a dispute.

Chasing debts or resolving disputes in any country can be difficult. In Spain, with its bureaucracy and slow court procedures, trying to resolve such issues can be even more difficult.

Debt Collection

Unless you run a business where cash is exchanged at the time the goods or services are supplied, at some stage you will have to deal with somebody who will not pay. You may issue an invoice with 28 days' payment terms, for example, and the person does not pay. There can be many reasons why somebody does not pay you. Sometimes they will not pay because they do not wish to. Or they might not pay because they cannot afford to. Alternatively, they may not pay for the simple reason that they have forgotten or are not good at sorting out their own paperwork. To be honest it doesn't matter what the reason is – if they haven't paid, this affects your business.

The first thing to do is to talk to the person who owes you money. This solves the vast majority of problems. Even if they still refuse to pay, at least you will now know that you have a problem. Resolving the situation without resorting to the courts is highly recommended.

If speaking to the debtor doesn't resolve the issue then you are going to have to think about how to proceed. Basically there are two ways – the traditional way and the more 'creative' way.

The Traditional Debt Collection Method

Contact your lawyer and get them to write to the debtor. This has two effects – it shows the debtor that you are serious about recovering the debt and it also acts as the first step of a court case if this is needed. Hopefully this will be the end of the matter and the debt will be repaid.

If the debtor still doesn't pay, you are then forced to make another decision – is it worth going to court? You need to consider whether the debtor can afford to pay, whether they have any assets, how much it is going to cost you in legal fees and also how long it is going to take to go to court. The size of the debt will determine how the court proceedings will work. The way the court case will proceed also determines whether or not the debtor admits that the debt is due.

All the way through the court proceedings, bear in mind what you are trying to achieve. Too many people get very personal about court cases and end up spending lots of money and time to win the battle but end up losing the war. Assuming that you win the court case and the debtor does not appeal, you will have to enforce the judgement. This means making the debtor do what the court ordered him or her to do. In some cases this can be just as difficult as the court case itself – especially if the debtor is determined to make your life difficult. Your lawyer can advise you on the best course of action based on your circumstances. An equivalent of the UK small claims court does exist in Spain and, as in the UK, this is where claims for smaller amounts of money are dealt with at a lower cost and, in theory, more quickly.

The More 'Creative' Way

Of course, Spain being Spain, there are more creative ways of debt recovery, which do not rely on the courts. A number of debt recovery agencies have been set up in Spain that basically embarrass the debtor into paying. The way this works is for the debt collector to dress up as a particular character – a knight, a Franciscan monk, or the Pink Panther. Dressed in this very conspicuous costume the debt collector will make his way to where the debtor is and demand payment. The theory is simple:

- **The costume is very obvious and everybody knows what it means. The debtor is therefore more likely to pay up in order to get rid of an embarrassing situation.**
- **Because the costume is obvious it means that other people can easily see that the person owes money to somebody else. In turn this is likely to affect their credit with other people.**
- **Because the costume is normally comical it is a non-threatening method and therefore less likely (although not guaranteed) to end up in a fight between the debt collector and the debtor.**

This method has been used in Spain since the 1960s. It has its origins in medieval times when a person who was found to be a debtor was paraded through the street wearing a bright costume.

Disputes

Not all disputes involve money. You may have agreed with someone to supply you with something and they have failed to do so, or purchased something and found it to be damaged or not in working order when it arrives. Alternatively, someone might be doing something that is affecting your business. Or you might find yourself in a situation where someone has a dispute against you. Often, if this is the case, you will feel that the other person is getting worked up unecessarily about something that you have done or not done. In most cases disputes can easily be resolved. In fact, as a foreigner in Spain you will probably think that many things are 'disputes' when in reality there is no issue. The Spanish can be quite excitable and enjoy arguing. You must therefore first of all establish whether or not there really is a problem.

If there is a problem then you need to decide what to do about it. This can be difficult. If possible try to talk to the person that you are having the dispute with. The best way of doing this is to go for a coffee and discuss what you can do to resolve the problem. Keep calm and explain what you see as the main issue and how it can be resolved. Be reasonable and try to explain that a solution would be best for both of you. In most instances this will be the end of the matter and you will both come away with the problem resolved and a new respect and understanding for each other. Unfortunately, this isn't always the solution. In some cases it may actually make the situation worse!

If the person that you are having a dispute with works for an organisation, it may be appropriate to talk to their supervisor or their complaints department. Firms have a complaints book (*libro de reclamaciónes*). It might make you feel better to fill in the complaints book, but don't expect it to resolve anything. Some businesses (for example, dentists, following a court case in 2001) are no longer required to have a complaints book.

If the matter is serious then you may decide to make a formal complaint to the police (*denuncia*). Again, this can have mixed results. This may resolve the matter permanently, or it may make the problem go away temporarily only to return much worse at a later stage. You will have to make a judgement call on this one.

If the dispute has a European element you could write to your MEP, who may be able to help, depending on the circumstances. Details of your MEP can be found at **www.europarl.eu.int**.

If you think that court cases in the UK are slow and cost too much money then you are in for a shock should you ever be involved in a court case in Spain. It can take years for a court dispute to be settled. Then, when you think that you have got to the end of the matter, you discover that probably 80 per cent of court cases in Spain are appealed and the whole process starts again. In fact, so many court cases are appealed that there is a very good argument for saying that the court of first instance might as well be scrapped completely in order to save time! In short, court cases are to be avoided if possible.

Lawyers

It is advisable to get a lawyer involved in any dispute as soon as it looks serious. This can avoid your making mistakes that actually make the situation worse. A good lawyer can help you find a practical solution to a dispute.

Unfortunately, many lawyers in Spain take the traditional approach to resolving disputes and want to 'issue proceedings in the court'. They often pay little regard to the cost and time involved in court proceedings. But things are changing and more Spanish lawyers are taking the more British approach to resolving disputes, which involves practical solutions for practical problems; *see* 'Alternative Dispute Resolution', p.212.

Getting Your Paperwork Right

Debt recovery and disputes in Spain can be difficult to resolve. It is much better to try to avoid such situations in the first place, and a good way of doing this is to get your paperwork right in the first place as this will avoid problems in the future.

When you run a business in Spain there is always going to be paperwork – not necessarily the type or amount of paperwork that you want, but there will be paperwork. If you are in any doubt as to what paperwork you need, or whether it is correct, seek advice from somebody who can assist you – the body who issues the paperwork, a lawyer, an accountant or a *gestor*. Do not assume that the paperwork is correct – this will only come back to bite you in the end.

The Courts

With a bit of luck and by making the right moves you should never need this section, but it is important to understand how the Spanish court system works 'just in case'.

The courts in Spain are even slower than they are in the UK. Nevertheless, Spanish courts have some very good ideas – for example, court cases are recorded on video. The video is transferred to a CD-Rom which is then given to the lawyers representing the two parties for their records. In this way there is an exact record of what went on at the court and the clients can see exactly what their lawyers did for them even if they were not present.

Spain has different courts and different levels of courts. In Spain the courts range from the court of first instance up to the supreme court. After the supreme court comes the European courts, as Spain is part the EU. The different levels of courts in Spain are outlined in the box opposite (with the highest court at the top). In addition to the above there are several other courts, which relate to specific actions such as the *Juzgado de Menores* (Children's Court), *Juzgados de lo Social* (Labour Courts), *Juzgado de lo Contensioso Administrativo* (Administrative Courts) and the *Juzgados de lo Penal* (Criminal Courts).

Trial by jury exists for criminal trials, and the jury is made up of nine people. In order to be found guilty, seven out of the nine jurors must agree.

Alternative Dispute Resolution (ADR)

You have a dispute with somebody and have tried taking them for a coffee and it hasn't worked. You still need to resolve the problem, but would rather avoid going to court. A possible solution is Alternative Dispute Resolution (ADR). There are various different types of ADR – the most well-known being arbitration. Arbitration (*arbitraje*) is where the two sides to the dispute ask a third party who has no connection with either of them to consider the matter and to

The main courts

Court	Equivalent	Parts of the Court	Comments
Tribunal Supremo	Supreme Court	1. Civil Chamber 2. Criminal Chamber 3. Administrative Chamber 4. Labour Chamber 5. Military Chamber	The highest court in the land. Jurisdiction over the country. Based in Madrid.
Tribunal Constituciónal	Constitutional Court		At the same level as the Tribunal Supremo but only hears cases involving constitutional matters.
Audiencia Naciónal	National Court	1. Criminal Chamber 2. Labour Chamber 3. Administrative Chamber 4. Central Examining Courts 5. Central Criminal Courts	Second highest court in the land. Jurisdiction over the whole country. Based in Madrid.
Tribunal Superior de Justicia de la Comunidades Autonomas	Regional High Court	1. Civil Chamber 2. Criminal Chamber 3. Administrative Chamber 4. Labour Chamber	The highest court in each autonomous region of Spain.
Audiencia Provincial	Provincial Court	1. Civil Chamber 2. Criminal Chamber	Highest court in each province. The court will be located in the capital of each province.
Juzgado de Primera Instancia	Court of First Instance		Hears Civil cases at first instance and also appeals on judgements passed by Justices of the Peace.
Juzgado de Paz	Justice of the Peace		Small-town court that hears minor civil cases.

reach a decision. This decision is binding on the two parties. Arbitration is not a court – it is much more informal than going to court and will therefore cost less and be faster. Alongside arbitration there is a whole range of other ADR possibilities including mediation (*mediación*), conciliation (*conciliación*), evaluation by a neutral party (*evaluacion neutral*) and Online Dispute Resolution (ODR).

The ARyME (*Arbitraje y Mediación*) website at **www.aryme.com** is a useful source for finding out about institutions offering ADR.

Who Can Go to Arbitration?

Most but not all disputes can go to arbitration. You cannot go to arbitration if:

- **a court case has already started or there has already been a court decision**
- **an offence has been committed**
- **one or more of the parties is a minor**

Your own industry may have an organisation that provides arbitration services. There are also general arbitration bodies, for example, the consumption arbitration board (*Junta Arbitral de Consumo*) and the college of arbitration (*Colegio Arbitral*). An arbitrator or any organisation carrying out arbitration must be independent of the parties and must have knowledge of the issues involved. More than one person can act as arbitrator in any one case, but the number of arbitrators must always be uneven – for obvious reasons.

How Does Arbitration Work?

First the two sides must agree to arbitration. They choose a person or a body to act as the arbitrator. The arbitrator writes to the parties confirming that they have agreed to arbitration. The two sides sign a document in which they agree to be legally bound by the outcome of the arbitration. The arbitrator decides on the location of the hearing and informs the relevant parties. The language of the arbitration hearing is agreed. Any relevant documentation or evidence is submitted to the arbitrator. The arbitrator considers the matter and issues his decision in writing within six months of the start of arbitration. The decision will be signed by a notary and notified to the parties. The arbitrator's decision is binding. If one of the parties does not wish to comply with the decision then the other party can force the judgement through the courts.

Arbitration tends to be cheaper than going to court, but everything still has a price. Obviously somebody needs to pay the arbitrators for their time and assistance. The arbitrators have the right to ask the parties to pay their reasonable fees and expenses. It is important to establish what these are likely to be at the beginning of the arbitration procedure.

Bankruptcy

The laws on bankruptcy in Spain were recently changed (September 2004). In addition, new courts were set up to deal with bankruptcies (*Juzgados de Mercantil*). The idea behind the rules was to make the whole process simpler and also to assist companies who find themselves in such a situation to work through the problems and to carry on trading. Unfortunately, the new rules do appear to some to make it easier for companies to be made bankrupt.

Applications for Bankruptcy

An application for bankruptcy can be initiated in two ways. First of all the person who is running the company and who owes the debts (the debtor) may make the application himself. This is called 'voluntary bankruptcy'. The second way is for the people who are owed money (the creditors) to make the application. This is called 'forced bankruptcy'. A creditor can make an application for bankruptcy of the debtor in one of the following situations:

1. If the debtor has not paid taxes and social security payments for the last three months.
2. If the debtor has not paid his staff wages for the last three months.
3. If the debtor is in default of his payment obligations.
4. If the debtor has had goods seized from him.
5. If the debtor has transferred assets or goods in a fraudulent way – for example, selling assets at undervalue in order to keep those assets outside future bankruptcy proceedings. If this is the case then the courts can set aside such transactions if they occurred within the last two years.

In both voluntary and forced bankruptcies the procedure is the same from that moment onwards. The judge will appoint trustees to analyse both the assets and the debts of the debtor. Once they have done this the judge will be able to decide one of two courses of action. First, the judge can arrange an agreement between the debtor and his creditors for the repayment of the debts. This is intended to resolve the problem of the debts while also attempting to keep the debtor trading. The new law encourages anybody who is showing the first signs of bankruptcy to file for bankruptcy. In fact, you must file for bankruptcy within two months of knowing that you are going to be insolvent. Failure to do so can carry severe penalties.

If the court judges that the debtor can carry on with the business while the bankruptcy proceedings are taking place, then the social security payments that they have to make are reduced by 50 per cent, making it easier for them to repay the debts they owe. Interest on any debts is also frozen during the time of the bankruptcy proceedings.

The second option is for the debtor's assets to be sold and for the money realised from the sale to be distributed among the creditors.

Generally speaking, the debtor will be allowed to carry on trading despite the bankruptcy proceedings. This has two advantages – the creditors are more likely to be paid and the debtor has more chance of surviving the bankruptcy.

Different creditors will have different preferences over any assets of the debtor. A person who initiates the bankruptcy proceedings will have priority rights. There are basically three types of creditors. In order of preferential treatment they are privileged creditors, subordinate creditors and ordinary creditors. The person who starts the bankruptcy proceedings can count up to a quarter of their debt as a privileged credit.

References

Spain at a Glance 214
Further Reading 215
Contacts 216
Spanish Area Telephone Codes 223
Regional Climate Chart/Rainfall 224
Largest Cities 225
Dictionary of Useful and Technical Terms 226
Public Holidays and Celebrations 233

09

Spain at a Glance

Capital city: Madrid
Official name of country: Reino de España (Kingdom of Spain)
Head of state: Juan Carlos I
Type of government: Constitutional monarchy
Head of government: Jose Luis Rodriguez Zapatero
Area: 504,782 sq km
Length: Distance from San Sebastián to Cádiz (far north to far southwest): 1,132km; from Girona (northeast) to Huelva (southwest): 1,240km
Maximum width: Distance from Lugo (far northwest) to Girona (northeast): 1,120km
Geographic highlights: Picos de Europa in Asturias; the Pyrenees, on the French border; the Sierra Nevada, south of Granada; rolling plains with big skies in La Mancha and with the addition of cork trees and bulls grazing in Extremadura; striking landscapes of the meseta in Castilla y León; deserts once used as locations for 'spaghetti westerns' in Almería; green, fertile and hilly Galicia, complete with dramatic (if oil-stained) coastline; many other mountain ranges throughout the country such as the Sierras de Madrid, Cazorla (in Jaén) and Cádiz
Independent states within Spain: None but the country has 17 'Autonomous Communities' (*Comunidades Autónomas*), each with its own Assembly, plus the North African enclaves of Ceuta and Melilla. Some have had a greater range of powers devolved than others. These are: Andalucía; Aragón; Asturias; Ceuta (an enclave in Morocco); Canarias (Canary Islands); Cantabria; Castilla-La Mancha; Castilla y León; Catalunya (Catalonia); Comunitat Valencià (Community of Valencia); Extremadura; Euskadi (the Basque country's name in Basque, referred to in Castilian as País Vasco); Galiza (Galicia in its own language); Illes Balears (Balearic Islands in the dialect of Catalan spoken there); La Rioja; Madrid; Melilla (an enclave in Morocco); Murcia; Navarra
Languages and dialects: Castilian Spanish (Castellano); Catalan (Català); Galician (Galego) and Basque (Euskera)
Bordering countries: France, Portugal, Gibraltar, Andorra, Morocco
Surrounding seas: Mediterranean, Atlantic
Population: 40,217,413 (July 2003 estimate)
Religion: Roman Catholic 94 per cent; other 6 per cent
GDP purchasing power parity: $838 billion (2004 estimate); €699 billion
GDP growth rate: 2 per cent (2002 estimate)
GDP per capita: $23,300 (2004 estimate) €19,187
Unemployment: 10.5 per cent (2004 estimate)

Further Reading

Reference

Nick Rider, Harvey Holtom, John Howell, *Buying a Property in Spain* (Cadogan Guides).
Harvey Holtom, *Working and Living in Spain* (Cadogan Guides).
Alec and Erna Fry, *Finca – Renovating an Old Farmhouse in Spain* (Santana Books).
David Searl, *You and The Law in Spain* (Santana Books).
John Howell, *Guide to Buying a Property Overseas* (Moneycorp).
Facaros, Dana and Michael Pauls, *Spain* (Cadogan Guides); *Andalucia* (Cadogan Guides); *Northern Spain* (Cadogan Guides); *Bilbao and the Basque Lands* (Cadogan Guides); *Madrid* (Cadogan Guides); *Barcelona* (Cadogan Guides).

History

Brenan, Gerald, *The Spanish Labyrinth* (CUP).
Carr, Raymond, *The Spanish Tragedy* (Weidenfeld).
Fletcher, Richard, *Moorish Spain* (Phoenix).
Orwell, George, *Homage to Catalonia* (Penguin).
Preston, Paul, *Franco, a Biography* (Harper-Collins).
Thomas, Hugh, *The Spanish Civil War* (Penguin).
Vilar, Pierre, *Spain, a Brief History.*

Modern Spain

Carr, Raymond, *Modern Spain* (Opus).
Elms, Robert, *Spain, A Portrait After the General* (Mandarin).
Hooper, John, *The New Spaniards* (Penguin Books).
Preston, Paul, *The Triumph of Democracy in Spain* (Routledge).

Magazines

A Place in the Sun, Brooklands Magazines
Everything Spain, Brooklands Magazines
Homes Overseas, Blendon Communications
International Homes Magazine, International Property
Living Spain, Albany Publishing
Spain Magazine, The Media Company
Spanish Homes Magazine, Future Publishing
Spanish Magazine, Merricks Media
Viva España, Blendon Communications
World of Property, Outbound Media

Contacts

Emergency Numbers

Guardia Civil emergencies t 062

Police (*Policia*) emergencies t 091

Ambulance (*Ambulancia*) t 061

Fire service (*Bomberos*) t 080

National Police (*Policia*) t 091

General purpose emergency number t 112

Directory inquiries t 1003

International operator t 1008

Maritime rescue and security (*Salvamento y seguridad maritino*) t 900 202 202

Business Contacts

Ministries & Agencies
ICEX – Instituto Español de Comercio Exterior
Spanish Ministry of Economy,
Paseo de la Castellana 14–16, 28046 Madrid
t 91 349 61 00
f 91 349 61 20
icex@icex.es
www.investinspain.org

Inland Revenue
Centre for Non-Residents, Longbenton, Newcastle Upon Tyne, NE98 1ZZ
Pensions and Benefits Overseas Directorate **t** 0191 218 7777
Centre for Non-Residents Helpline
From the UK: **t** 0845 9154811, **f** 0845 9157800 (calls are charged at BT local rate)
From outside the UK: **t** 0044 191 2254811, **f** 0044 191 2257800

Instituto Nacional de la Seguridad Social
Ministry of Social Security
Padre Damian 4, 28036 Madrid
t 915 688 300
www.seg-social.es/inicio

Ministerio de Agicultura, Pesca y Alimentación
Ministry of Agriculture, Fishing and Food
www.mapa.es

Ministerio de Economía Dirección General de Comercio e Inversiones
General Directorate for Trade & Investment, at the Spanish Ministry of Economy
Paseo de la Castellana 162 Planta 7 28071 Madrid
t 91 349 39 83
f 91 349 35 62
Buzon.Oficial@SGIEX
www.mineco.es

Ministerio de Educación y Ciencia
Ministry of Education and Science Information Service
c/ Alcala 36, 28071 Madrid
t 91 221 85 00
www.mec.es

Ministerio de Sanidad y Consumo
Ministry of Health and Consumer Affairs
Pº del Prado 18-20 (planta baja) 28014 Madrid
t 901 400 100
f 915 964 480
www.msc.es/home.jsp

Ministerio del Interior
Spanish Ministry of Interior
c/ General Pardinas, 90 Bis, 28071 Madrid
t 91 402 81 00
f 91 402 39 92
www.mir.es

Business Organisations
Dirección General de Aviación Civil
Paseo de la Castellana, 67, 28071 Madrid
t 91 597 70 00
f 91 597 70 00
www.mfom.es/aviacioncivil

Federación de Hostelería
Co de las Huertas 18 – 1ª Plta, 28223 Pozuelo de Alarcón, Madrid
t 91 352 91 56
f 91 352 90 26
www.fehr.es

International Franchise Association
1350 New York Avenue, NW Suite 900 Washington DC 20005-4709
t (202) 628 8000
f (202) 628 0812

Investment Promotion Bureau of SEPI
c/ Velázquez, 134, 28006 Madrid
t 91 396 10 84/14 73
f 91 396 12 26

Organización de Consumidores y Usuarios
Organisation for Consumers and Users
c/ Albarracin 21, 28037 Madrid
t 902 300 187
www.ocu.org

Servicio de Reclamaciónes Dirección General de Seguros y Fondos de Pensiones
Department for Complaints Against Insurance Companies
Paseo de la Catellana, 44, 28046 Madrid
t 91 339 70 70

Spanish Chamber of Commerce in Great Britain
126 Wigmore Street, London W1U 3RZ
t 020 7009 9070
f 020 7009 9088
www.spanishchamber.co.uk

UK Trade and Investment Information Centre
Kingsgate House, 66–74 Victoria Street, London SW1E 6SW
t 020 7215 8000
f 020 7215 4231
www.uktradeinvest.gov.uk

Intellectual Property
Centro de Documentación de la Propiedad Intelectual
Documentation Centre for Intellectual Property
Plaza del Rey 1, 1ª Planta, 28071 Madrid
t 91 701 70 00 Ext-32138
f 91 701 73 85

Oficina Española de Patentes y Marcas
Spanish Office of Patents and Trade Marks

c/ Panamá, 1, 28071 Madrid
t 91 792 58 04
f 91 349 55 97
www.oepm.es

Registro de Propiedad Intelectual Registro Central
Intellectual Property Registry
c/ Serrano, 150 – 4ª planta, 28006 Madrid
t 91 550 54 00
f 91 550 59 36

Subdirección General de la Propiedad Intelectual
Plaza del Rey 1, 1ª Planta, 28071 Madrid
t 91 701 70 00
f 91 701 73 85
www.mcu.es

Market Analysis
Business Monitor International
Mermaid House, 2 Puddle Dock, Blackfriars, London EC4V 3DS
t 020 7248 0468
f 020 7248 0467
www.businessmonitor.com

Datamonitor Europe
Charles House, 108–110 Finchley Road, London NW3 5JJ
t 020 7675 7000
f 020 7675 7500
euroinfo@datamonitor.com
www.datamonitor.com

Euromonitor Plc
60–61 Britton Street, London EC1M 5UX
t 020 7251 8024
f 020 7608 3149
info@euromonitor.com
www.euromonitor.com

Other Organisations
Blevins Franks
Tax and Financial Planners

Barbican House, 26–34 Old Street, London EC1V 9QQ
t 020 7336 1000
f 020 7336 1100
info@blevinsfranks.com
www.blevinsfrank.com

British Chamber of Commerce in Spain
Bruc 21, 10, 40, 08010 Barcelona
t 93 317 32 20
f 93 302 48 96
britchamber@britchamber.com www.britishchamberspain.com

Entidad Estatal de Seguros Agrarios
National Farming Insurance Body
c/ Miguel Angel, 23 – 5ª planta, 28010 Madrid
t 91 308 10 30/32
f 91 308 54 46

Fundación Institito de Propietarios Extranjeros (FIPE)
Institute of Foreign Property Owners
Apartado 418, 03590 Altea
t 96 584 23 12
f 96 584 15 89
www.fipe.org

John Howell & Co
Solicitors and International Lawyers
22 Endell Street, Covent Garden, London WC2H 9AD
t 020 7420 0400
f 020 7836 3626
www.europelaw.com

Spanish Embassies and Consulates in the United Kingdom and Republic of Ireland

Spanish Embassy, United Kingdom
39 Chesham Place, London SW1X 8SB
t (020) 7235 5555
f (020) 7259 5392
embespuk@mail.mae.es

Spanish Consulate General
20 Draycott Place, London SW3 2RZ
t (020) 7589 8989
f (020) 7581 7888
conspalon@mail.mae.es

Spanish Consulate: Manchester
Suite 1A, Brook House, 70 Spring Gardens, Manchester M2 2BQ
t (0161) 236 1262
f (0161) 228 7467
conspmanchester@mail.mae.es

Spanish Consulate: Edinburgh
63 North Castle Street, Edinburgh EH2 3LJ
t (0131) 220 1843/220 1439/220 1442
f (0131) 226 4568
cgspedimburgo@mail.mae.es

Spanish Embassy: Ireland
17 Merlyn Park, Ballsbridge, Dublin 4, Republic of Ireland
t (01) 269 1640/ 269 2597/ 283 8827/ 283 9900
f (01) 269 1854/ 269 2705
www.mae.es/embajadas/dublin/

United Kingdom Embassy and Consulates in Spain

British Embassy in Madrid
c/ Fernando el Santo 16, 28010 Madrid
t 91 700 82 00
f 91 700 82 72
presslibrary@ukinspain.com
www.ukinspain.com

British Consulates, Vice-Consulates and Honorary Consuls in Spain

For a full listing, see **www.ukinspain.com**

Republic of Ireland Embassy and Consulates in Spain

Embassy of Ireland
Ireland House, Paseo de la Castellana 46, 4°, 28046 Madrid
t 91 576 3500
f 91 435 1677
embajadairlanda@terra.es

Honorary Vice-Consul: Barcelona
Gran Vía Carlos III 94, 08028 Barcelona
t 93 451 9021
f 93 411 2921

Honorary Consul: Málaga
Galerías Santa Mónica, Avenida Los Boliches 15, 29640 Fuengirola, Málaga
t 95 246 6783
f 95 246 6783

Other Foreign Embassies and Consulates in Spain

Australian Embassy
Plaza del Descubridor Diego de Ordas 3, 28003 Madrid
t 914 416 025
f 914 425 362
www.spain.embassy.gov.au

Australian Consulate, Barcelona
Gran Via Carlos III 98, 9°, 08028 Barcelona
t 93 490 9013
f 93 411 0904
habitat@habitat-sa.es

Australian Consulate, Seville
c/ Federico Rubio 14, 41004 Sevilla
t 95 422 0971
f 95 421 1145

Canadian Embassy
c/ Núñez de Balboa 35, 28001 Madrid
t 91 423 3250
f 91 423 3252
www.canada-es.org

New Zealand Embassy
Plaza de la Lealtad 2, 3°, 28014 Madrid
t 91 523 0226
www.nzembassy.com/home.cfm?c=27

United States of America Embassy
c/ Serrano 75, 28006 Madrid
t 91 587 2200
f 91 587 2303
www.embusa.es

For a full listing of US Consulates in Spain, *see* www.embusa.es

Spanish Area Telephone Codes

Aguilas	968	Lorca	968
Albacete	967	Lugo	982
Alcira	96	Madrid	91
Alcoy	96	Mahon	971
Algeciras	956	Málaga	95
Alicante	96	Marbella	95
Almería	950	Merida	924
Arrecife	928	Murcia	968
Avila	920	Orense	988
Aviles	98	Oviedo	98
Badajoz	924	Palencia	979
Barcelona	93	Palma de Mallorca	971
Benidorm	96	Pamplona	948
Bilbao	94	Pontevedra	986
Burgos	947	Reus	977
Caceres	927	Sabadell	93
Cádiz	956	Sagunto	96
Cartagena	968	Salamanca	923
Castellon de la Plana	964	San Feliu de Llobregat	93
Ceuta	956	San Sabastian	943
Ciudad Real	926	Santa Cruz de Tenerife	922
Córdoba	957	Santander	942
Cuenca	969	Santiago de Compostela	981
Gandia	96	Segovia	921
Gerona	972	Sevilla	95
Gijon	98	Tarragona	977
Granada	958	Tarrasa	93
Guadalajara	949	Tenerife	922
Huelva	959	Terval	978
Ibiza	971	Toledo	925
Irun	943	Torremolinos	95
Jaen	953	Tortosa	977
Jerez de la Frontera	956	Valencia	96
La Coruna	981	Valladolid	983
Lanzarote	928	Vigo	986
Las Palmas	928	Vitoria	945
León	987	Zamora	980
Lerida	973	Zaragoza	976
Linares	953		
Logrono	941		

Regional Climate Chart/Rainfall

Average monthly temperatures °Centigrade (daily maximum and
minimum) and Rainfall (monthly mm)

	Jan	Feb	Mar	Apr	May	June	July	Aug	Sept	Oct	Nov	Dec
Málaga												
Max	17	15	18	20	24	27	30	30	28	23	20	17
Min	11	7	12	11	14	17	20	20	18	16	13	10
Rainfall	8	8	7	9	6	3	1	1	3	8	9	9
Alicante												
Max	18	19	22	26	28	31	34	31	24	24	18	17
Min	7	8	13	15	19	20	21	22	18	14	12	8
Rainfall	9	6	9	9	6	6	3	5	7	8	10	7
Majorca												
Max	17	10	17	18	23	25	31	32	29	22	19	17
Min	4	0	7	7	8	14	16	18	18	13	8	7
Rainfall	13	11	9	11	5	5	3	4	9	11	11	10
Madrid												
Max	9	11	15	18	21	27	31	30	25	19	13	9
Min	2	2	5	7	10	15	17	17	14	10	5	2
Rainfall	8	8	10	9	7	6	3	3	4	7	8	9
Las Palmas												
Max	13	14	16	18	21	25	28	28	25	21	16	13
Min	6	7	9	11	14	18	21	21	19	15	11	8
Rainfall	7	7	9	8	6	6	4	5	7	8	6	6
Tenerife												
Max	21	22	23	22	23	23	27	28	27	26	24	22
Min	16	16	16	16	17	17	21	22	22	21	19	17
Rainfall	3	3	4	3	2	2	0	1	2	2	5	4
Barcelona												
Max	13	14	16	18	21	25	28	28	25	21	16	13
Min	6	7	9	11	14	18	21	21	19	15	11	8
Rainfall	31	39	48	43	54	37	27	49	76	86	52	45
A Coruña												
Max	13	13	15	16	18	20	22	23	22	19	15	13
Min	7	7	8	9	11	13	15	15	14	12	9	8
Rainfall	118	80	92	67	54	45	28	46	61	87	124	135
Santander												
Max	12	12	14	15	17	20	22	22	21	18	15	13
Min	7	7	8	10	11	14	16	16	15	12	10	8
Rainfall	119	88	78	83	89	63	54	84	114	133	125	159

Largest Cities

By Population of Municipality	By Population of Metropolitan Area
1. Madrid 3,092,759	1. Madrid 5,603,285
2. Barcelona 1,582,738	2. Barcelona 4,667,136
3. Valencia 780,653	3. Valencia 1,465,423
4. Seville 709,975	4. Seville 1,294,081
5. Zaragoza 626,081	5. Málaga 1,019,292
6. Málaga 547,105	6. Bilbao/Bilbo 946,829
7. Murcia 391,146	7. Gijón/Avilés/Oviedo 850,097
8. Las Palmas de Gran Canaria 377,600	8. Alicante 676,237
9. Palma de Mallorca 367,277	9. Zaragoza 656,922
10. Bilbao/Bilbo 353,567	10. Las Palmas de Gran Canaria 609,628
11. Valladolid 321,143	11. Murcia 557,583
12. Córdoba 318,628	12. Palma de Mallorca 462,010
13. Alicante/Alacant 305,911	13. Granada 450,439
14. Vigo 292,566	14. Vigo 420,672
15. Gijón/Xixón 270,875	15. Santa Cruz de Tenerife 409,621
16. L'Hospitalet de Llobregat 246,415	16. Cádiz 406,095
17. A Coruña 243,902	17. San Sebastian/Donostia 395,758
18. Granada 237,663	18. A Coruña 388,692
19. Vitoria/Gasteiz 223,257	19. Valladolid 377,562
20. Santa Cruz de Tenerife 220,022	20. Tarragona 348,921
21. Badalona 214,440	21. Córdoba 318,628
22. Oviedo/Uvieú 207,699	
23. Elche/Elx 207,163	
24. Móstoles 201,789	

Dictionary of Useful and Technical Terms

For useful vocabulary relating to finding accommodation *see* **Living in Spain**, 'Housing Jargon', p.176. For reasons of space I have concentrated on Castilian (or 'Spanish' as it is most commonly known) to the detriment of Catalan, Galician and Basque.

Everyday Words and Phrases

Hola	Hello
Adiós/hasta luego	Goodbye
Buenos días/Buenas tardes	Good morning/afternoon
Buenas noches	Goodnight
Por favor	Please
(muchas) gracias	Thank you (very much)
De nada	You're welcome
Con permiso/¿Me permite?	Excuse me
Disculpe/Perdón	I am sorry (apologising)
Lo siento (mucho)	I am sorry (expressing regret)
No importa	It doesn't matter
De acuerdo/Está bien	All right
Vale	Okay
Sí	Yes
No	No
Nada	Nothing
No (lo) sé	I don't know
No hablo español (castellano)	I don't speak Spanish (Castilian)
Hablas/Habla usted inglés?	Do you speak English?
¿Hay alguien que hable ingles?	Does anyone here speak English?
Por favor, hable más despacio	Please, speak slowly
¿Me puede(s) ayudar?	Can you help me?
¡Socorro!	Help!
¿Cómo estás/está usted?	How do you do?
Bien, gracias, ¿y tú/usted?	Well, and you?
¿Cómo te llamas/se llama?	What is your name?
Yo me llamo ...	My name is ...
¿De donde eres/es usted?	Where are you from?
Yo soy de ...	I am from ...
¿Qué es esto/eso?	What is this/that?
¿Qué?	What?
¿Quién?	Who?
¿Dónde?	Where?
¿Cuándo?	When?
¿Por qué?	Why?
¿Cómo?	How?

¿Cuánto/a?	How much?
¿Cuántos/as?	How many?
Me he perdido	I am lost
Tengo hambre/sed	I am hungry/thirsty
Estoy cansado/a	I am tired
Me siento mal	I am ill
Bueno/Malo	Good/bad
Despacio/Rápido	Slow/fast
Grande/Pequeño	Big/small
Caliente/Frío	Hot/cold

Los Números   Numbers

Uno/una	1
Dos	2
Tres	3
Cuatro	4
Cinco	5
Seis	6
Siete	7
Ocho	8
Nueve	9
Diez	10
Once	11
Doce	12
Trece	13
Catorce	14
Quince	15
Dieciséis	16
Diecisiete	17
Dieciocho	18
Diecinueve	19
Veinte	20
Veintiuno	21
Veintidós	22
Treinta	30
Cuarenta	40
Cincuenta	50
Sesenta	60
Setenta	70
Ochenta	80
Noventa	90
Cien	100
Ciento uno	101
Doscientos/as	200
Trescientos/as	300

Cuatrocientos/as	400
Quinientos/as	500
Seiscientos/as	600
Setecientos/as	700
Ochocientos/as	800
Novecientos/as	900
Mil	1,000
Un millón	1 million

La Hora   The Time

¿Qué hora es?	What's the time?
¿Tienes/llevas la hora?	Have you got the time?
Es la una	It's one o'clock
Son las dos/tres/cuatro etc...	It's two/three/four etc. o'clock
Son las ... y cinco/diez/veinte/veinticinco	It's 5/10/20/25 past ...
Son las ... menos cinco/diez/veinte/ veinticinco	It's 5/10/20/25 to ...
Son las ... y cuarto/media	It's quarter/half past ...
Son las ... menos cuarto	It's quarter to ...
El amanecer	Dawn
La madrugada	The early hours
(La) mañana	Morning
(El) mediodía	Noon
(La) tarde	Afternoon
(La) tarde/noche (before/after sundown)	Evening
La noche	Night
Ayer	Yesterday
Mañana	Tomorrow
La semana pasada/el mes/año pasado	Last week/month/year
Anteayer	The day before yesterday
Ahora	Now
Más tarde	Later
Temprano/pronto	Early
Tarde	Late
La semana/el mes/año que viene	Next week/month/year

Las Estaciones   Seasons

La primavera	Spring
El verano	Summer
El otoño	Autumn
El invierno	Winter

Los Días

Lunes	Monday
Martes	Tuesday
Miércoles	Wednesday
Jueves	Thursday
Viernes	Friday
Sábado	Saturday
Domingo	Sunday

Days

Los Meses

Enero	January
Febrero	February
Marzo	March
Abril	April
Mayo	May
Junio	June
Julio	July
Agosto	August
Septiembre	September
Noviembre	November
Octubre	October
Diciembre	December

Months

De Viaje

Avión	Aeroplane
Aeropuerto	Airport
Reservación/Reserva/Reservar un billete	Booking/to book a ticket
Autobús/Autocar	Bus/coach
Estación de autobuses/trenes	Bus/railway station
Aduana	Customs
Vuelo	Flight
Viaje	Journey/trip
Andén	Platform
Asiento	Seat
Barco	Ship
Billete	Ticket
Viaje de ida/ida y vuelta	One way/return trip
Tren	Train
Consigna	Left luggage
Horario	Timetable/schedule
¿Dónde está el/la ...?	Where is the ...?
¿Cómo puedo llegar al/a la ...?	How can I get to the ...?

On the Move

¿A qué hora sale el próximo ...?	When is the next ...?
¿A qué hora sale/parte?	What time does it leave/arrive?
¿De dónde sale/parte?	Where does it leave from?
Quiero un billete a/un billete de ida y vuelta a ...	I want a single/return ticket to ...
¿Cuánto cuesta el billete?	How much is the fare?
Aquí/allí/allá (the last one means 'even further')	Here/there
Cerca/lejos	Near/far
A la izquierda/derecha	Left/right
Todo recto/directo	Straight on
La primera/segunda a la izquierda/ derecha	First/second left/ right
Calle	Street
Plaza	Square
Esquina	Corner

En el Camino

On the Road

Coche	Car
Bicicleta	Bicycle
Moto	Motorbike
Gasolina	Petrol
Aceite	Oil
Gasolinera	Garage (for petrol)
Taller (mecánico)	Garage (for car repairs)
Carretera	Road
Autopista	Motorway
Autovía	Main road/highway
Carretera comarcal	Back/country road/lane
Permiso de conducir	Driving licence
Salida	Exit
Entrada	Entrance
Peligro	Danger
No aparcar/estacionar or estacionamiento prohibido	No parking
Límite de velocidad	Speed limit
Disminuir velocidad	Slow down
Ceda el paso	Give way
Obras	Roadworks
Alquiler de coches	Rent (cars)

De Compras, Por la Ciudad, Servicios y Personas Utiles

Shopping, Around Town, Services and Useful People

Banco	Bank
Grandes almacenes	Department store
Tiendas	Shops (of all types)
Mercado	Market
Centro comercial	Shopping centre/mall
Correos	Post office
Sellos	Stamps
Abierto/a/cerrado/a	Open/closed
Farmacia	Chemist's (for prescriptions)
Ambulatorio	Health centre
Urgencias	Emergency ward/out patients
¿Cuánto es/son ...?	How much is/are ...?
¿Dónde está el/la ... mas cercano/a?	Where is the nearest ...? or Is there a ... near
Or ¿Hay un/a ... cerca de aquí?	here?
¿Puede cambiar un billete (de cincuenta euros?)	Can you change a (€50) note?
¿Tiene/Me puede dar cambio para el teléfono/tabaco etc.?	Have you got any change (for the telephone/cigarette machine, etc.)?
Comisaría	Police station
Bomberos	Fire service
Museo	Museum
Teatro	Theatre
Cine	Cinema
Oficina de turismo	Tourist office
Taquilla	Box/booking office
Agencia de viajes	Travel agency
Servicios/aseos	Toilets
Hombres/Caballeros	Men
Mujeres/Damas	Women
Fontanero	Plumber
Electricista	Electrician
Mecánico	Mechanic
Carpintero	Carpenter
Albañil	Builder/bricklayer
Abogado	Lawyer
Gestor	'Administrative service provider' (no real translation exists, see p.132)
Trámites	Red tape/bureaucratic procedures
La Hacienda	Tax office
Oficina de Empleo (INEM)	Employment office
Ministerio de(l) educación/justicia/ interior etc. ...	Ministry of education/justice/the interior (home office), etc. ...

Comer Fuera

Restaurante	Restaurant
Menú del día	Fixed-price set menu
Carta	Menu
Lista de vinos	Wine list
Comer a la carta	To eat *à la carte*
Camarero/a	Waiter/waitress
Entradas/primer plato	Starters
Segundo	Main course
Verduras	Vegetables
Ensalada	Salad
Carne	Meat
Pescado	Fish
Mariscos	Seafood
Postre	Sweet
La cuenta	Bill
¿Tiene una mesa para una/ dos persona(s)?	Have you got a table for one/two?
¿Me puede dejar la lista de vinos, por favor?	Can I see the menu/wine list?
¿Me trae la cuenta, por favor?	Can you bring me the bill please?
¿Puedo pagar con tarjeta?	Can I pay by credit card?
Or *¿Admiten/Aceptan tarjetas?*	Do you take credit cards?

Eating Out

Internet Vocabulary

Base de datos	Database
Borrar/Suprimir/Cancelar	Delete
Arroba	@
Descifrar	Decode
Barra barra/doble barra	//
Dos puntos	: (colon)
En línea	Online
Dirección de correo electrónico/correo-e/e-mail	Email address
Guión bajo	_ (underline)
Punto	. (dot)
Red (La red)	Network
Buscar	To browse
Barra	/ (forward slash)
Apagar (el equipo)	Shut down
Guión	- (hyphen)
Usuario	User
Uve doble, uve doble, uve doble/tres uve dobles	www

Public Holidays and Celebrations

Days celebrated nationwide are asterisked; others are celebrated almost everywhere:

1 January*	New Year's Day (Año Nuevo)
6 January	Epiphany or Kings' Day (Reyes Magos)
19 March	San José (Día de San José)
March/April*	Good Friday, Viernes Santo
Easter (Holy Week)*	Semana Santa
Easter Monday	
1 May*	International Labour Day (Fiesta del Trabajo)
May/June	Corpus Christi, on the 2nd Thursday after Whitsun
	Ascension Day (Ascensión) 40 days after Easter
15 August*	Assumption of the Virgin (Asunción)
12 October*	Virgin of Pilar, National Day (Día de la Virgen del Pilar)
8 December*	Immaculate Conception (Inmaculada Concepción)
25 December*	Christmas (Navidad)

Spain's fiestas are rightly famous worldwide. Every city, town and village has fiestas in honour of its patron saint while many others are national events. Local tourist offices provide full information of fiestas in every town. Some major celebrations are:

31 December	New Year's Eve: a large family dinner, everyone eats a grape with each chime of the clock just before midnight to bring good luck for the new year.
1 January	New Year's Day is quiet but is a public holiday.
5 January	In most of Spain processions celebrate the coming of the Reyes Magos (the Three Kings), who will bring children presents the next morning.
6 January	Reyes or Epifanía. More important than Christmas for many; children receive their 'big' presents, and naughty children are threatened with just a piece of coal, usually made of sugar (few really go without presents).
January–February	Carnival, Carnaval, an occasion for dressing up and revelling. Most spectacular in Cádiz and Tenerife, the latter considered second only to Rio de Janeiro's.
March or April	Easter, Semana Santa, a major fiesta throughout Spain. The most spectacular processions are in Andalucía.
19 March	Fallas, in Valencia, during the week before San José (19 March) paper-maché caricature statues of celebrities adorn the streets and are then burnt. Impressive fireworks.
April	Feria de Abril, Seville. The April Fair is a week-long party. Womenfolk wear traditional flamenco dresses, singing, dancing and sherry-drinking into the small hours.

23 April	*Sant Jordi* (Saint George in Catalan). Men give their loved one a rose, she (or he) responds with a book. Now common throughout Spain.
Whitsuntide	Fifty days after Easter Sunday this colourful mass pilgrimage goes to the shrine of El Rocío in the village of Almonte, Huelva. Traditional Andalucian garb and two days of merry-making in Doñana park.
1 May	International Labour day, less significant politically nowadays but large union-organised marches throughout Spain.
June	Corpus Christi is celebrated nationally but the processions and other festivities are especially colourful in Andalucía, Salamanca, Toledo and Barcelona.
June	*San Juan*, the shortest night of the year, celebrated throughout Spain. People jump over bonfires three times (an act of purification). Most spectacular in Alicante.
6 July	*San Fermín*, a week-long fiesta in Pamplona. The main attraction is bull-running (*encierros*). Bullfights every afternoon plus dances, processions and copious eating and drinking.
July–August	During the summer practically every village in Spain celebrates its local fiestas with concerts and dances in the main square.
15 August	The Assumption of the Virgin, *Asunción*, is celebrated nationally.
12 October	A national fiesta, known as *El Día de la Raza* (Day of the Race) or *El Día de la Hispanidad* (Day of the Hispanic World). The Virgin of Pilar is venerated, particularly in Zaragoza.
1 November	All Saints' Day, *Día de Todos los Santos*.
2 November	All Souls' Day, when people take flowers to the tombs of their dead relatives.
8 December	Immaculate Conception, *La Inmaculada Concepción*.
25 December	*Navidad,* Christmas. Celebrated with gifts and, more recently, a tree, but tradition calls for a *Belén*, a Nativity scene with handmade figurines. The big family meal is on Christmas Eve, *Noche Buena*, roast lamb is preferred to turkey. Boxing Day is not a holiday.

Spain touring atlas

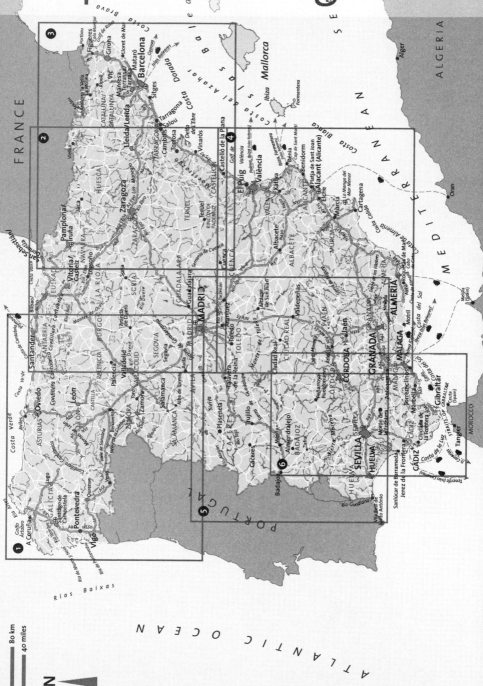

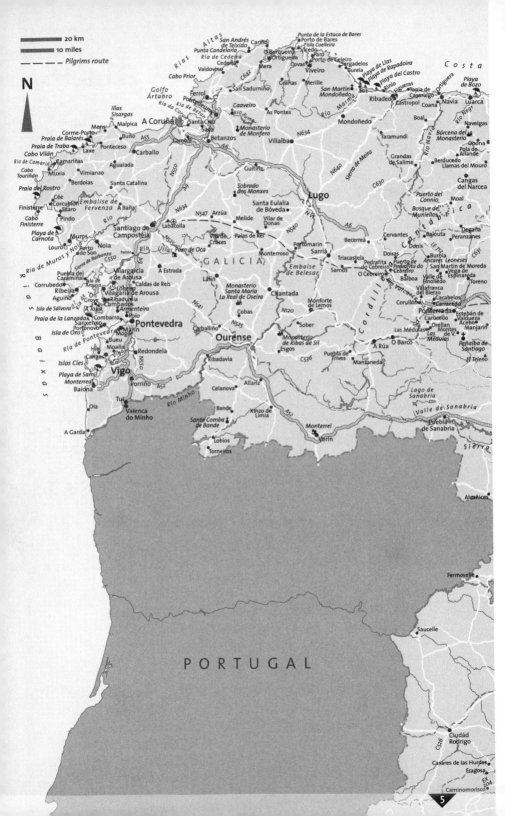

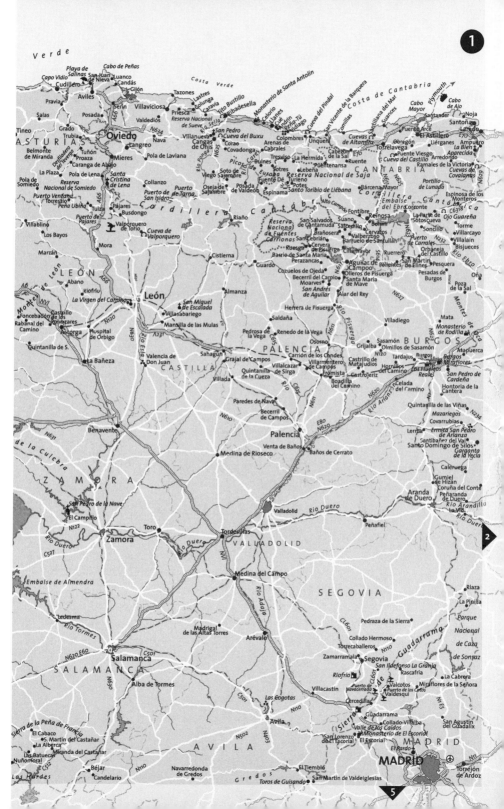

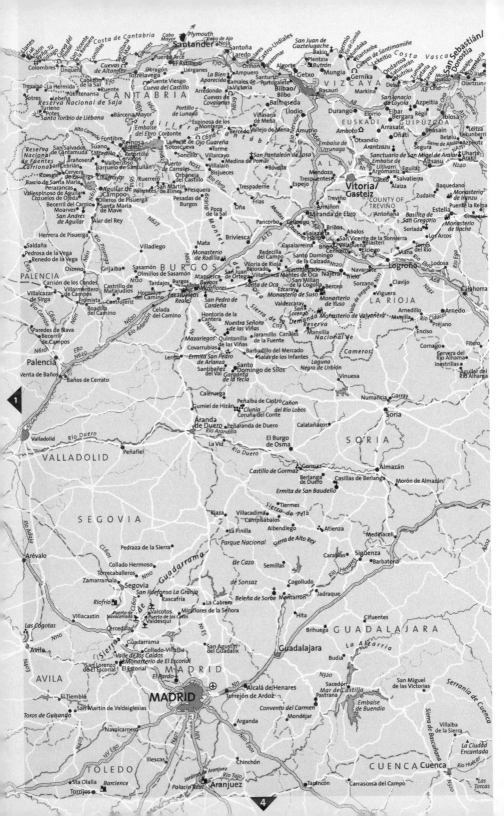

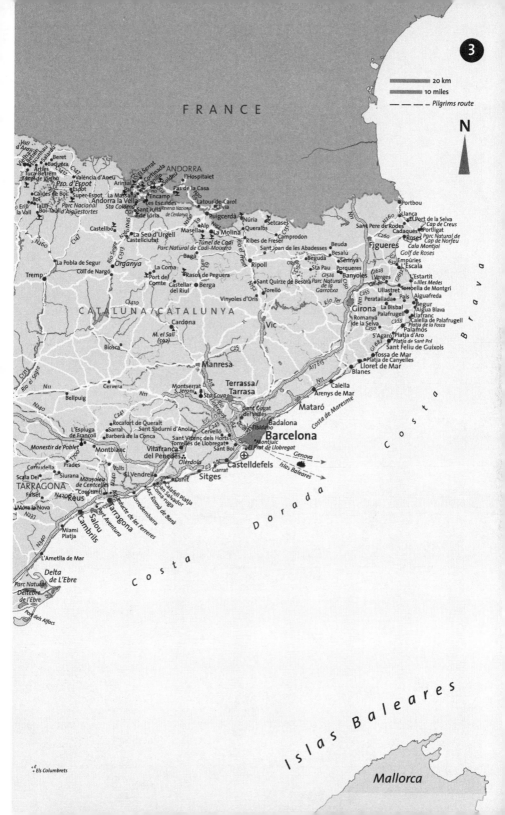

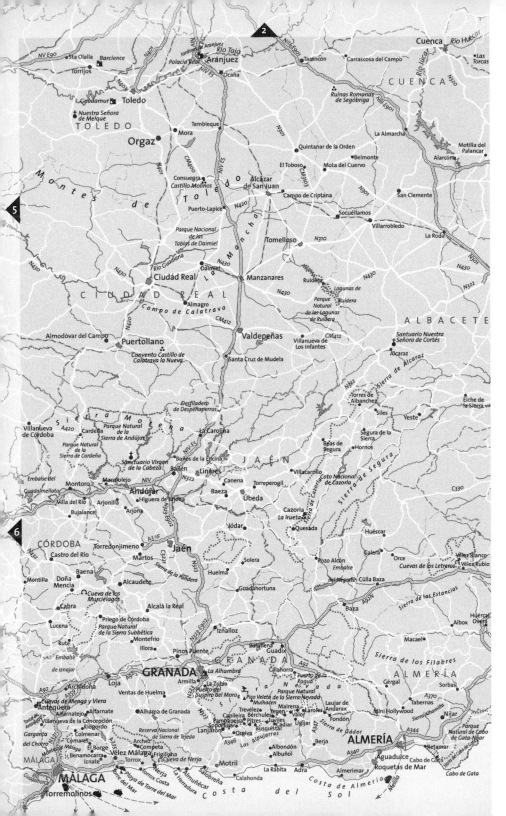

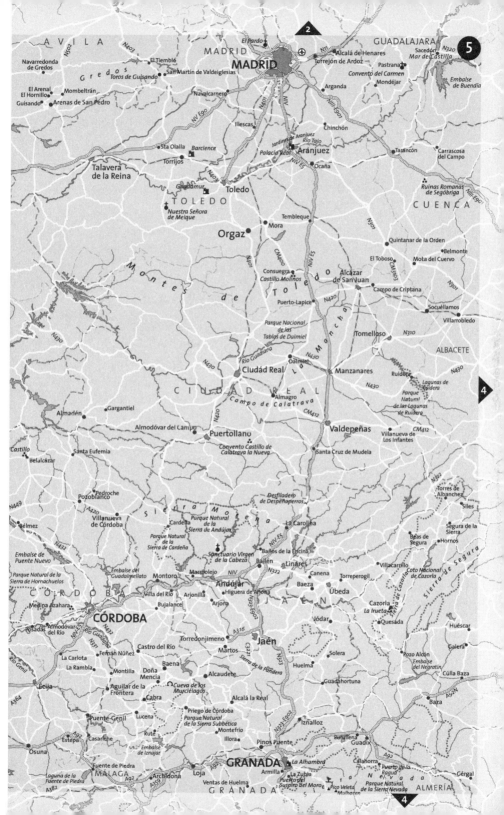

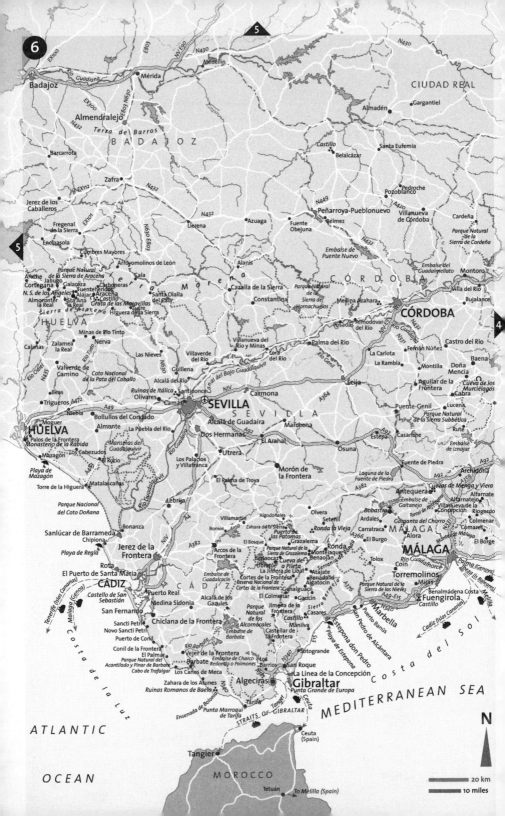

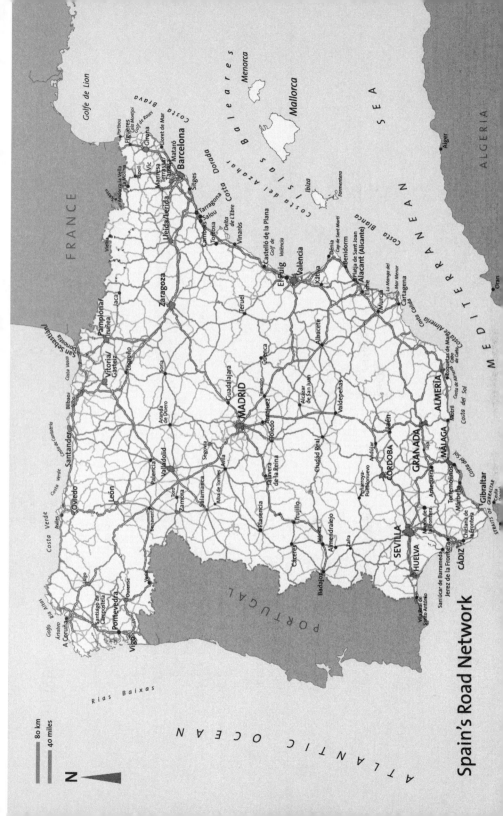

Spain's Road Network

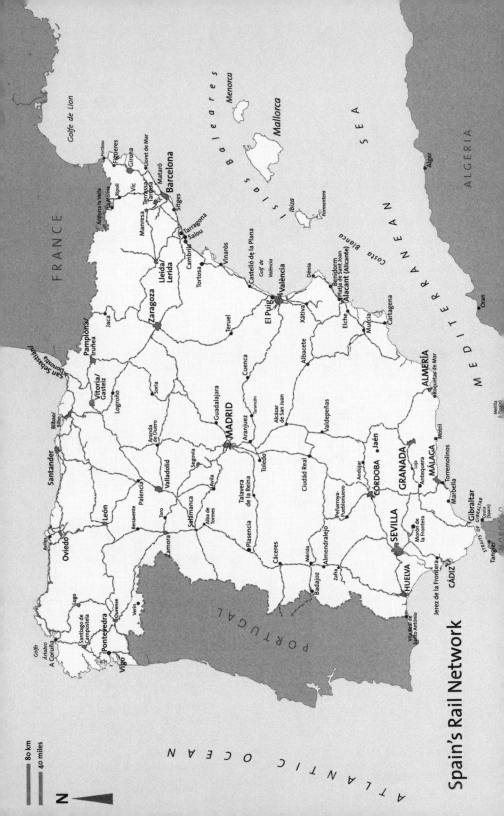

Spain's Rail Network

Appendices

Appendix 1 250
Sample CV in Spanish 250

Appendix 2 251
Sample Job Application Letter 251

Appendix 3 253
Spanish Business Plan 253

Appendix 4 259
Types of Spanish Business Structure 259

Appendix 5 261
Wealth and Inheritance Tax 261

10

Appendix 1

Currículum vitae

DATOS PERSONALES
Nombre: Insert your name
Lugar y fecha de nacimiento: Insert your place and date of birth
Nacionalidad: Insert your nationality
Estado Civil: Insert your marital status
Dirección: Insert your address
Teléfonos de contacto: Insert your contact telephone numbers
e-Mail: Insert your email address

FORMACIÓN ACADÉMICA
Insert your academic history, e.g.:
    Masters in Electrical Engineering at Staffordshire University, England, 1995
    Degree in Electronics at Keele University, England, 1994. 2:1 achieved.
Notes: A degree is a *licenciatura*
    A B.A. is roughly translated as *licenciatura en letras*
    A B.Sc. is roughly translated as *licenciatura en ciencias*
    'A' levels are roughly translated as *bachillerato superior*
    The grades will also require explaining.

FORMACIÓN COMPLEMENTARIA
Insert any additional education and courses that you may have received, e.g.:
    Course on the relevance of electrical engineering in modern day society, 1997
    Marketing course at Stockport College, England, 1996

IDOMAS
Insert any languages spoken and the level, e.g.:
English – mother tongue.
Spanish written and oral to advanced level.

INFORMÁTICA
Insert any IT skills, e.g.:
Advanced use of Microsoft Office (Word, Outlook, Power Point)
Advanced use of Windows XP.
Advanced use of internet and intranet.

EXPERIENCIA PROFESIONAL
Insert professional working experience, e.g.:
june 1999 – april 2003: Team leader ABC S.A. Bilbao.
september 1996 – june 1999: Project manager at XYZ S.L., Madrid.
Note: Names of months use lower case initial letters.

OTROS DATOS DE INTERÉS
Insert other important details, e.g.:
Full driving licence

Appendix 2

Sample Job Application Letter

If you send a CV on its own it will end up in the bin. You need to enclose a covering letter. This should be addressed to the person listed in the advertisement or the director of human resources (*El Director de Personal*) if sent 'on spec'.

Insert your name:
Insert your address:

Enter the date:

Enter the address that the letter is being sent to:

Estimado señor,

En respuesta al anuncio publicado en [name of place where the advertisement was placed] con fecha [insert date], referente al puesto de [insert job description], me dirijo a usted para presentar mi candidatura a dicho puesto.

Soy recién Licenciada en [insert your degree] y me gustaría, si es posible, trabajar en vuestra compañía. Considero las actividades de vuestra compañía muy interesante y considero mi experiencia útil para vuestras actividades.

Agradezco su atención y quedo a su disposición para cualquier aclaración.

Le saluda cordialmente,

Stephen Allan

Anexo: Currículum vitae

A rough translation of the above letter can be found over the page:

Insert your name:

Insert your address:

Enter the date:

Enter the address that the letter is being sent to:

Dear Sir,

In response to your advert placed in [name of place where the advertisement was placed] dated [insert date], relating to the position of [insert job description], I present myself as a candidate for the said post.

I have recently graduated in [insert your degree] and I would like, if it is possible, to work at your firm. I consider the activities carried out by your firm very interesting and also consider my experience useful for those activities.

I thank you for your attention and am at your disposal for any clarification that you may require.

Yours sincerely,

Stephen Allan

Enclosed: Curriculum vitae

Appendix 3

Spanish Format Business Plan

Basic details

1. Name of the business, i.e. the name of the company and any trading name.

2. A description of the area where the business is going to operate (province, town, etc.)

3. Confirmation of the date when the business started, or if the business hasn't started yet when it is intended to start the business.

4. Type of business – whether it is going to be a partnership, a limited company or any other type of business structure. See 'Business Structures', p.94.

5. A brief description of the activities that the business is going to carry out. This should state the type of business, its characteristics, the sector that the business is going to operate within and any competitive advantages that the business has over its competition.

6. The number of staff and employees that the business envisages that it will need.

7. A summary of the investment required in the business. This should set out how much is needed as an investment along with a description of how this finance is to be raised – i.e. whether the finance is coming from your own funds or whether it is coming from an external source.

Total investment required
.... euros

Own capital invested
.... euros

Other finance required
.... euros

Owners of the business

You should identify the owners of the business and provide their personal details, such as full names, addresses, identity or passport numbers and any other relevant personal details.

You should set out a brief professional history of the owners of the business. The aim of this is to show the credibility of the people running the business. This is a sort of mini CV and should include;

1. Profile of the owners, including education, professional experience, success in their working life and so on.

2. Experience of the owners that is specifically relevant to the project.

Description of the goods or services that the business will provide
Identification of the goods or services
In this section you must fully describe the products or services that you are going to offer.

Description of the technical characteristics of the products or services
What is the basic concept and technical characteristics of the products or services? Set out the advantages that your product or services have.

Description of any innovative elements
Set out any specifications which are innovative and which make your product different from any existing competitors that is currently in the marketplace.

Production plan
This sets out all the technical and organisational details relating to the production of the goods or services.

Technical description
In this section you must include details of design and production of the goods (if there is to be any production of goods). If you are going to provide a service then you should set out the details of any technical aspects involved in the provision of the service.

In the case of production of goods you must start off discussing the timescale for investigation into the production of the goods, discussing the necessary investment in labour, equipment, prototypes, customer clinics, and any other steps that are necessary in order to produce the final product.

You must set out all the risks and difficulties inherent in the process, possibility of improvements in the short or medium term, any new products that will need to be developed, the production costs and any intellectual property rights that come from the product.

Description of the production process
You must give attention to the following aspects of the production process:
- Geographical location of the production, cost of production, environmental issues, proximity to raw materials and so on.
- Buildings and land necessary for the business, any expansion plans, description of how the buildings and land are to be acquired, maintenance costs, layout and cost of fixtures and fittings.
- Equipment necessary for the production of the goods or the provision of services, characteristics, method of sale, production capacity, estimated cost, calendar of stock purchase and life of any equipment.
- Detailed description of the production process from the delivery of the raw materials to the stocking of the finished products. A comparison with

other companies in the same business and any competitors, as well as a description of any advantages that you have over them.

• Production strategy and any plans to sub-contract part of the production. If there is going to be sub-contracting of part of the production process, details of how the sub-contracting is going to work, cost and so on. Description of the production in terms of volume, cost, labour, raw materials and so on.

• Description of the quality-control issues that affect the production process. Inventory control. Details of how you are going to minimise costs. Details of how to minimise problems that would affect both you and your customers.

Market analysis

This part of the business plan sets out the details of whether there is a demand for the product or service that you intend to offer. Once it has been established that there is a demand for such a product or service then a strategy for market penetration is established. In addition, this helps to decide how to make your product or service different from others in the marketplace. A market analysis must consider the following points:

General description of the market sector

Give a description of the market sector in which your product or service will be placed. This should include an analysis of what the sector is like at the moment and also how it might develop in the future. Is the market expanding? What are the main influences on the sector? What are the latest developments in the sector? What is the size of the sector?

Who are your potential clients?

You should set out who your potential clients are, how receptive your potential clients are to new players in the market as well as the main factors that influence them to buy a particular item or service over another. Are your potential clients mainly influenced by price, quality, service or any other factors?

Analysis of the competition

Carry out a study of your competition. You should set out their strengths and weaknesses. Provide details of their location, their products or services, prices, quality, distribution methods, market share, and any other relevant information.

Any barriers to entry

There may be certain barriers to entry in a market sector. You need to discuss whether these barriers are going to cause any problems. If they are likely to cause a problem, then you need to set out an analysis of these barriers and any steps you are intending to put into place to get around them.

Marketing plan

This sets out your marketing strategy for your products or services.

Price strategy

It is obviously important to be price competitive with your rivals in the sector, but it is also important to make a profit. In this section you must set out your pricing structure with particular reference to the competition and set out how much profit you still intend to be making with that pricing structure.

If your prices are going to be less than the competition then you must explain how this is going to be achieved – through lower production costs, more efficient production methods, lower labour costs, lower distribution costs, etc.

If your prices are going to be higher than the competition then you need to explain why you feel that you can justify higher prices. This is likely to focus on greater quality, better service, innovation, a better product or service, better guarantees, etc.

Sales policy

In this section you would set out any policies that you have for sales. Are you going to be selling direct to the public or selling through other forms (distributors, agents, etc.)? What are your plans for sales in both the medium and long term? You must include details of how you are going to distribute your goods and services and how this is going to work. Yet again you must compare this with what your competition is doing and set out the advantages and disadvantages your way has over your competition. If you are going to use third-party distributors you must explain how this form of distribution is going to work, what incentives they will be given, targets, etc. In this section you must also set out details of how often you are going to charge clients, any discounts that you anticipate giving to good clients and any other relevant points relating to sales.

Advertising and publicity

How do you intend to attract potential new clients? What are you going to be doing in terms of advertisements, direct mailing, seminars, articles in magazines and newspapers, trade fairs and any other methods of attracting clients and bringing your products or services to the attention of any potential new customers. You must compare your advertising and publicity strategy with that of your competition and explain why you feel that your method is going to be more effective in terms of market awareness and costs.

Post-transaction service and guarantees

In this section you must set out any aspects of your business that relate to the customer after they have purchased your product or service. Are there any guarantees that come with the product? What is the after-sales support like? If there are any guarantees, how long do these last and what do they cover? You must set out how the after-sales support is structured and the costs involved in providing this. What does the competition do in terms of after-sales support and how are you going to be different from them?

Organisation and personnel

Set out the structure of the business in terms of the people who will be working there. Describe the different roles of the people working in the business and how they interact with each other. For each person in the business you must set out the necessary qualifications, experience and characteristics that you need them to have. What are the jobs and responsibilities of the different people in the organisation? How many staff do you envisage needing to start with (in the short term) and how do you envisage this changing over time – both in the medium and long term? You must set out how the staff are to be employed and give details of their remuneration. When talking about staff you must make some reference to human resources and any structures that you have in place for promotion of staff in the future.

Investment plan

In this section you must set out all the different aspects of the investment that both you and any potential investors need to put into the business in order to make it a success.

Your own investment

In this section you must set out any investment that you will be putting into the business and any investment that any business partners will be putting into the business, in the short, medium and long term.

You should discuss any points that are relevant to production or supply, for example:
1. Distance to your target market.
2. Distance to any raw materials and supplies.
3. Cost of transport.
4. Availability of qualified staff.
5. Description of lines of communication.
6. Possibility for future expansion.
7. Machinery – do you need any? If so, what do you need?

You should also consider here whether it is better to buy or rent premises, equipment, etc. Give a resumé of property and premises.

You must discuss any intangible investments. These may include:
1. Investment in development.
2. Administrative costs.
3. Intellectual property costs.
4. Research.
5. Legal fees – lawyers, notaries, land registries, etc.

You must mention any investment that has already gone into the business – loans (from banks and other sources), existing stock, taxes due, etc.

Budget

In this section you would set out the budget for the business. It is advisable to get your Spanish accountant to help you with this to make sure that it is done in the Spanish format. Basically this is a prediction of the financial status of the business. The budget will help you to identify whether or not the business is financially viable. You will set out all the costs of the business, balance these up against the predicted income and then identify whether you make a profit at the end or not. Obviously the aim is to make a profit! Doing the budget will also help you concentrate on a number of other things – cash flow, for example.

Finance

In this section you should address the financial situation that is highlighted by the budget. If the budget is showing a loss then you need to discuss any finance that you need. This discussion should include subjects such as:

1. How much finance you need.
2. How this is going to be raised.
3. Who is going to assist with the finance.
4. How it is going to be secured.
5. How it is going to be repaid, etc.

Risk

There should be some discussion of risk. The discussion should include such items as:

1. Risk to the business of the proposed course of action.
2. Risk to staff.
3. Risk to the public.
4. Risk and effect of delay to the project.
5. Risk of change in the market and demand for the product.
6. Risk of competition.

Appendix 4

Types of Spanish Business Structure

Type of structure	Description	No. of partners	Working capital	Liability	Taxation	Comments
Empresario individual	Individual. Equivalent of UK sole trader	1	No minimum	Unlimited	Individual income taxation	Tends to be used when one person is just starting up a small business
Communidad de bienes	Individual. Equivalent of UK partnership	2 or more	No minimum	Unlimited	Individual income taxation	Tends to be used when several people are just starting up a small business
Sociedad de Responsabilida Limitada	Corporate. Equivalent of UK limited company	1 or more	Minimum of €3,005.06	Limited	Corporate taxation	Limited liability structure, which is still relatively flexible
Sociedad Anónima	Corporate. Equivalent of UK Plc.	1 or more	Minimum of €60,101.21	Limited	Corporate taxation	Tends to be for large organisations such as banks and insurance companies
Sociedad colectiva	General partnership	Minimum of 2	No minimum	Unlimited	Corporate taxation	Simple structure using partners
Sociedad Limitada Nueva Empresa	Limited Company for New Businesses	Maximum of 5	Minimum of €3,012. Maximum of €120,202	Limited to the capital put into the business	Corporate taxation	Designed to be set up quickly and cheaply and targets new businesses
Sociedad comanditaria por acciones		Minimum of 2	Minimum of €60,101.21		Corporate taxation	Similar to *Sociedad colectiva* but some of the partners will have limited liability

Type of structure	Description	No. of partners	Working capital	Liability	Taxation	Comments
Sociedad comanditaria simple		Minimum of 2	No Minimum	Some partners have unlimited liability while others have limited liability	Corporate taxation	
Sociedad laboral		Minimum of 3	Minimum of €60,121.21 (SAL) Minimum of €3,005.06 (SLL)	Limited to the capital put into the business	Corporate taxation	
Sociedad cooperativa		Minimum of 3	The minimum set out in the statutes of the company	Limited to the capital put into the business	Corporate taxation (Special scheme)	
Sociedad de garantía recíproca		Minimum of 150	Minimum of €1,803,036.30	Limited	Corporate taxation	
Entidades de capital-riesgo		Minimum of 3	*Sociedades de Capital-Riesgo:* Minimum €1.202.024,20 *Fondos de Capital-Riesgo:* Minimum €1.652.783,30	Limited	Corporate taxation	
Agrupación de interés económico		Minimum of 2	No minimum	Limited to the capital put into the business	Corporate taxation	

Appendix 5

Wealth and Inheritance Tax

Wealth Tax 2004

Wealth from	Up to	Tax Rate	Total Tax Payable to Top of this Band
Nil	€167,129	0.11%/0.2%	€334
€167,129	€334,253	0.3%	€836
€334,253	€668,500	0.6%	€2,507
€668,500	€1,337,000	0.9%	€8,523
€1,337,000	€2,673,999	1.3%	€25,904
€2,673,999	€5,347,998	1.7%	€71,362
€5,347,998	€10,695,996	2.1%	€183,670
Over €10,695,996		2.5%	

Inheritance Tax 2004

From	To	Tax Rate	Tax Payable to Top of this Band
Nil	€7993	7.65%	€611.50
€7,993.46	€15,980.91	8.50%	€1,290.43
€15,980.91	€23,968.36	9.35%	€2,037
€23,968.36	€31,955.81	10.20%	€2,851.98
€31,955.81	€39,943.26	11.05%	€3,734.59
€39,943.26	€47,930.22	11.90%	€4,685.04
€47,930.22	€55,918.17	12.75%	€5,703.50
€55,918.17	€63,905.62	13.60%	€6,789.80
€63,905.62	€71,893.07	14.45%	€7,943.98
€71,893.07	€79,880.52	15.30%	€9,166.06
€79,880.52	€119,757.67	16.15%	€15,606.22
€119,757.67	€159,634.83	18.70%	€23,063.25
€159,634.83	€239,389.13	21.25%	€40,011.04
€239,389.123	€398,777.54	25.50%	€80,655.09
€398,777.54	€797,555.10	29.75%	€199,291.41
Over €797,555.08		34.00%	

Note: These figures are correct as of 2004. Certain relatives have a tax-free allowance. For example, your husband/wife or children will each be entitled to inherit €15,911 tax free. Your uncle or aunt would be entitled to €7,955 tax free. The rates above apply to the balance in excess of those amounts.

Index

accountants 76
activity-based businesses
    7–8, 52–3
administrative system
    20–2
advertising 61, 123–4
    camping/caravan sites
        36
    job vacancies 120–1,
        140–1
    see also marketing
after-sales support 256–7
age distribution 19
agriculture *see* farming
air-conditioning 59, 181
Almería 18
Alternative Dispute
    Resolution (ADR)
    208–9
alternative medicine
    186–7
Andalucía 18
arbitration 208–10
arguments 138
    see also disputes
Atlantic Spain 16–17
auctions 168–9
autonomous regions 20
ayuntamiento (town hall)
    20, 21

Balearic Islands 18
banker's drafts 102
bankruptcy laws 210–11
banks
    cheques 104
    choosing a bank
        103–4
    IBAN numbers 101
    offshore accounts 104
    opening an account
        103
    opening hours 105

types of accounts 104
    see also finance
bars 5–6, 31–3
Basque language 23–4,
    25–6, 157–8
bathrooms 59
BBC World Service 177
bed and breakfast
    businesses 7, 38
bedrooms 59
benefits 150–1
bilateral contracts 195–6
black economy 108–9
boats 160
body language 135
borrowing limits 164–5
bottled gas 181–2
branch offices 81–2
breach of contract 195,
    197
brokers 199–200
budgets 258
building/alteration
    licences 130
buildings insurance 202
business etiquette 138
business ideas 30–41,
    76–7
    bars 5–6, 31–3
    construction industry
        8–9
    estate agencies 9, 54,
        137
    farming 44–6
    fishing 48–9
    gaps in the market
        10–13
    golf-based services 8
    holiday
        accommodation
        6–7
        bed and breakfast
            7, 38

camping/caravan
    sites 34–7
    hotels 38–40, 64
    see also rental
        properties
internet-based
    companies 10, 44
IT-based businesses
    12, 42–3
pilots 51–2
restaurants 5–6, 34, 67
service businesses
    9–10, 41–2
shops 9–10, 41–2
spas 53
stress-busting
    businesses 53
success criteria 66–7
teaching 49–51
tourism services 7–8,
    52–3
translation work 51
waste disposal 12
business law 194–9
    contract law 194–7
    intellectual property
        rights 198
    product liability 198–9
business names 68
business partners
    99–100
business plans 77–9, 124,
    253–8
    after-sales support
        256–7
    budgets 258
    investment plan
        257–8
    market analysis 255
    marketing plans 256
    ownership structure
        253
    personnel 257

product description
254
production plan 254–5
risk assessment 258
business structures 90–7,
259–60
capital requirements
93, 94, 96
cooperatives 95
and credibility 97
limited companies
92–5, 111–12
limits on liability 96
partnerships 91–2
property ownership
111–12
red tape 96–7
small and medium-
sized enterprises
(PYME) 92
sole traders 90–1
and taxation 96
buying a business 83–9
anti-competition
clauses 84
assistance from
previous owner 84
due diligence 88–9
Economic Interest
Groups (EIG) 88
finding a business
85–6
franchises 86–7
informing employees
85
joint ventures 87–8
licences 84
reasons for selling 83
reputation 83–4
temporary business
association 88
buying a property 110–18,
162–70
auctions 168–9
civil state 117–18
finding a property
168–70
general inquiries 117
lawyers 114–16
mortgages 111, 163–7

notaries 114–15
ownership structure
111–12
payment procedures
116–17
price declaration 116
price negotiations 116
property law 113–14
property market 162
special inquiries 117
taxes 106
see also estate agents

camping/caravan sites
34–7
advantages 35
advertising 36
charging structure 35
disadvantages 36
legal requirements 37
location 37
off seasons 35
rating systems 34–5
registration 36
Canary Islands 18–19
cannabis 187
capital gains tax 107
capital for limited
companies 93, 94, 96
caravan sites *see*
camping/caravan sites
cars 159, 182
classic car tours 52–3
driving licences 183
insurance 204
taxation 159
cash 102–3
Castilian 22–3
Catalan 23–5, 157
Central Spain 17
chambers of commerce
76, 100
cheques 104
children
as employees 119
schools 189–92
civil state 117–18
claims on insurance
policies 201
classic car tours 52–3

climate 16–19, 55
rainfall chart 224
temperature chart 224
clinics 185
community of owners 64
company hierarchies
134–5
competition clauses 84
complaints books 199
complementary
medicine 186–7
computer ownership 10,
42–3
constitution 20
construction industry
8–9
consulates 220–2
consultancies 12, 43
contacts and networking
69, 123, 134, 141
contents insurance 202
contracts 194–7
bilateral 195–6
breach of contract 195,
197
employment 121–2,
146–8
exchange contracts
196
leasing 196
legal elements 195
limitation periods 197
penalty clauses 195
performance
guarantees 196–7
tenancy agreements
66, 174, 196
unilateral 195–6
cooperatives 95
corporation tax 108
Costa Blanca 17–18
Costa Brava 17
Costa de la Luz 18
Costa del Sol 18
costs
of mortgages 165
of moving 109–10
of property ownership
6
courts 208, 209

see also disputes
credibility 97
currency dealers 102,
    166–7
current accounts 104
CVs (curriculum vitae)
    144–5, 250

debt collection 205–6,
    208
deeds of incorporation
    92–3
dentists 186
dialling codes 223
directories 61
disciplinary actions
    148–9
dismissal of employees
    148–9
disputes 204–10
    Alternative Dispute
        Resolution (ADR)
        208–9
    arbitration 208–10
    breach of contract 195,
        197
    courts 208, 209
    debt collection 205–6,
        208
    with insurance
        companies 201
    lawyers 207
    paperwork 208
dividend payments 93
doctors 184
double taxation treaties
    106
dress codes 135, 137
driving licences 183
due diligence 88–9

e-commerce 10, 44
Economic Interest
    Groups (EIG) 88
economy 19–20
    agricultural sector
        44–5
    small business
        statistics 4
education 148, 189–92

teaching work 49–51
elections 20, 21
electricity 179–80
electronic transfer of
    funds 101–2
embassies 220–2
emergency numbers 216
employees 39, 67–8, 85,
    118–23, 257
    children 119
    contracts of
        employment 121–2,
        146–8
    dismissal 148–9
    entitlements 123
    finding staff 119–20
    minimum wage 122
    probation periods 122
    redundancy 148–9
    social security
        payments 122–3,
        129, 184
employer's liability
    insurance 203
employment agencies
    119–20, 139, 140
employment contracts
    121–2, 146–8
equipment for rental
    properties 58–60
estate agents 9, 54, 137,
    170
    buying a business
        from 85
    fees 110
etiquette 138
European Employment
    Service (EURES)
    119–20, 140
Euskera 23–4, 25–6, 157–8
exchange contracts 196
exchange controls 103
exchange rates 101–2,
    103, 166–7
experience 72–3
eye tests 186

family and friends 61–2,
    99
family-owned businesses

135
farming 44–6
    forestry 48
    grants 45
    illegal workers 46–7
    insurance 46, 202–3
    irrigation 45
    livestock 48
    organic farming 48
    vineyards 47–8
fax machines 176
festivals 233–4
finance 98–103
    banker's drafts 102
    business partners
        99–100
    cash 102–3
    electronic transfer of
        funds 101–2
    exchange controls 103
    exchange rates 101–2,
        103, 166–7
    forward-buying
        currencies 167
    from friends and
        family 99
    grants 100–1
    limited company
        capital
        requirements 93,
        94, 96
    money transfers
        101–2, 166–7
    own funds 98–9
    re-mortgages 98
    Spanish lenders 98
    subsidies 100–1
    and taxation 98–9
    see also banks;
        mortgages
finding a business 85–6
finding a job/staff 119–21,
    139–45
    advertisements 120–1,
        140–1
    employment agencies
        119–20, 139, 140
    European
        Employment
        Service (EURES)

119–20, 140
HR consultants 119,
139–40
Internet advertising/
searches 120, 140
registering job
vacancies 119
finding a property
168–70
fishing 48–9
fixed-term contracts
121–2, 146–7
forestry 48
forward-buying
currencies 167
franchises 86–7
fraud 77
friends and family 61–2,
99
furniture 160

Galician 23–4, 25, 157
gaps in the market 10–13
gas 181–2
general inquiries 117
geography 16–19
gestores 128
golf-based services 8
governmental system
20–2
grants 45, 100–1

healthcare 183–7
alternative medicine
186–7
clinics 185
dentists 186
doctors 184
emergency numbers
216
hospitals 185
opticians 186
private health
insurance 187
qualifying for free
state healthcare 183–4
heating 59
hierarchies 134–5
holiday accommodation
6–7

bed and breakfast 7, 38
camping/caravan sites
34–7
hotels 38–40, 64
see also rental
properties
holiday entitlements
147–8
public holidays 233–4
homeworking 80–1
honour 139
hospitals 185
hotels 38–40, 64
authorizations 40
contracts with holiday
companies 39
guest registration 40
leisure facilities 39
maintenance 39
rating system 40
registering with guide
books 40
staff 39
house books 58
HR (human resources)
consultants 119,
139–40

IAE 130–1
IBAN numbers 101
identity numbers 127
illegal workers 46–7, 144
immovable property 113
income tax 107
infant education 190
inflation 19
information and research
68–71, 76–7
inheritance tax 107, 261
insurance 199–204
brokers 199–200
buildings 202
claims 201
contents 202
disputes 201
duration of policies
200
employer's liability
203
farm 46, 202–3

life 203
notice periods 200
private health 187
professional
negligence 203
public liability 201–2
salary 204
termination of
policies 200
third party liability
201–2
unemployment 204
vehicle 204
intellectual property
rights 198
Internet 62, 69, 71
advertising job
vacancies 120
computer ownership
10, 42–3
grant websites 101
internet-based
companies 10, 44
job vacancies 120, 140
property websites 170,
171
service providers
176–7
useful phrases 232
internships 142
interviews 145–6
introductions 135
investment plan 257–8
irrigation 45
IT-based businesses
consultancies 12, 42–3
programming 43
IVA (*Impuesto de Valor
Anadido*) 108

job application letters
251–2
joint ventures 87–8

kitchens 59

land ownership 113–14
land register 114
language 22–8, 74,
226–30

Basque 23–4, 25–6, 157–8
Castilian 22–3
Catalan 23–5, 157
Galician 23–4, 25, 157
language schools 50–1
learning Spanish 74, 154–6
teaching English 50
tests 145
translation work 51
useful phrases 26–8, 226–30
hospitals 185
housing 172–3
Internet 232
numbers 227–8
restaurants 232
shopping 231
time 228–9
travel 26, 229–30
lawyers 71–2, 76, 114–16, 207
leasing contracts 196
legal system
bankruptcy laws 210–11
business law 194–9
contract law 194–7
courts 208, 209
employment law 121–2
intellectual property rights 198
product liability 198–9
property law 113–14
see also disputes
Leonardo da Vinci scholarships 142
letting agencies 55, 64–6
licences 84, 97, 129–30
life insurance 203
life plans 79
limitation periods in contracts 197
limited companies 92–5, 111–12
capital requirements 93, 94, 96
livestock 48

local property taxes 106
local representative offices 82

magazines see newspapers and magazines
management agencies 55, 64–6
mañana 136
market analysis 255
market research 70–1
marketing 123–4
directories 61
on the Internet 62
mutual assistance groups 63
plans 256
a rental property 60–3
to friends and family 61–2
see also advertising
maternity benefits 150–1
matrimonial regime 117–18
mayors 20, 21
medical tests 145
Mediterranean Spain 17
meetings 136
minimum wage 122
Ministry of Labour and Social Affairs 131
mobile food-vending 11
mobile phones 176
money transfers 101–2, 166–7
mortgages 98, 111, 163–7
applications 165
borrowing limits 164–5
costs 165
exchange rate risk 166–7
offers 165
on Spanish properties 163–4
movable property 113
moving to Spain 158–61
costs 109–10
Murcia 18

mutual assistance groups 63

names
of businesses 68
of people 135–6, 144
national authorities 22
negligence insurance 203
networking 69, 123, 134, 141
newspapers and magazines 77, 178
businesses for sale 85–6
property adverts 168, 174
situations vacant 120–1, 140–1
NIE 127
notaries 114–15

objective dismissal 149
offshore accounts 104
offshore companies 112
opening hours 105
operating licences 129–30
opticians 186
organic farming 48
ownership of property 111–12

parent companies 81–2
part-time contracts 121
partnerships 91–2
business partners 99–100
penalty clauses 195
pensions 188–9
performance guarantees 196–7
permits 126–7
personal contacts 69, 123, 134, 141
pets 161
pilots 51–2
planning see business plans; life plans
population 19
foreigners living in

Spain 4–5, 11
largest cities 225
postal system 176
pre-visit packs 58
premises
    renting 109–10
    working from home
        80–1
    see also buying a
        property
primary education 190
private health insurance
    187
private schools 191–2
probation periods 122
product description 254
product liability 198–9
production plans 254–5
professional occupations
    9–10
    negligence insurance
        203
    qualifications 131–2
programming 43
property investment
    11–12
    see also rental
        properties
property law 113–14
    building/alteration
        licences 130
property market 162
property ownership
    structure 111–12
    see also buying a
        property
provincial authorities 22
public holidays 233–4
public liability insurance
    201–2

qualifications 131–2

radio 177–8
rainfall chart 224
re-mortgages 98
red tape 96–7
redundancy 148–9
regional authorities 22
registration

of boats 160
of branch offices 81–2
of businesses 97
of camping/caravan
    sites 36
with a consulate 132
of hotels 40
of intellectual
    property rights 198
of job vacancies 119
with labour and social
    affairs ministry 131
with tax authorities
    130–1
removal companies 158
rental agreements 66,
    174, 196
rental properties 53–66
    access 56
    air-conditioning 59
    bathrooms 59
    bedrooms 59
    choice of property
        57–8, 60
    cleanliness 58
    contracts 66, 174, 196
    equipment 58–60
    heating 59
    house books 58
    kitchens 59
    letting agencies 55,
        64–6
    living areas 59
    location 55
    maintenance 63–4,
        65–6
    management
        agencies 55, 64–6
    marketing 60–3
    pre-visit packs 58
    swimming pools 60
    target market 54
    tenancy agreements
        66, 174, 196
    to friends and family
        61–2
    tourist attractions
        56–7
    washing machines 59
    welcome packs 58

welcoming guests 58
    yields 60
    see also buying a
        property; holiday
        accommodation
rented accommodation
    170–5
    contracts 66, 174, 196
    finding a property
        174–5
    inventories 174
    security deposit 170
renting business
    premises 109–10
representative offices 82
reputation 83–4
research and information
    68–71, 76–7
residence permits 126–7
residence for tax 105–6
restaurants 5–6, 34, 67
    useful phrases 232
retirement 151, 188–9
risk assessment 258

salary insurance 204
satellite TV 177–8
scholarships 142
schools 189–92
    teaching jobs 49–51
seasonal work 143
secondary education 190
senators 20
service businesses 9–10,
    41–2
shops 41–2
    useful phrases 231
sickness benefits 150
siestas 136
small and medium-sized
    enterprises (PYME) 92
    statistics 4
social security 122–3, 129,
    184
    welfare benefits 150–1
socialising at work 138
sociedad anónima (SA)
    93–4
sociedad colectiva 95
sociedad limitada (SL)

92–3
sociedad unipersonal de responsabilidad limitada 93
software programming 43
solar power 180
sole traders 90–1
solicitors *see* lawyers
spas 53
special inquiries 117
staff *see* employees
StopStress 53
stress-busting businesses 53
strikes 152
subsidies 100–1
surnames 135–6, 144
SWIFT transfer 101–2
swimming pools 60

taxation 96, 98–9, 105–9
    black economy 108–9
    of branch offices 82
    capital gains tax 107
    of cars 159
    corporation tax 108
    double taxation treaties 106
    income tax 107
    inheritance tax 107, 261
    local property taxes 106
    of pensions 189
    of property purchase 106
    registering with authorities 130–1
    residence 105–6
    VAT 108, 159
    wealth tax 107, 261
teaching 49–51
    English 50
telephones 175–6
    dialling codes 223
    emergency numbers

216
television 177–8
temperature chart 224
temporary business association 88
temporary work 141–2
tenancy agreements 66, 174, 196
third party liability insurance 201–2
time 228–9
tour businesses 52–3
tourism services 7–8, 52–3
town halls (*ayuntamiento*) 20, 21
trade shows 77
training 148, 190
translation work 51
travel, useful phrases 26, 229–30
trusts 112

unemployment insurance 204
unemployment statistics 19
unilateral contracts 195–6
unions 151–2
utilities 179–82
    air-conditioning 181
    electricity 179–80
    gas 181–2
    water 182

VAT 108, 159
Vauxhall 68
vehicle insurance 204
vineyards 47–8
voltage 180
voluntary work 142–3

waste disposal 12
water 182
wealth tax 107, 261
weather *see* climate

websites *see* Internet
welcome packs 58
welfare benefits 150–1
wine 47–8
wiring 180
women
    in business 136
    maternity benefits 150–1
work experience contracts 147
working from home 80–1
working hours 147
working in Spain 134–52
    arguments 138
    business etiquette 138
    company hierarchies 134–5
    contracts of employment 121–2, 146–8
    CVs (*curriculum vitae*) 144–5, 250
    dismissal 148–9
    dress codes 135, 137
    family-owned businesses 135
    finding a job 139–45
    honour 139
    illegal working 144
    internships 142
    interviews 145–6
    introductions 135
    job application letters 251–2
    language tests 145
    medical tests 145
    meetings 136
    personal contacts 69, 123, 134
    redundancy 148–9
    seasonal work 143
    socialising 138
    temporary work 141–2
    voluntary work 142–3
    women in business 136